ASVAB AFQT

FOR

DUMMIES®

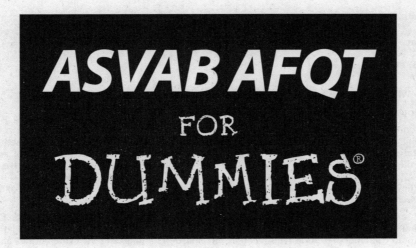

ASVAB AFQT FOR DUMMIES®

by Rod Powers

WILEY

Wiley Publishing, Inc.

ASVAB AFQT For Dummies®

Published by
Wiley Publishing, Inc.
111 River St.
Hoboken, NJ 07030-5774
www.wiley.com

For general information on our other products and services, please contact our Customer Care Department within the U.S. at 877-762-2974, outside the U.S. at 317-572-3993, or fax 317-572-4002.

For technical support, please visit www.wiley.com/techsupport.

Wiley also publishes its books in a variety of electronic formats. Some content that appears in print may not be available in electronic books.

Library of Congress Control Number: 2009941349

ISBN: 978-0-470-56652-7

Manufactured in the United States of America

10 9 8 7 6 5 4 3

WILEY

About the Author

Rod Powers joined the Air Force in 1975 intending to become a spy. He was devastated to learn that he should've joined the CIA instead, because the military services don't have that particular enlisted job. Regardless, he fell in love with the military and made it both a passion and a career, retiring with 23 years of service. Rod spent 11 of those years as an Air Force first sergeant, helping to solve the problems of the enlisted corps.

Since his retirement from the military in 1998, Rod has become a world-renowned military careers expert. Through his highly popular U.S. Military Information Web site on About.com (http://usmilitary.about.com), Rod has advised thousands of troops about all aspects of U.S. armed forces career information. This is Rod's fourth military book. Two of his previous books, *ASVAB For Dummies* and *Veteran Benefits For Dummies,* were published by Wiley.

Rod is the proud father of twin girls, both of whom are enjoying successful careers in the Air Force. He currently resides in Daytona Beach, Florida, where he is attempting to prove that there is no such thing as too much sunshine.

Even today, Rod tries to run his life according to long-lived military ideals and standards, but he gets a bit confused about why nobody will obey his orders anymore.

Dedication

To Maloni, the love of my life, and the best granddaughter a granddaddy could ever hope for.

Author's Acknowledgments

I would like to thank Linda Parker for the hours she spent reviewing the practice exams and pointing out that I divided when I should have multiplied. Thanks also to Jane Burstein, Patrick Long, and Carolyn Wheater for reviewing the final manuscript for technical accuracy.

Special thanks also to Mike Baker, my acquisitions editor; Barb Doyen, my wonderful literary agent; and Elizabeth Kuball, editor extraordinaire.

More special thanks to the recruiting commands of the Army, Air Force, Navy, Marine Corps, and Coast Guard for providing invaluable resource information.

Publisher's Acknowledgments

We're proud of this book; please send us your comments at http://dummies.custhelp.com. For other comments, please contact our Customer Care Department within the U.S. at 877-762-2974, outside the U.S. at 317-572-3993, or fax 317-572-4002.

Some of the people who helped bring this book to market include the following:

Acquisitions, Editorial, and Media Development

Project Editor: Elizabeth Kuball

Acquisitions Editor: Mike Baker

Copy Editor: Elizabeth Kuball

Assistant Editor: Erin Calligan Mooney

Editorial Program Coordinator: Joe Niesen

Technical Editors: Jane Burstein, Patrick Long, Mary Jane Sterling, Carolyn Wheater

Senior Editorial Manager: Jennifer Ehrlich

Editorial Supervisor and Reprint Editor: Carmen Krikorian

Editorial Assistant: Jennette ElNaggar, David Lutton

Cover Photos: © iStock

Cartoons: Rich Tennant (www.the5thwave.com)

Composition Services

Project Coordinator: Katie Crocker

Layout and Graphics: Claudia Bell, Carrie A. Cesavice, Christine Williams, Erin Zeltner

Proofreaders: Rebecca Denoncour, Mildred Rosenzweig

Indexer: Valerie Haynes Perry

Publishing and Editorial for Consumer Dummies

    Diane Graves Steele, Vice President and Publisher, Consumer Dummies

    Kristin Ferguson-Wagstaffe, Product Development Director, Consumer Dummies

    Ensley Eikenburg, Associate Publisher, Travel

    Kelly Regan, Editorial Director, Travel

Publishing for Technology Dummies

    Andy Cummings, Vice President and Publisher, Dummies Technology/General User

Composition Services

    Debbie Stailey, Director of Composition Services

Contents at a Glance

Table of Contents

Introduction

$\mathcal{B}$ecause you're reading this book, there's a very good chance that you're interested in joining the U.S. military. I say that because the military recruiting commands are the only people in the entire world who care about the Armed Forces Qualification Test (AFQT) score. The AFQT score is derived from four of the nine Armed Services Vocational Aptitude Battery (ASVAB) subtests. It's used to determine your overall qualification to join the military branch of your choice.

Perhaps you've read my best-selling *ASVAB For Dummies*, or some other ASVAB prep book, and you want more practice so that you can achieve the highest possible AFQT score. Maybe you've already taken the ASVAB, you want to retest for a higher AFQT score, and you're looking for an advantage. In either case, you've chosen the right book!

Ever since *ASVAB For Dummies* hit the bookshelves, I've received hundreds of e-mails from readers, asking for ways to score higher on the AFQT portion of the ASVAB. That's why I decided to write this book. Although the entire ASVAB is important in order to qualify for the military job you want, the four subtests that make up the AFQT score are ultra-important, because the AFQT score determines whether you can even get into the military.

Long gone are the days when someone could just walk into a recruiter's office and get into the military as long as he had a pulse. Today's all-volunteer military members are the cream of the crop. For example, did you know that, under current regulations, you need a minimum of a high school education to join, and that no more than 10 percent of all recruits can have a GED?

Something else you may not know: The military services can't just grow to whatever size they want. Like any other government agency, they have a budget, and they have to operate within that budget. Every year, when Congress passes the annual Defense Authorization Act, it tells each military branch how many members it's allowed to have at any given time. By law, the services can't go over the size mandated by our congressional leaders (who hold the military purse strings).

Did you also know that, of every ten people who walk into a military recruiter's office, only three ultimately are allowed to enlist? Sure, some are disqualified because of medical history or criminal history, but many are turned away because their AFQT scores are too low, or because other qualified applicants have higher AFQT scores.

Today's military is high tech. Even the "common" infantry soldier has to learn how to use and maintain complicated electronic gadgets in order to survive on today's battlefield. The services use the AFQT to determine whether someone is "trainable" in the new, high-tech military.

About This Book

Full-disclosure doctrine requires me to inform you that much of the information in this book can be found in *ASVAB For Dummies*. The AFQT is, after all, part of the ASVAB, and I wouldn't cheat you by putting part of the information in one book and part of the information in another.

So, why should you spend some of your hard-earned money on this book, particularly if you've already bought *ASVAB For Dummies?* Because here you find expanded, more-detailed information about the AFQT and the four subtests that make up the AFQT score. If you're worried about your AFQT score, I guarantee this book will help you get the highest score possible.

Even if you're not worried about your AFQT score, this book contains four — count 'em, four! — additional practice tests for the four most important subtests of the ASVAB. Extra practice is never a bad thing, as my high school football coach was fond of saying.

Conventions Used in This Book

I don't use many special conventions in this book:

- Whenever I use a new term, I *italicize* the term and define it nearby, often in parentheses.
- I put Web addresses and e-mail addresses in monofont, so that you can easily distinguish them from the surrounding text.

When this book was printed, some Web addresses may have needed to break across two lines of text. If that happened, rest assured that I haven't put in any extra characters (such as hyphens) to indicate the break. So, when using one of these Web addresses, just type in exactly what you see in this book, pretending as though the line break doesn't exist.

What You're Not to Read

This book has a few *sidebars* (shaded gray boxes) sprinkled throughout. They're full of interesting information about topics described in those chapters, but you don't have to read them if you don't want to — they don't contain anything you *must* know about the AFQT, so if you're in a hurry, you can skip them.

You can also skip anything marked with a Technical Stuff icon. (For more on icons, see "Icons Used in This Book," later in this Introduction.)

Foolish Assumptions

While writing this book, I made a few assumptions about you — namely, who you are and why you picked up this book. I assume the following:

- **You aren't a dummy.** You just want information to help you get the highest AFQT score possible.
- **You're a high school graduate, or have a GED or at least 15 college credits.** You just want to brush up on your high school math and/or English skills, as they apply to the AFQT. (If you aren't a high school graduate, or you don't have a GED or at least 15 college credits, you need to get back to school, because you're not eligible to enlist in the military.)
- **You want to join the U.S. military and want to take advantage of all the enlistment goodies, such as enlistment bonuses, that are available.** Depending on current recruiting needs, the services often tie enlistment incentives, such as bonuses or additional education benefits, to high AFQT scores.

How This Book Is Organized

There is a method to my madness — a reason why this book is organized the way you see it today. I've organized this book according to subject matter. Information relating to communicative skills is located in one part, math skills are grouped in another part, and so on. Here's what I cover in each part.

Part 1: Taking the AFQT Tour

Part I presents you with an overview of the AFQT and explains which of the four ASVAB subtests are used to compute your AFQT score. You also learn how the score is computed, the minimum score required to join each military branch, and how you can request a retest if your score is too low.

For your added reading enjoyment, I also include a chapter with advice for getting the most out of your study time and maximizing your AFQT score.

Part 11: English as a First Language

If you already know that you need help on a particular language-related subtest, turn to Part II where I show you how to pump up your vocabulary and reading comprehension skills, two important ASVAB subtests that contribute to your AFQT score.

Part 111: Calculating Better Math Knowledge

If you feel comfortable about your Word Knowledge and Paragraph Comprehension skills but you know that you're far from a math whiz, flip straight to Part III to start boning up on math concepts. In this part, you also find some tips and techniques for deciphering those tricky math word problems.

Part 1V: AFQT Practice Exams

Most AFQT preparation books give you two or three practice tests. Here you get *four* full-length AFQT practice exams! If you want to get a feel for the test and figure out what areas you need to brush up on, turn to Part IV and take the first full-length practice test. After you take the test and check your answers, you can determine which subtests are a piece of cake for you and where you need help. Taking this approach lets you tailor a study plan to your individual needs. (Even if you don't have a lot of time for studying, taking the practice tests will help you prepare for the exam.)

Part V: The Part of Tens

This is a *For Dummies* book, so it wouldn't be complete without a Part of Tens. If you want to get right down to it and find out some of the most important information for doing well on the AFQT, and you like your info presented in easily digestible lists, turn to Part V. This part gives you test-taking tips and directs you to additional resources if you need them.

Icons Used in This Book

Throughout this book you find *icons* — little pictures in the margins — that help you use the material in this book to your best advantage. Here's a rundown of what they mean to you:

The Tip icon alerts you to helpful hints regarding the subject at hand. Tips can help you save time and help you score higher on the AFQT.

The Remember icon reminds you of important information you should read carefully.

The Warning icon flags information that may prove hazardous to your plans of acing the AFQT. Often, this icon accompanies common mistakes people make when taking the test or qualifying for enlistment. Pay special attention to the Warning icon so you don't fall into one of these pitfalls.

The Example icon points out sample questions that appear in the review chapters.

The Technical Stuff icon points out information that's interesting, enlightening, or in depth but that isn't necessary for you to read. You don't *need* this information to maximize your AFQT score, but knowing it may make you a better informed test taker — or at least help you impress your friends!

Where to Go from Here

You don't have to read this book from cover to cover in order to maximize your AFQT score. You may want to brush up on word problems but already know that you'll ace the Paragraph Comprehension subtest. If so, head to Chapters 10 and 11, but skip Chapters 6 and 7.

If you decide to skip around, look over the table of contents and choose which topics you're interested in.

You may want to jump straight to Chapter 12 and take the first AFQT practice exam — that way, you can get an idea of what subjects you need to study more. Early on in your reading of the book, check out Chapter 2, which provides invaluable information regarding how the AFQT score is computed and how the score applies to military enlistment.

No matter where you start, I wish you all the best in your future military endeavors. I enjoyed every single second of my 23-year military career, and I'm confident you'll enjoy your time in the military as well.

Part I
Taking the AFQT Tour

The 5th Wave   By Rich Tennant

"I always get a good night's sleep the day before a test so I'm relaxed and alert the next morning. Then I grab my pen, eat a banana, and I'm on my way."

In this part . . .

To score well on the AFQT, you need to know what it's about, and that's why I'm here. Believe me — you do want to do well on the AFQT portion of the ASVAB. The score you earn on the AFQT determines whether you can join the military service branch of your choice. Each of the services has a different minimum standard. Depending on their current recruiting needs, some of the services may even use the AFQT score to determine what kind of enlistment bonuses and incentives you may qualify for.

Even if you can't control yourself and you want to jump right in by reviewing the principles of algebra and memorizing word lists, chill out and take a few minutes to read through Part I. This part gives you an overview of the AFQT, tells you how the score is derived, and lets you know under what circumstances you can request a retest. I also give you tips on getting the best possible score. Armed with the information in this part, you can devise a strategy for defeating the enemy.

Chapter 1

Examining the AFQT

*I*f you're thinking about joining the U.S. military, your AFQT score may well be the most important score you achieve on any military test. Sure, other tests determine which military jobs you may get or whether you get promoted, but what good are those if you can't get into the military in the first place? You need a qualifying score on the AFQT, or your plans for enlistment come to a dead end. The military is not flexible on this point. You could be a young Rambo in the making, in perfect health, able to run 3 miles in 3 minutes, and it wouldn't matter if you didn't have a qualifying AFQT score.

The services have years and years of research to back up their policy. Study after study has shown that an individual's AFQT score is the single most significant factor in determining whether a recruit will make it through basic training and the first enlistment period. Considering the fact that it costs the military more than $25,000 to process a new recruit for enlistment and send that person through basic training, you can see how the services want to maximize their chances of getting their money's worth.

But, with a little review, there is absolutely no reason that you shouldn't be able to score well on the AFQT. The score is, after all, composed of four areas that you studied intensely during your high school years: basic math, math word problems, vocabulary, and reading. That's where *ASVAB AFQT For Dummies* comes in. Other preparation books try to prepare you for the entire Armed Services Vocational Aptitude Battery (ASVAB), but this book is specifically designed to help you boost the most important ASVAB score of all — the AFQT score.

A Close-Up View of the AFQT

The AFQT is not a stand-alone test. You can't just walk into a recruiter's office and say you want to take the AFQT. You have to take the entire ASVAB, which consists of nine separate subtests. Four of those subtests make up the score that's known as the AFQT score. The AFQT score determines whether you're qualified to join the service of your choice. (Turn to Chapter 2 for the minimum qualifying scores for each service.)

In the beginning, there was no AFQT

When you start basic training, you'll learn about military history. Why not start a little sooner and find out where this whole testing thing came from?

The Army began general testing of draftees during World War I. In order to provide a method for classifying these soldiers, the Army developed the Army Alpha Test, which consisted of 212 multiple-choice and true/false questions, including common-sense questions and vocabulary and arithmetic problems. But many of the draftees couldn't read or write, so the Army developed the Army Beta Test, which required little word knowledge and relied on pictures and diagrams. Nearly 2 million solders took one of these tests during World War I.

During World War II, the Army General Classification Test (AGCT) replaced the Alpha and Beta tests. The new test had 150 questions — mostly vocabulary and arithmetic. The AGCT was used by the Army and Marine Corps to assign recruits to military jobs. Of the 9 million soldiers and marines who took this test during World War II, just over 60 percent could read and write above a third-grade level. During this time, a completely separate aptitude test was given to Navy recruits; it was called the Navy General Classification Test (NGCT). (The Air Force didn't have a test because the United States technically didn't have an Air Force as you know it today — the Air Force was part of the Army back then.)

In 1948, Congress required the Department of Defense to develop a uniform screening test to be used by all the services. In 1950, the Department of Defense came up with the Armed Forces Qualification Test (AFQT). This test consisted of 100 multiple-choice questions in areas such as math, vocabulary, spatial relations, and mechanical ability. The military used this test until the mid-1970s. In addition to the AFQT, there were service-specific tests required to classify prospective recruits into jobs. The Army Classification Battery, the Navy Basic Test Battery, and the Airman Qualification Examination (to name a few), were used for classification purposes from the late 1950s to the mid-1970s.

In the 1960s, as military jobs began getting more diverse and technical, the Department of Defense decided to develop a standardized military selection and classification test and administer it in high schools. That's where the ASVAB enters the picture. The first ASVAB test was given in 1968, but the military didn't use it for recruiting purposes for several years. In 1973, the draft ended and the nation entered the contemporary period in which all military recruits are volunteers. That year, the Air Force began using the ASVAB; the Marine Corps followed in 1974. From 1973 to 1975, the Navy and Army used their own test batteries for selection and classification. In 1976, the ASVAB became the official military job classification test used by all services, and the AFQT score became the official entry standard.

Here are the four subtests that make up your AFQT score:

- ✔ **Arithmetic Reasoning:** The Arithmetic Reasoning subtest consists of 30 math word problems. The subtest is multiple choice. You're given 36 minutes to correctly solve as many of the 30 problems as you can. Chapter 10 leads you step-by-step through solving math word problems. Take a look at Chapter 11 for some tips on doing well on this subtest.

- ✔ **Word Knowledge:** The Word Knowledge subtest is a vocabulary test, plain and simple. You have to find words that are "closest in meaning" to underlined words in the question stem. There are 35 words to define in 11 minutes. You can boost your vocabulary knowledge by following the advice in Chapter 4 and get an idea of what the subtest is all about in Chapter 5.

- ✔ **Paragraph Comprehension:** The Paragraph Comprehension subtest requires you to read a paragraph, and then answer one to four questions about information contained in that paragraph. There are 15 questions in all, and you're expected to complete the subtest in 13 minutes. Chapter 6 can help you improve your reading comprehension skills, and you can get a little practice with the Paragraph Comprehension subtest in Chapter 7. (*Note:* Many other standardized tests refer to this type of question as "reading comprehension." The military likes to do things its own way, so it refers to them as "paragraph comprehension" questions. Different name, same thing.)

✔ **Mathematics Knowledge:** This subtest measures your ability to solve high school–level math problems. You have to solve 25 basic math problems in 24 minutes. Like the other subtests of the AFQT, all the questions are multiple choice. To make sure your math skills measure up, see Chapter 8. Chapter 9 gives you an idea about the test format, as well as a little added math practice.

The AFQT isn't the only qualifying standard used by the military. You have to meet all the set standards in order to qualify for enlistment, including age, weight, number of dependents, medical history, education level, and criminal history.

Some standards can be waived, depending on the service's current recruiting needs. However, the minimum AFQT score (see Chapter 2) is rarely waived. A high AFQT score can help with other waivers. The higher your AFQT score, the more likely it is that a service branch will favorably consider a waiver for other disqualifying factors. For example, if you have too many criminal misdeeds in your past, and require a waiver to enlist, a service is much more likely to grant the waiver if you score 85 on the AFQT, than if you score 45.

Why You Want the Highest Possible Score

Chapter 2 gives you the minimum AFQT qualifying scores for each service. But you don't want to be satisfied with making just the minimum. You want to score as high as possible.

The services put great stock in your AFQT score. Not only does a high AFQT score give you a greater chance of enlistment, but it means you might have access to special treats, such as the following:

✔ **Enlistment incentives:** Depending on current recruiting needs, individual services often tie the AFQT score to enlistment incentives, such as monetary bonuses or education benefits. For example, the Army often requires a minimum AFQT score of 50 to qualify for a bonus or to qualify for the Army College Fund (a monetary incentive that increases the value of the G.I. Bill).

✔ **Enlistment programs:** Most military jobs are tied to individual line scores derived from the entire ASVAB, but certain enlistment programs sometimes require a minimum AFQT score, which is significantly higher than the minimum score needed for a regular enlistment. For example, some Navy jobs (such as those in the nuclear field) require a higher AFQT score.

✔ **Education level:** In order to join any of the services, a high school diploma is required. The services are, however, allowed to take a limited number of GED applicants each year. In order to qualify with a GED, you must score higher on the AFQT than a qualified high school diploma holder.

✔ **Quotas:** During times when the services are doing well meeting their recruiting goals, they often get more people who want to join than they have room for. At these times, the services get to pick and choose who they let join and who they don't. It's not unusual for a branch to temporarily raise its AFQT minimum score in order to separate the best-qualified applicants from the rest. For example, at the time this book went to print, the Army National Guard wasn't accepting anyone with an AFQT score less than 50.

✔ **Waivers:** One recent study indicated that only four out of ten people who walked into a recruiter's office were qualified for enlistment. Certain factors — such as criminal history, age, education level, number of dependents, or medical history — made them ineligible. Some of these eligibility criteria can be waived. However, when the military grants a waiver, it's taking a chance on an otherwise ineligible recruit. The military is much more likely to take a chance on someone with a high AFQT score than someone who has a low (but qualifying) score.

Enlistment standards, programs, quotas and incentives change — sometimes on a week-by-week basis, depending on the service's current recruiting needs. For the latest information, check with a military recruiter or visit `http://usmilitary.about.com`.

The AFQT is scored as a *percentile*. That means, for example, that if you score 70, you've scored higher than 70 percent of the thousands of people who've taken the test before you. The highest possible score on the AFQT is 99.

The AFQT isn't a one-shot deal. If you don't achieve a qualifying score, you can retest. After your first test, you have to wait at least 30 days to take a second test. After the second test, in most cases, you have to wait *six months* before you can test again. Keep trying until you get the score you want and deserve.

Establishing a Study Program

If you're not planning to make a study plan, you should plan again. A study plan is essential if you want to score well on the AFQT.

There is no one best way to prepare a study plan. Each person has different ways of study and learning that work the best for him. Still, people can generally be divided into three categories when it comes to learning:

- **Auditory learners:** These people learn best by hearing something. They do really well in lecture classes, and they love listening to audiobooks.
- **Visual learners:** These folks prefer to learn by seeing something. They prefer to read a book or look at a diagram.
- **Tactical learners:** These people get the best results by doing something. Instead of listening to an explanation or reading an instruction manual, they need to do it in order to learn it.

Try to figure out what type of learner you are before developing a plan of study. Chapter 2 can help with this. Chapter 2 also includes some tips about what to include in your study plan, based on your own individual learning style.

Most people don't look forward to sitting down for a study session. Because of that, they try to make study more enjoyable by spending time on the subjects they're already good at. After all, studying familiar information is much easier than learning something new. Try not to fall into this trap! If you're already an avid reader, you probably don't need to spend much of your time improving your reading comprehension skills. You're already going to ace that portion of the AFQT, right? Instead, spend most of your time boning up on the areas where you need improvement, such as math and math word problems.

Try to dedicate one to two hours per day to your AFQT studies. Pick a time and place where you won't be interrupted. Having your dad yell at you to cut the grass probably won't be beneficial to your study session. Also, turn off your cellphone. Is that call as important as your future military career? You won't be allowed to use your cellphone in basic training anyway, so this is a good time to get into the practice of not texting your BFF that OMG, J4I, UBD is making me AAK.

Having raised twin daughters, I happen to be an expert on this texting stuff. Your BFF is your "best friend forever." And "OMG, J4I, UBD is making me AAK" translates to "Oh my God, just for info, user brain damage is making me asleep at the keyboard."

Guessing Smart

All the questions on the ASVAB/AFQT are multiple-choice with four possible answers. That means if you answer eeny-meeny-miny-mo, by the law of averages, you'd get one-fourth of the questions right.

Of course, you can increase these odds immensely by studying. But the chances are good that no matter how much time you put into advanced study, you'll come across at least one question on the test that leaves you scratching your head.

When this happens, you can improve your odds of guessing correctly by guessing smart. See Chapter 5 for tips on intelligent guessing for the Word Knowledge subtest, Chapter 7 for techniques you can use on the Paragraph Comprehension subtest, Chapter 9 for Mathematics Knowledge subtest guessing plans, and Chapter 11 to learn how to make intelligent guesses on the Arithmetic Knowledge subtest. Chapter 3 includes tips and techniques about smart guessing in general.

Using the Practice Exams to Your Advantage

This book includes four full-length AFQT practice exams, with questions that are very similar to the ones you'll see on the ASVAB subtests that comprise the AFQT score. The practice exams included in this book can help increase your confidence and ensure that you're ready to take the actual ASVAB, but you have to use them correctly.

When I wrote my first book, *ASVAB For Dummies,* many readers contacted me. Some were disappointed that the practice tests included in the book were not the *exact same* as the questions they found on the actual ASVAB. I'll let you in on a little not-so-secret secret: No ASVAB or AFQT preparation book will include the exact same questions as what you'll find on the actual test. Not only would that be unethical, but it would probably result in several federal law-enforcement agents knocking on the author's door — not my idea of a good time. Actual ASVAB test questions are *controlled items* — that means that the military keeps them to themselves. If you see any questions on the actual ASVAB or AFQT that are the exact same as the ones you find in this book (or any other preparation guide), it's pure coincidence.

However, just because the practice exams don't include the exact same questions that you'll see on the AFQT doesn't mean that the practice exams aren't valuable — just use them the way they were designed to be used:

- ✔ **Practice Exam 1:** The first practice test is designed as an initial assessment tool. Take this test before you set up your study plan. You can use the results of Practice Exam 1 to determine which areas of the AFQT you need to spend the most time on.
- ✔ **Practice Exam 2:** Use this test as a progress check after a week or two of study. Adjust your study plan accordingly.
- ✔ **Practice Exam 3:** Take this practice exam about a week before you're scheduled to take the actual ASVAB. Use the results to determine which AFQT subjects need a little extra attention.
- ✔ **Practice Exam 4:** Take the final practice exam a day or two before the ASVAB to make sure you're ready, and to boost your confidence. If you don't score well, you may want to consider asking your recruiter to reschedule your ASVAB test for a later date, to give you more time to study.

You may find your recruiter trying to rush you to take the ASVAB and medical exam, so he can get you signed up quickly. Recruiters live and die off their recruiting goals. Make sure you don't let the recruiter schedule your exam until you're sure you're ready to take the test.

The mini-AFQT computerized test (see Chapter 2) that recruiters have in their offices is a pretty good indicator of whether you're ready for the real test. Usually, people's AFQT score is within five or six points of what the mini-AFQT predicts.

Although you can't equate scores on the practice exam with actual AFQT scores (because of the method of scoring the AFQT; see Chapter 2), shoot for a minimum of 80 percent on each subtest:

- **Arithmetic Reasoning:** This subtest has 30 questions. If you miss more than 6, you should dedicate more study time to solving math problems.

- **Word Knowledge:** There are 35 questions on the Word Knowledge Subtest. You need to focus more attention on this area if you miss more than 7 questions.

- **Paragraph Comprehension:** If you miss more than 3 of the 15 Paragraph Comprehension questions, dedicate more study time to your reading skills.

- **Mathematics Knowledge:** Missing more than 5 questions on this 25-question subtest indicates the need for further study.

Chapter 2

Facing the AFQT Head-on

*I*n order to enlist in the U.S. military, everyone has to take the Armed Services Vocational Aptitude Battery (ASVAB). The ASVAB consists of nine separately timed subtests, which are primarily used by the military to determine your aptitude to learn various military jobs.

Four of the ASVAB subtests are used to compute the Armed Forces Qualification Test (AFQT) score. This score determines whether you're qualified to join the military service of your choice. Each branch of military service has its own minimum AFQT score standards. Your AFQT score tells the military what your chances are of making it successfully through your enlistment period. The services have conducted countless studies over the years, and the results are very clear: The higher your AFQT score, the greater the chances that you'll successfully complete your enlistment contract.

As you can imagine, the AFQT score is very important to the military recruiting commands. If you have a high AFQT score, you can expect your recruiter to be wining and dining you, offering you all kinds of enlistment incentives, and telling all his co-workers that you're his very best friend. On the other hand, if your AFQT score is below the minimum standards set by that service, you can expect your recruiter to say, "Don't call us — we'll call you." If you have a qualifying AFQT score that's mediocre, you can probably still enlist, but you'll most likely miss out on many enlistment goodies, such as enlistment bonuses. (Maybe you'll get a free T-shirt.)

In this chapter, I explain which of the four ASVAB subtests are used to compute your AFQT score and how the military calculates the score. I also tell you the minimum qualifying AFQT scores for each service branch, and explain how you can request a retest if your score is too low.

ASVAB: The Big Picture

There are several versions of the ASVAB, depending on where, and for what purpose, you take the test. However, for the purposes of this discussion, I can separate them into just two: the computerized version, and the pencil-and-paper version.

The computerized version of the ASVAB contains nine separately timed subtests. The paper format of the test has only eight subtests: The Assembling Objects (AO) subtest is not included on any of the paper versions. In Table 2-1, I outline the nine ASVAB subtests in the order that you take them.

Table 2-1	The ASVAB Subtests in Order		
Subtest	**Number of Questions**	**Time (in Minutes)**	**Content**
General Science	25	11	General principles of biological and physical sciences
Arithmetic Reasoning *	**30**	**36**	**Math word problems**
Word Knowledge *	**35**	**11**	**Correct meaning of a word and best synonym for a given word**
Paragraph Comprehension *	**15**	**13**	**Questions based on paragraphs (usually a few hundred words) that you read**
Mathematics Knowledge *	**25**	**24**	**High school math**
Electronics Information	20	9	Electricity and electronic principles and terminology
Mechanical Comprehension	25	19	Basic mechanical and physical principles
Auto and Shop Information	25	11	Knowledge of automobiles, shop terminology, and tool use
Assembling Objects **	16	9	Spatial orientation

Used to calculate the AFQT score
*** Only included on the computer version of the ASVAB*

You can't take just the four AFQT subtests of the ASVAB. You have to take all nine subtests in order to get a qualifying AFQT score. The military isn't set up to give *partial* ASVAB tests. For example, if you take the ASVAB and get line scores that qualify you for the military job(s) you want, but your AFQT score is too low to join, you have to retake the entire ASVAB — not just the four subtests that make up the AFQT — to get a higher AFQT score.

During the initial enlistment process your service branch determines your military job or enlistment program based on minimum line scores they've established. Line scores are computed from the various subtests of the ASVAB. If you get an appropriate score in the appropriate areas, you can get the job you want — as long as that job is available and you meet other established qualification factors.

The computerized ASVAB

Nobody really cares about the AFQT score except the military — and they care *a lot!* So, because you're reading this book, it's a safe bet that you're interested in joining the military. And if you're interested in joining the military, there is a greater than 90 percent chance that you'll take the computerized version of the ASVAB. That's because more than 90 percent of those taking the ASVAB for the purpose of joining the military take it at a Military Entrance Processing Station (MEPS), and all of these places use the computerized test.

The computerized version of the ASVAB — called the CAT-ASVAB (CAT stands for Computerized Adaptive Testing) — has the same questions as the paper version. The CAT-ASVAB adapts the questions it offers you based on your level of proficiency. (That's why it's called *adaptive.*) The first test item is of average difficulty. If you answer this question correctly, the next question is more difficult. If you answer the first question incorrectly, the computer gives you an easier question. (By contrast, on the pencil-and-paper ASVAB, hard and easy questions are presented randomly.) On the ASVAB, harder questions are worth more points than easier questions, so you want to get to them sooner, to maximize your score.

Pros

Maybe it's because young people today are more comfortable in front of a computer than they are with paper and pencil, but military recruiters have noted that, among applicants who have taken both the paper-based version and the computerized version of the ASVAB, recruits tend to score slightly higher on the computerized version of the test.

When you take the CAT-ASVAB, the computer automatically calculates and prints your standard scores for each subtest and your line scores for each service branch. (If you're interested in line scores, which are used for military job-classification purposes, you may want to pick up a copy of *ASVAB For Dummies.*) This machine is a pretty smart cookie — it also calculates your AFQT score on the spot. With the computerized version, you usually know if you qualify for military enlistment on the same day you take the test and, if so, which jobs you qualify for.

Cons

Unlike the pencil-and-paper version, you can't skip questions or change your answers after you enter them on the CAT-ASVAB. This restriction can make taking the test harder for some people. Instead of being able to go through and immediately answer all the questions you're sure of and then come back to the questions that require you to do some head scratching, you have to answer each question as it comes. Also, judging how much time to spend on a difficult question before guessing and moving on can be tough. Finally, if you have a few minutes at the end of the test, you can't go back and check to make sure you marked the correct answer to each question.

The pencil-and-paper test

Most people take the pencil-and-paper version of the ASVAB under the *Institutional ASVAB Program,* a cooperative program between the Department of Education and the Department of Defense at high schools all across the United States. Although the results of this version can be used for military enlistment purposes (if taken within two years of enlistment), its primary purpose is to serve as a tool for high school guidance counselors to use when recommending possible careers to high school students.

The pencil-and-paper version can also be taken for purposes of enlistment through a recruiter, but that's not done very often these days. In unusual circumstances, when it's impractical for an applicant to travel to a MEPS location, arrangements can be made to administer the pencil-and-paper version locally.

A final pencil-and-paper version of the ASVAB is the Armed Forces Classification Test (AFCT). This version of the ASVAB is used by folks already in the military who want to improve their ASVAB scores for the purposes of retraining into a different military job. Except for the name of the exam, the AFCT is exactly the same as the other versions of the ASVAB.

Pros

The paper-based test allows you to skip questions that you don't know the answer to and come back to them later. You can't do this on the CAT-ASVAB. This option can be a real help when you're racing against the clock and want to get as many answers right as possible. You can change an answer on the subtest you're currently working on, but you can't change an answer on a subtest after the time for that subtest has expired.

The mini-AFQT

There is sort of a "mini-AFQT" you may take in the recruiter's office. This test is called the Computer Adaptive Screening Test (CAST). Another version in use is called the Enlistment Screening Test (EST).

The CAST and EST are not qualification tests — they're strictly recruiting tools. These tests may be administered at the discretion of a recruiter. The CAST and EST contain questions similar (but not identical) to questions appearing on the ASVAB. They're used to help estimate an applicant's probability of obtaining a qualifying AFQT score. If you take one of these "mini-tests" and score low, you probably don't want to take the actual ASVAB until you've put in some extensive study time. In fact, many recruiters won't even schedule you for the ASVAB unless you score well on the CAST or EST.

You can mark up the exam booklet as much as you want. If you skip a question, you can circle the number of the question in your booklet to remind yourself to go back to it. If you don't know the answer to a question, you can cross off the answers that seem unlikely or wrong to you and then guess based on the remaining answers.

Cons

On the pencil-and-paper version, harder questions are randomly intermingled with easier questions, so you may find yourself spending too much time trying to figure out the answer to a question that's too hard for you, and you may miss answering some easier questions at the end of the subtest because you ran out of time. The result: Your overall score will be lowered.

The paper answer sheets are scored using an optical scanning machine. The machine has a conniption when it comes across an incompletely filled-in answer circle or stray pencil marks and will often stubbornly refuse to give you credit for these questions, even if you answered correctly.

Finally, it may take a week or more (sometimes up to a month — remember, we're talking military efficiency here) to get your scores.

Scoring the AFQT

If the military would simply score the subtests of the ASVAB as "number correct," or even "percent correct," a recruiter's life would be much easier. But, the military being the military, it does it the hard way.

The AFQT is often mistakenly called the "overall ASVAB score." It's not uncommon to hear someone say, "I got a 67 on the ASVAB," or "My ASVAB score was 92." That's not correct — it implies that the AFQT is derived from all nine subtests of the ASVAB, and it's not. The AFQT score is computed from just four of the ASVAB subtests — the four subtests of the ASVAB that measure your math and communicative ability (see "ASVAB: The Big Picture," earlier in this chapter).

In this section, I explain how the AFQT is scored.

Understanding raw scores

The military scores each subtest of the ASVAB using a raw score. A *raw score* is the total number of points you receive on each subtest of the ASVAB. Although you won't see your raw scores on the ASVAB score cards, they are used to calculate the other scores that the military uses, such as line scores used for job qualification.

You can't use the practice tests in this book (or any other ASVAB or AFQT study guide) to calculate your probable ASVAB scores. ASVAB scores are calculated using raw scores, and raw scores are not determined simply from the number of right or wrong answers. On the actual ASVAB, harder questions are worth more points than easier questions.

Computing the verbal expression score

The verbal expression (VE) score is used by the military to measure your communicative ability. The score is used not only when computing the AFQT score, but also to compute many of the military's *line scores* (scores that determine military job qualifications). The military brass (or at least their computers) determine your VE score by first adding the value of your Word Knowledge (WK) raw score to your Paragraph Comprehension (PC) raw score. The result is then converted to a scaled score, ranging from 20 to 62.

The AFQT score formula

To get your *AFQT raw score,* the computer doubles your VE score, and then adds your Arithmetic Reasoning (AR) score and your Mathematics Knowledge (MK) score to it. Here's the formula:

AFQT raw score = 2VE + AR + MK

You won't get to see what your AFQT raw score is on your ASVAB score sheet. The computer converts the score into a percentile score.

Normalizing the percentile score

Your AFQT raw score is converted to an AFQT *percentile score,* ranging from 1 to 99. How is that done? In 1997, the Department of Defense conducted a "Profile of American Youth" study, which examined the AFQT raw scores of a national probability sample of 18- to 23-year-olds who took the ASVAB during that year.

Your AFQT percentile score is derived by comparing your AFQT raw score to those of the approximately 14,000 young people who took part in the study. For example, an AFQT percentile score of 50 means that you scored better than 50 percent of the individuals included in the 1997 study.

Minimum Qualifying Scores

The primary purpose of the AFQT percentile score is to determine whether you qualify for the military service of your choice. Each of the branches has its own priorities, so they all have different minimum qualifying scores.

The AFQT tier categories

AFQT scores are grouped into five categories based on the percentile score ranges shown in Table 2-2. People who score in Categories I and II tend to be above average in trainability; those in Category III, average; those in Category IV, below average; and those in Category V, markedly below average.

Table 2-2	AFQT Tiers
Category	*Percentile Score*
I	93–100
II	65–92
III A	50–64
III B	31–49
IV A	21–30
IV B	16–20
IV C	10–15
V	0–9

If your AFQT percentile score falls into Category I, all the military services want you — and want you very badly. They also want you if your score falls into Category II or Category IIIA.

If your score falls into Category IIIB, you may or may not be able to enlist, depending in large part on how the branch is currently doing on making its recruiting goals.

Congress has directed that the military cannot accept Category V recruits or more than 4 percent of recruits from Category IV. If you're in Category IV, you must have a high school diploma to be eligible for enlistment; you can't do it with a GED. Even so, if your score falls into Category IV, your chances of enlistment are small — very small.

Making the military cut

Each of the services has established minimum AFQT qualification scores within its respective recruiting regulations:

> ✔ **Army (including Army National Guard and Army Reserves):** The Army requires a minimum AFQT score of 31 for those with a high school diploma and 50 for those with a GED. At times when the Army is experiencing high recruiting and reenlistment rates, it has been known to temporarily increase its qualifying AFQT score minimum to as high as 50.

✔ **Air Force (including Air National Guard and Air Force Reserves):** Air Force recruits must score at least 36 points on the AFQT to qualify for enlistment. In actuality, the vast majority (over 70 percent) of those accepted for an Air Force enlistment score 50 or above. For those who have a GED, rather than a high school diploma, the minimum is 65.

You're more likely to be struck by lightning than enlist in the Air Force without a high school diploma. Only about 0.5 percent of all Air Force enlistments each year are GED holders.

✔ **Navy:** Navy recruits must score at least 35 on the AFQT to qualify for enlistment. For GED holders, the minimum score is 50.

✔ **Navy Reserves:** The Navy Reserves requires a minimum score of 31 on the AFQT for those with a high school diploma and 50 for those with a GED.

The Navy is the only branch for which the requirements for the Reserves are different from the requirements for the branch itself.

✔ **Marine Corps (including Marine Corps Reserves):** Marine Corps recruits must score at least 32. Very few exceptions are made (about 1 percent) for some otherwise exceptionally qualified recruits with scores as low as 25. Those with a GED must score a minimum of 50 on the AFQT to be considered. The Marine Corps limits GED enlistments to no more than 5 percent per year.

✔ **Coast Guard (including Coast Guard Reserves):** The Coast Guard requires a minimum of 40 points on the AFQT. A waiver is possible for applicants with prior service if their ASVAB line scores (which are computed from the various ASVAB subtests) qualify them for a specific job and they're willing to enlist in that job. For the very few people (less than 5 percent) who are allowed to enlist with a GED, the minimum AFQT score is 50.

Just because you've met the minimum qualifying score for the service of your choice, that's no guarantee of enlistment. During good recruiting times, it's not uncommon for a military branch to get more qualified applicants than it has slots for. During these times, the military has to pick and choose which applicants to accept, and which ones to turn away. Quite often, they do this based on AFQT scores.

Also, enlistment incentives, such as enlistment bonuses and college funds (educational assistance) are often tied to minimum AFQT scores. As with quotas, this is subject to change at any time, based on the service's current recruiting needs.

Retaking the Test

You can't actually "fail" the AFQT, but you can fail to achieve a high enough score to enlist in the service you want. If this happens, that means your AFQT score was too low, which, in turn, means that you need to work on one (or more) of four areas: math knowledge, arithmetic reasoning, reading comprehension, and word knowledge. These are the four subtests that are used to calculate your AFQT score. Parts II and III of this book are specifically designed to help you improve your scores on these four subtests.

When you're sure that you're ready, you can apply (through your recruiter) for a retest.

ASVAB tests are valid for two years, as long as you aren't in the military. In most cases, after you join the military, your ASVAB scores remain valid as long as you're in. In other words, except in a few cases, you can use your enlistment ASVAB scores to qualify for retraining years later.

After you take an initial ASVAB test (taking the ASVAB in high school doesn't count as an initial test), you can retake the test after 30 days. After the retest, you must wait at least six months before taking the ASVAB again.

When you retake the ASVAB, it's not your highest score that counts, but rather the score on your *most recent* test. If you score lower on the retest, that is the score that will be used for your military enlistment.

The bad news is that you can't retake the ASVAB on a whim or whenever you feel like it. Each of the services has its own rules.

Army

The Army will allow a retest only if

- Your previous ASVAB test has expired. ***Remember:*** Test scores are valid for two years.
- You failed to achieve an AFQT score high enough to qualify for enlistment.
- Unusual circumstances occur. For example, if you're called away from the test because of an emergency, you can retake the test.

Army recruiters are not allowed to schedule a retest for the sole purpose of increasing scores in order to qualify for enlistment incentives, job qualifications, or other special enlistment programs.

Air Force

The Air Force does not allow you to retest after you've enlisted in the Delayed Entry Program (DEP). Current policy allows retesting of applicants who are not in the DEP, but already have a qualifying AFQT score. Retesting is authorized when the applicant's current *line scores* (job qualification scores) limit the ability to match an Air Force skill with his qualifications.

These days, you can just take the ASVAB and a medical examination and head straight out to basic training. You have to wait your turn. The military only has so many basic training slots each month, and they have to reserve a slot for you (often several months in the future). To ensure your commitment, the services enlist you in the DEP. Under this program, you're enlisted in the inactive reserves, while waiting for your basic training date to arrive.

Navy

The Navy allows you to retake the test if your previous ASVAB test has expired, or you've failed to achieve a qualifying AFQT score for enlistment in the Navy.

In most cases, individuals in the DEP cannot retest. One notable exception is the Navy's DEP Enrichment Program. This program provides for the provisional DEP enlistment of high school diploma graduates with AFQT scores between 28 and 30. Individuals enlisted under the program are enrolled in academic enhancement training, retested with the ASVAB, and accessed onto active duty as long as they score 31 or higher on the subsequent ASVAB retest.

Marine Corps

The Marine Corps will authorize a retest if your previous test is expired. Otherwise, recruiters can request a retest as long as the retesting is being required because the initial scores (considering your education, training, and experience) do not appear to reflect your true capability.

Additionally, the retest cannot be requested *solely* because your initial test scores did not meet the standards prescribed for specific military job qualification.

Coast Guard

For Coast Guard enlistments, six months must elapse since your last test before you may retest solely for the purpose of raising scores to qualify for a particular enlistment option. The Coast Guard Recruiting Center may authorize retesting after 30 days have passed from an initial ASVAB test if substantial reason exists to believe that your initial AFQT score or subtest scores do not reflect your education, training, or experience.

Chapter 3
The Art of Studying and Test Taking

• •

In This Chapter

▶ Reading the right way

▶ Discovering your learning style

▶ Making time to study

▶ Sitting down to the test

• •

A military career is all about taking tests. You take tests to enter the military, you take tests in basic training, you take tests when learning your new military job, you take tests to re-certify in your military job every few years, and you even take tests to earn promotions!

As a first sergeant, if I had a dime for every time I heard someone say, "I just can't take tests," then, well, then I'd have a lot of dimes. I said it then to the troops, and I'll say it to you now: There's no such thing. If you couldn't take tests, you never would've made it through high school or gotten a GED, and one of the two is required in order to join the military. The truth of the matter is that, when people get out of a school environment, they quickly lose the motivation and skills to study properly. Lack of success in test taking has more to do with ineffective study skills and techniques than intellectual ability.

Effective studying doesn't happen overnight. Studying requires time and patience. Getting the highest possible AFQT score is very much an individual affair — there is no one path that will always produce the best results for everyone. Studying is a process that you learn through trial and error — you have to discover a strategy that works for you.

By incorporating the reading rules, study strategies, and test-taking techniques covered in this chapter, you should increase your chances of achieving the study and test-taking goals you set for yourself.

Reading for Study

I know what you're thinking: "Wait a minute. You talk about reading comprehension in Chapter 6. Why am I reading about reading here?" Reading for the purposes of study is a different kind of reading. Reading comprehension only requires you to place information into short-term memory long enough to answer a question about it a few seconds later. In order to read for the purposes of study, you need to commit important information to your long-term memory — at least long enough to take the ASVAB.

Survey, question, read, recall, and review

This method is affectionately known as the SQR[3] method by those who make a living teaching students how to study. This method helps you separate the important information from the chaff.

Survey

The first step is to survey the material to get the big picture. This quick preview allows you to focus your attention on the main ideas and to identify the sections you want to read in detail. The purpose is to determine which portions of the text are most applicable to your task. Read the table of contents, introduction, section headings, subheadings, summaries, and the bibliography. Skim the text in between. Be sure to look at any figures, diagrams, charts, and highlighted areas.

Question

After you've gained a feel for the substance of the material, compose questions about the subject you want answered. First, ask yourself what you already know about the topic. Next, compose your questions.

Read

Now go back and read those sections you identified during your survey and search for answers to your questions. Look for the ideas behind words.

Recall

To help retain the material, make a point to summarize the information you've read at appropriate intervals — such as the end of paragraphs, sections, and chapters. Your goal is not to remember *everything* you've read — just the important points. Recite these points silently or aloud. Reciting the points will help you improve your concentration. You can also jot down any important or useful points. Finally, determine what information you still need to obtain.

Review

This last step involves reviewing the information you've read. Skim a section or chapter immediately after you finish reading it. You can do this by skimming back over the material and by looking at any notes you made. Go back over all the questions you posed and see if you can answer them.

Taking notes

Reading something once is not enough to really learn it. That's why note taking is so important. Clearly written, accurate notes help to capture information for later study and review. Taking notes also helps you to focus and learn during your study time.

Here are some note-taking and note-studying tips:

- ✔ **Organize the information.** Arrange data or ideas into small groups that make sense to you. The smaller groups will make it easier to remember the information.

- ✔ **Make the information relevant.** Connect the new information with the information you already know. Recalling the information you already know about a subject makes it easier to recall the new stuff.

- ✔ **Learn actively.** Use all your senses. Don't just speak aloud when reviewing your notes — get your entire body into the act. Get up and move around as if you're practicing for a speech.

- ✔ **Use your long-term memory.** To commit information to your long-term memory, review the material several times. Take advantage of your ability to remember best what you read last by changing the order of the information you recite during your review.

Putting Study Strategies to Work for You

Knowing how to study is like knowing how to fish. It's a set of learning skills that lasts a lifetime and brings many rewards. Just as there are many ways to fish, there are many ways to study. The key is finding the techniques that work best for you.

Working with your own learning style

Individuals learn best in individual ways. Some people may learn faster by hearing something. For others, seeing something may be the way. Still others may learn best by doing something. No one style of learning is better than another. However, by identifying your dominant learning style, you can adjust your study techniques to your individual learning abilities.

Auditory learners

Auditory learners use hearing to process information. When given a choice, strong auditory learners will sit where they can easily hear the speaker and where outside sounds will not interfere. Some auditory learners sit to one side, on the side of their strongest ear. Many times, auditory learners have an easier time understanding the words from songs on the radio and announcements on public address systems than other people do.

Here are some characteristics of auditory learners:

- ✔ They prefer to hear information.

- ✔ They have difficulty following written directions.

- ✔ They have difficulty with reading and writing.

- ✔ They may not look the speaker in the eye; instead, they may turn their eyes away so they can focus more on listening.

If you're an auditory learner, keep in mind the following study suggestions:

- ✔ Use audiotapes or CDs for reading and lectures (when available).

- ✔ Participate in discussions, ask questions, and repeat given information.

- ✔ Summarize or paraphrase written material, and record the information.

- ✔ Discuss the material with someone else.

Visual learners

Visual learners need to see the big picture. They may choose a seat where they can see the whole stage or the whole screen. They may like the back seat so everything is out in front and they can see it all. Visual learners survey the scene, like to sightsee, and see the forest despite the trees.

Visual learners share the following characteristics:

- They need to see it to learn it — they must have a mental picture.
- They have artistic ability.
- They have difficulty with spoken directions.
- They find sounds distracting.
- They have trouble following lectures.
- They may misinterpret words.

If you're a visual learner, follow these suggestions:

- Use visuals (graphics, films, slides, illustrations, doodles, charts, notes, and flashcards) to reinforce learning.
- Use multicolored highlighters to organize your notes.
- Write down directions.
- Visualize words, phrases, and sentences to be memorized.
- Write everything down; review often.

Tactile learners

Tactile learners have the need to touch and feel things. They want to feel or experience the lesson themselves. Given a choice, strong tactile learners will be right in the middle of the action. They tear things apart to see how they work and put them back together without the directions. Tactile learners immediately adjust the seat, mirror, radio, and temperature when they get in the car.

Here are some characteristics of tactile learners:

- They prefer hands-on learning or training.
- They can put a bicycle together without the directions.
- They have difficulty sitting still.
- They learn better when they can get involved.
- They may be coordinated and have athletic ability.

If you're a tactile learner, try the following strategies:

- Make a model, do lab work, role-play, "be the ball."
- Take frequent breaks.
- Copy letters and words to learn how to spell and remember facts.
- Use a computer to study as much as possible.
- Write facts and figures over and over.
- Read and walk, talk and walk, repeat and walk.

Getting the most out of your study time

Whether you're studying for the ASVAB, the AFQT, military promotion tests, or a college course, proper study techniques will help you attain your goals.

Staying motivated

Studying and learning can take you so far in life, yet it can feel so hard to get down to it. Whether studying for college or to advance your career, studying can be one of the most important things you should be doing. Modern life — whether commercials, the Internet, friends, or TV — continually demands your attention, and all these things can feel easier to attend to than study. So, what can you do to help stay motivated?

- ✔ **Give your study the attention it deserves.** If you were totally isolated, say on a desert island, where there was absolutely nothing else to do other than study, you'd study every last morsel of your subject until you were completely versed in it because there would be nothing else to distract you. Imagine being in a cell with no TV and nothing except *ASVAB AFQT For Dummies.* You'd certainly read it cover to cover — and maybe many times! You'd know this book inside out because it's all you'd have to do. Having too much choice, too much possibility over what you pay attention to means that now, more than ever before in history, you need to exert willpower to stay motivated.

- ✔ **Think about your goals.** Consider why you're studying and what you're studying for because, presumably, it connects to what you want your life to be. All kinds of things may distract you when you're not studying. But ask yourself, do you want your life to be about drinking coffee, playing computer games, watching TV, and chatting with friends, or do you have bigger fish to fry? Your life is about what you do with it, day in and day out.

- ✔ **Feed and develop your mind.** We live in a culture of entertainment where everything is supposed to be fun and exciting. If you buy into this idea too much, then you stop benefiting from the more subtle stimuli, because they don't immediately excite you. Your mind needs the rigor of study as well as the relaxation of entertainment. When you study well, you find it has its own subtle pleasures and satisfactions above and beyond the good results it can bring into your life. Imagine what it would be like to feel compelled to study hard and well.

Managing your time

You may have all the time in the world, but if you don't use it wisely, it won't help you to meet your goals. Procrastination is a problem for many people studying for the ASVAB or AFQT. The following tips will help you deal with this issue:

- ✔ **Clear your schedule.** Recognize that your obligations and the resulting stress are as important as other people's needs. Set limits around being interrupted or rescheduling your work time to accommodate others. Omit or reschedule some of your other obligations. You want to give full concentration to your studies without feeling guilty about what you're *not* doing.

- ✔ **Create a work area that is free from distractions and commit to staying there for at least one to two hours.** If you get side-tracked, remind yourself how this activity will help you to meet your goals.

- ✔ **Prioritize.** What has to be done first? What is worth more in terms of your AFQT score? (Chapter 2 can help you with this.) What is worth more in terms of your personal, educational, or career goals?

✔ **Use a daily to-do list.** This list will help you reach your goals and prioritize your daily tasks. As soon as you've completed a task, check it off your list. If you like keeping things on your computer, check out Remember The Milk (www.rememberthemilk.com), a free online to-do list.

✔ **Break down your study into chunks.** Estimate how much time you'll need to complete the task. Don't try to do it all at once. Break it down so that it's doable and not so overwhelming. Stay up to date on assignments to help avoid overload.

✔ **Recognize that you don't have to be perfect.** Some people are so afraid that they won't perform perfectly that they don't do anything at all. Make sure you understand your goals. Then evaluate how important your study is and what level of performance is acceptable to you. Then just do it!

If you score better than the 50th percentile on the AFQT, you become a very attractive candidate to the military. You don't need a perfect score to get recruiters to chase you all over town.

✔ **Make study enjoyable.** Work on this task first, while you have more energy. Reward yourself when you check tasks off your daily to-do list.

You're only human, so you'll probably gravitate toward studying the subject areas that you have an interest in or that you're good at. If you're an avid reader, don't spend too much of your time studying reading comprehension. (You're already going to ace that part of the test.) On the other hand, if you had a hard time in math in high school, you'll want to spend extra time brushing up on your arithmetic skills.

Finding the right place to study

After you've found the time to study, commit to a time and place that meets your needs. In order to do this, ask yourself whether the environment in which you're studying matches your learning style. If you don't know your dominant learning styles, refer to the "Working with your own learning style" section, earlier in this chapter. Here are some aspects of the study environment you may need to consider:

✔ **Time of day:** Whenever possible, schedule your most challenging courses and most intense study sessions during the time of day when you're most alert. Some people are at their best in the morning; others don't get rolling until late afternoon. You know how you work, so plan to study when you can give your best to it.

✔ **Posture and mobility:** Some people prefer to sit at a table or desk (in a formal posture) in order to concentrate and study effectively. Others are able to learn more easily while sitting comfortably on a sofa or lying on the floor (in an informal posture). Still others need to move about in order to learn; reading while walking on a treadmill may be appropriate for them. Some people can sit and study for long periods of time (they have high persistence), while others need to take frequent breaks (they have low persistence). Recognizing your posture and mobility needs will help you to plan where and when you should study.

✔ **Sound:** Contrary to popular belief, not everyone needs to study in a perfectly quiet environment. If you do choose to study to music, choose baroque classical music, such as Johann Sebastian Bach and Antonio Vivaldi. The tempo and instrumentation of this music seems to be most compatible with study and learning.

Several studies have shown that baroque music, with a 60 beats-per-minute beat pattern, activates the left and right brain. The simultaneous left- and right-brain action maximizes learning and retention of information, according to one study conducted by the Center for New Discoveries in Learning.

- **Lighting:** Studies have shown that some people become depressed because of light deprivation during the winter months. If you're one of those people, try to study and spend as much time as possible in highly lit places.

  Other studies have shown reading ability can be affected by the light contrast between print and paper color. There is a high contrast between black letters printed on white paper. Some people find it easier to read black print on blue or gray paper, which has less contrast and is easier on their eyes. (You can't always choose the paper your study material is printed on, but you can choose it for note-taking and reviewing purposes.) Light does make a difference, so study in the environment that best matches your learning preferences.

- **Temperature:** You can't always control the temperature of a room, but you should be aware of your preference for either a cool or warm environment. Dress in layers so that you can adjust to differences in room temperatures. Study in the environments in which you feel most comfortable.

Setting goals

Setting goals is a good way to accomplish a particularly difficult task. Developing study skills is one such task that takes time and effort to master. By setting *S.M.A.R.T.* goals related to an area of your study skills that needs improvement, you'll be studying like a pro in no time! S.M.A.R.T. goals are

- **Specific:** After you decide what you want to work on, narrow it down to one thing. Be as specific as possible. Working out one problem at a time will make it much easier to reach your goal without spreading yourself too thin. "I want to be a better reader" is too broad. Be more specific — for example, you might say, "I want to improve my reading speed." Write down this specific goal.

- **Measurable:** Goals can only be achieved if they can be measured in some way. For example, instead of "I want to improve my reading speed," a measurable goal would be "I want to improve my reading speed by ten words per minute."

- **Action:** This is where you decide how you're going to achieve your goal. Write this part as an "I will" statement. Following the example I give in the last bullet, your goal would now look something like, "I want to improve my reading speed by ten words a minute. I will do this by skimming over words like *the* and *an*."

- **Realistic:** Make sure your goals are within reach. "I will improve my reading speed by memorizing every word in the dictionary" is not reasonable for most people. Everyone has limits due to time, resources, or ability. Don't ignore these restraints or you'll be setting yourself up to fail.

- **Timeline:** Set a date to accomplish the goal. Make sure this date is both specific and realistic for you. "I will meet this goal sometime over the summer" is vague. Try something more like, "I will meet this goal by the first day of school next fall." This gives you a definite time to shoot for and will help keep you working toward the goal. Goals can take only a few days to achieve, or they may take months or years. Just be sure to make it a realistic timeline for you and your lifestyle.

Taking the Test: Putting Your Best Foot Forward

Sooner or later, the time for you to actually sit down and take the ASVAB will arrive. It may arrive before you think you're ready. Or you may think that test day can't get here fast enough. Regardless of which group you fall into, by understanding test-taking techniques, keeping a positive attitude, and overcoming your fears, you'll improve your test-taking ability.

Approach the big test as you'd approach a giant jigsaw puzzle. It may be tough, but you can do it! A positive attitude goes a long way toward success. Use the practice tests in Part IV to familiarize yourself with the test structure and to build your confidence in the subject matter. Although the questions are not the exact questions you'll see on the ASVAB, they are very, very similar. If you score well on the practice tests, you'll score well on the AFQT.

Some of the tricky problems can knock you off balance. However, if you prepare a plan of attack for what to do if you get stuck, you won't get worried or frustrated. In each of the chapters where I describe the individual tests (Chapters 5, 7, 9, and 11), I give you tips about what to do when all looks bleak. Go over these individual techniques before the test and make sure you have them down pat.

The night before

Cramming doesn't work. If you've followed a study plan, the night before the test you should do a quick review and get to bed early. *Remember:* Your brain and body need sleep to function well, so don't stay up late!

On the afternoon or evening before the test, get some exercise. Exercise can help you remain mentally sharp.

The night before the test is not the best time to go out for a few beers with your friends — headaches and the ASVAB don't work well together.

Test day

In the military, there is a saying that "If you're on time, you're late." You hear this more than once in basic training. If you're taking the ASVAB for the purposes of joining the military (chances of that are pretty good, if you're reading this book), then there is a better than 90 percent chance you'll be taking the test at a Military Entrance Processing Station (MEPS), and your recruiter has arranged your transportation.

At most stations, they conduct the ASVAB test in the afternoon, then set you up with a hotel room to continue processing (medical examination, job selection, security clearance interview, and so on) early the next morning.

Arrive prepared

Your recruiter should brief you about what to expect and, in some cases, may even drive you to the MEPS herself. In other cases, depending on how far you live from the closest MEPS, you may be provided with public transportation. In any case, you want to make sure you're on time and ready:

- ✓ **Eat a light meal before the test (breakfast or lunch, depending on the test time).** You'll be better able to think when you have some food in your stomach. However, don't eat too much. You don't want to be drowsy during the test. Also, don't drink too much water. The test proctors will allow you to use the bathroom if you need to, but if you need to go in the middle of one of the subtests, the clock doesn't stop.

- ✓ **If possible, arrange to arrive at the test site a little early, find a quiet place (such as your recruiter's car), and do a ten-minute power-study to get your brain turned on and tuned up.**

- ✓ **Bring only the paperwork your recruiter gave you and a photo ID.** Don't bring a calculator, your iPod, a backpack, or a sack full of munchies to the testing site. You won't be allowed to have them with you.

✔ **Keep in mind that MEPS is owned and operated by the military, so it doesn't have much of a sense of humor when it comes to dress codes.** Dress conservatively. Don't wear clothes with holes in them or profanity written on them. The only ones at the MEPS who want to see your underwear are the doctors during the physical exam. Leave your hat at home, because, under the military civilian dress code, you can't wear hats indoors.

Read the directions

Although instructing you to read the directions may seem obvious, when you're in a hurry, you can sometimes *misread* the directions, and that won't help you get the right answer. Each subtest has a paragraph or two describing what the subtest covers and instructions on how to answer the questions.

Understand the question

Take special care to read the questions correctly. Most questions ask something like, "Which of the following equals 6?" But sometimes, a question may ask, "Which of the following does *not* equal 6?" You can easily skip right over the *not* when you're reading, and get the question wrong.

You also have to understand the terms being used. When a math problem asks you to find the product of two numbers, be sure you know what *finding the product* means. (It means you have to multiply the two numbers.) If you add the two numbers together, you arrive at the wrong answer.

Review all the answer options

Often, people read a question, decide on the answer, glance at the answer options, choose the option that agrees with their answer, mark it on the answer sheet, and then move on.

Although this approach usually works, it can sometimes lead you astray. On the ASVAB, you're supposed to choose the answer that is "most correct." (Now and then, you do the opposite and choose the answer that is "least correct.") Sometimes several answers are reasonably correct for the question at hand, but only one of them is "most correct." If you don't stop to read and review all the answers, you may not choose the one that is "most correct." Or, if you review all the answer options, you may realize that you hastily decided upon an incorrect answer because you misread it.

When in doubt, guess. On the ASVAB, guessing is okay. In fact, it's encouraged. If you choose the correct answer, that's the equivalent of +1 (or more, depending on how the question is weighted). If you don't answer a question, that's the equivalent of 0. If you guess on a question and get the question wrong, that's also the equivalent of 0, not –1. (No penalties here!) But, if you guess, and you guess correctly, that's +1 (or more).

In each of the chapters on a particular subtest (Chapters 5, 7, 9, and 11), I give you hints for making educated guesses that are specific to that topic. But here are some general rules:

✔ **Usually, an answer that has *always, all, everyone, never, none,* or *no one* is incorrect.**

✔ **If two choices are very similar in meaning, *neither of them* is probably the correct choice.**

✔ **If two answer options contradict each other, *one of them* is usually correct.**

✔ **The longer the answer, the more likely that it's the correct answer.** The test makers have to get all those qualifiers in there to make sure that it's the correct answer and you can't find an example to contradict it. If you see phrases like *in many cases* or *frequently,* that's a clue that the test makers are trying to make the answer "most correct."

✔ **Don't eliminate an answer based on the frequency of that answer coming up.** For example, if Choice B has been the correct answer for the last five questions, don't assume that it must be the wrong answer for the question you're on just because that would make it six in a row.

✔ **If all else fails, trust your instincts.** Often, your first instinct is the correct answer.

The Air Force Senior NCO Academy conducted an in-depth study of several Air Force multiple-choice test results, taken over several years. They found that when students changed answers on their answer sheets, they changed from a right to a wrong answer more than 72 percent of the time! The students' first instinct was the correct one.

Part II
English as a First Language

"What are you studying? Homonyms? Yeah, they're a real pane in the glass."

In this part . . .

Success in the military has a lot to do with how well you can read, understand what you're reading, and react to what you've read. The military loves writing things down. When you set sail for a military career, you'll find all kinds of written instructions to follow. If you don't read and follow instructions accurately, you may guide the sub you're navigating to Alaska instead of Hawaii.

In this part, I explain why doing well on the AFQT vocabulary and reading subtests is important, and I give you the tools to accomplish the mission. I include a review of basic vocabulary and reading information — rock-solid advice like how to find the main idea of a paragraph and ways to understand the definition of a vocabulary word based on context, roots, prefixes, and suffixes.

Chapter 4

Prefabricating a Voluminous Vocabulary

The military is in love with words. Military personnel write almost everything down in memos, manuals, regulations, standard operating procedures, and policy letters. They should hire a few *For Dummies* authors to write these, because the current writers seem to love fancy words. A hammer isn't a hammer in the military; it's a "manually operated nail impact implement." The boss of your duty section isn't "the boss," or even "the supervisor"; she's the "noncommissioned officer in charge" (NCOIC for short).

If you're going to be successful in the military, you have to have a solid vocabulary, and that's why the military includes a Word Knowledge subtest as part of the AFQT score. How will you be able to obey a regulation, if you don't know what the words mean? And, trust me, failure to obey a regulation is a big no-no in the military.

Your score on the Word Knowledge subtest, along with your score on the Paragraph Comprehension subtest (see Chapters 6 and 7), are used to compute what the military calls a *verbal expression* (VE) score. The VE score is then combined with your Arithmetic Reasoning score (see Chapters 10 and 11) and your Mathematics Knowledge score (see Chapters 8 and 9) to compute your AFQT score. (For more information on how these scores combine, turn to Chapter 2.)

The VE score is also used to determine qualification for many military jobs. If you're interested in which military jobs require a good VE score, you may want to consider picking up a copy of the bestselling *ASVAB For Dummies*, written by your friendly neighborhood ASVAB expert (me), and published by Wiley.

The good news is that anybody can improve his vocabulary. Ever since you first learned to talk, you've been learning new words and their meanings. In this chapter, I give you some hints, tips, and techniques that you can use to speed up the process.

Growing Your Vocabulary

Your vocabulary naturally grows throughout your life. Even grumpy old writers like me learn a new word once in a while through everyday life experiences. But if the ASVAB is staring you in the face, you may not want to wait for life's natural process. In the following sections, you descry omnifarious contrivances to expedite progression of a comprehensive phraseology. I'm sorry — I got carried away. What I mean is that you'll find some ways to improve your vocabulary.

The more you read, the more you learn

People who read a lot have larger vocabularies than people who don't read much. That sounds kind of obvious, but I'm sure the government has spent a few thousand dollars funding studies to confirm this.

It doesn't matter much what you read, as long as you make it a regular, daily practice. You don't have to read Homer or Keats. Leave that to the intellectuals in the Berkeley coffee shops. Your reading choices could be action-adventure or romance books for enjoyment, the daily newspaper, magazines, Internet articles and blogs, or even comic books. (If it weren't for Batman and Robin, I wouldn't know what "Zow!" means.)

When reading online, get into the habit of keeping an extra browser window open and pointed to an online dictionary site, such as www.dictionary.com. That way, if you run into a word you don't know, you can quickly highlight it and copy and paste it to the online dictionary.

Talking to people

Other people have vocabularies that differ from yours. If you speak to a variety of people, and you do it often, you'll be exposed to a variety of different cultures and occupations, all of which will expose you to new words.

Carry a small pocket notebook with you wherever you go. That way, when you come across a new word, you can write it down and look it up in a dictionary later.

Adding words to your vocabulary

Make it a goal to learn at least one new word per day. A great way to do this is to visit or subscribe to one of the many Internet word-of-the-day Web sites. Here are a few suggestions:

- **Dictionary.com:** You can visit the site daily, or subscribe to the word of the day via e-mail. Visit http://dictionary.reference.com/wordoftheday.

- **Merriam-Webster Online:** A new vocabulary word appears every single day. Point your browser to www.merriam-webster.com/cgi-bin/mwwod.pl.

- **A.Word.A.Day:** Provided by Wordsmith.org, this free service presents a new word for you to check out every day, or you can subscribe to its e-mail list. The site is www.wordsmith.org/words/today.html.

- ***The New York Times* Word of the Day:** *The New York Times* offers a new word every day, along with an example of how the word was used in a recent *New York Times* story. Visit www.nytimes.com/learning/students/wordofday/index.html.

- ***The Oxford English Dictionary:*** If you want more than just a word and definition, try the *Oxford English Dictionary* word of the day. In addition to definitions, the page also provides pronunciation, spelling, etymology, and a date chart, showing when the word was first used. The word of the day is also available by e-mail subscription and RSS feed. Check out www.oed.com/cgi/display/wotd.

RSS feeds have sprung up all over the Internet. Instead of clicking around all your favorite sites to check for anything new or interesting, subscribing to an RSS feed allows the site to send the information directly to you. You can read RSS feeds in a feed reader, like the free Google Reader (http://reader.google.com).

A crossword success story

My late father never finished high school. (That wasn't unusual in the 1940s, when many kids dropped out of school to work on family farms.) However, my dad had the most extensive vocabulary of anyone I've ever known. His secret? From the age of 20 on, my dad was hooked on the daily crossword puzzle that was published in the local newspaper. He did the crossword puzzle every single day of his life at the morning breakfast table, and if he didn't have time to finish, he would save it until he got home from work. Woe be to the family member who accidently threw away the paper if Dad hadn't finished the puzzle that morning.

Try to use your new word in conversation a couple of times. That will help you to remember the word. Writing a few example sentences using new vocabulary will help you remember the new words in context.

Using puzzles and games to improve your vocabulary

A fun way to increase your word knowledge is to do crossword puzzles or play word games. Scrabble and Mad Libs, for example, are great ways to reinforce new vocabulary words.

Microsoft has launched an online game site, called Club Bing (www.clubbing.com), where you can play many word games online and even win prizes! What more could you ask for? Practice your vocabulary, and maybe win an MP3 player to boot! Word games include Banana Shuffle, Chicktionary, Clink, Flexicon, Seekadoo, and more.

You're on my list: Word lists

Learning a new word every day won't do you much good if you forget it a week later. Learning often requires repetition, and that's especially true when it comes to memorizing new words.

Keep a list of all the new words you learn and go over that list at least two or three times a week, until you're sure the new words have become part of your vocabulary.

Just to get you started, I'll give you 50 free words (see Table 4-1).

Table 4-1		50 Vocabulary Words
Word	*Part of Speech*	*Meaning*
Abrupt	Adjective	Beginning, ending, or changing suddenly
Acrid	Adjective	Harshly pungent or bitter
Becalm	Verb	To make quiet
Buffoon	Noun	A clown
Chaos	Noun	Utter disorder and confusion
Cognizant	Adjective	Taking notice of something

(continued)

Table 4-1 *(continued)*

Word	Part of Speech	Meaning
Defer	Verb	To put off or delay to a later time
Derision	Noun	The act of ridiculing or making fun of something
Effulgence	Noun	Splendor
Enmity	Noun	Hatred
Famish	Verb	To cause extreme hunger or thirst
Fealty	Noun	Loyalty
Generalize	Verb	To draw general inferences
Grotto	Noun	A small cavern
Habitual	Adjective	According to usual practice
Hideous	Adjective	Extremely ugly or appalling
Ichthyic	Adjective	Fish-like
Icon	Noun	An image or likeness
Illusion	Noun	An unreal image
Irritate	Verb	To excite ill temper or impatience in something
Jovial	Adjective	Merry
Juxtapose	Verb	To place close together
Kernel	Noun	A grain or seed
Kinsfolk	Noun	Relatives
Laggard	Adjective or noun	Falling behind or one who lags behind
Laud	Verb	To praise
Maize	Noun	Native American corn
Malevolence	Noun	Ill will
Nestle	Verb	To adjust cozily in snug quarters
Novice	Noun	Beginner
Obese	Adjective	Exceedingly fat
Obtrude	Verb	To be pushed or to push oneself into undue prominence
Pare	Verb	To cut, shave, or remove the outside from anything
Pedagogue	Noun	A schoolmaster
Quadrate	Verb	To divide into quarters
Quiescence	Noun	Quietness
Rancor	Noun	Malice
Raucous	Adjective	Harsh
Sanguine	Adjective	Cheerfully optimistic or having the color of blood

Word	Part of Speech	Meaning
Sepulcher	Noun	A burial place
Teem	Verb	To be full to overflowing
Tenacious	Adjective	Unyielding
Umbrage	Noun	Injury or offense
Vacillate	Verb	To waver
Valid	Adjective	Founded on truth
Velocity	Noun	Speed
Wile	Noun	An act or a means of cunning deception
Wizen	Verb	To become or cause to become withered or dry
Yokel	Noun	Country bumpkin
Zealot	Noun	One who espouses a cause or pursues an object in an immoderately partisan manner

Flashing yourself with flashcards

Flashcards have been around for a long time. They're still in wide use in these days of electronics and computers because they work. And they work especially well for subjects that just require simple memorization.

You can make flashcards out of any stiff paper material, like index cards, construction paper, or card stock.

Take the words from your list and write them on flashcards. Use only one word per card. Write the word on the front of the card and a short definition on the back.

As far back as 1885, a psychologist named Hermann Ebbinghaus, who specialized in memory research, published a study that detailed the effective use of flashcards. According to his rules, you should follow these steps:

1. **Review all the cards in the set, looking at each front and back.**

   Go through the set several times.

2. **Test and sort.**

   Read the front of the card. Try to say what's written on the back. If you're wrong, put the card in a "wrong" pile. Do this for each card, until the cards are sorted into "right" and "wrong" piles.

3. **Review the "wrong" pile.**

   Read each card in the "wrong" pile, front and back. Go through the "wrong" pile several times.

4. **Test and sort with the "wrong" pile.**

   Go through the cards of the "wrong" pile, testing yourself with them and sorting them into "right" and "wrong" piles, just as you did with all the cards in Step 2. Keep working with the cards of the "wrong" pile until all of them are in the "right" pile.

Building a Word from Scratch

Many English words are created from building blocks called roots, prefixes, and suffixes. Not every word has all three, but many have at least one. The *prefix* is the part that comes at the front of a word, the *suffix* is the part that comes at the end of a word, and the *root* is the part that comes in the middle of a word. Think of roots as the base of the word and prefixes and suffixes as word parts that are attached to the base.

If you don't know the meaning of a word, you can often break it down into smaller parts and analyze those part. For instance, *introspect* is made up from the root *spect,* which means to look, and the prefix *intro,* which means within. Taken together, *introspect* means "to look within." Wasn't that fun?

If you memorize some of these word parts, you'll have a better chance of figuring out the meaning of an unfamiliar word when you see it on the Word Knowledge subtest — and that's a good thing. Figuring out the meaning of unfamiliar words is how people with large vocabularies make them even larger. (They look up words in the dictionary, too.)

Rooting around for roots

A root is a word part that serves as the base of a word. If you recognize a root, you can generally get an idea of what the word means, even if you're not familiar with it. As Mr. Miyagi said in *Karate Kid,* "Root strong, tree grow strong." All right, Daniel-san, in terms of your vocabulary, think of it this way: If your knowledge of word roots is strong, your vocabulary will be much larger.

In Table 4-2, I list some common roots. Memorize them. When you sit down to take the ASVAB, you'll be glad that you did.

Table 4-2		Roots
Root	*Meaning*	*Sample Word*
anthro or anthrop	relating to humans	anthropology
bibli or biblio	relating to books	bibliography
brev	short	abbreviate
cede or ceed	go, yield	recede
chrom	color	monochrome
circum	around	circumnavigate
cogn or cogno	know	cognizant
corp	body	corporate
dic or dict	speak	diction
domin	rule	dominate
flu or flux	flow	influx
form	shape	formulate
frac or frag	break	fragment

Root	Meaning	Sample Word
graph	writing	biography
junct	join	juncture
liber	free	liberate
lum	light	illuminate
oper	work	cooperate
pat or path	suffer	pathology
port	carry	portable
press	squeeze	repress
scrib or script	write	describe
sens or sent	think, feel	sentient
tract	pull	traction
voc or vok	call	revoke

Prefixes and suffixes

A prefix is a group of letters added before a word or base to alter the base's meaning and form a new word. In contrast, a suffix is a group of letters added after a word or base. Prefixes and suffixes are called *affixes* because they are attached to a root.

Tables 4-3 and 4-4 list some common prefixes and suffixes. Each list has the word part, its meaning, and one word that uses each word part. Writing down additional words that you know for each word part will help you memorize the list.

Table 4-3	Prefixes	
Prefix	**Meaning**	**Sample Word**
a-	no, not	atheist
ab- or abs-	away, from	absent
anti-	against	antibody
bi-	two	bilateral
con- or contra-	against	contradict
de-	away from	deny
dec-	ten	decade
extra-	outside, beyond	extracurricular
fore-	in front of	foreman
geo-	earth	geology
hyper-	excess, over	hyperactive

(continued)

Table 4-3 *(continued)*

Prefix	Meaning	Sample Word
il-	not	illogical
mal- or male-	wrong, bad	malediction
multi-	many	multiply
nom-	name	nominate
omni-	all	omnibus
ped-	foot	pedestrian
que-, quer-, or ques-	ask	question
re-	back	return
semi-	half	semisweet
super-	over, more	superior
tele-	far	telephone
trans-	across	translate
un-	not	uninformed

Table 4-4   **Suffixes**

Suffix	Meaning	Sample Word
-able or -ible	capable of	agreeable
-age	action, result	breakage
-al	characterized by	functional
-ance	instance of an action	performance
-ation	action, process	liberation
-en	made of	silken
-ful	full of	helpful
-ic	consisting of	alcoholic
-ical	possessing a quality of	statistical
-ion	result of act or process	legislation
-ish	relating to	childish
-ism	act, practice	Buddhism
-ist	characteristic of	elitist
-ity	quality of	specificity
-less	not having	childless
-let	small one	booklet

Suffix	Meaning	Sample Word
-man	relating to humans, manlike	gentleman
-ment	action, process	establishment
-ness	possessing a quality	goodness
-or	one who does a thing	orator
-ous	having	dangerous
-y	quality of	tasty

A Word by Any Other Name: Synonyms and Antonyms

English is a complicated language. It would probably be easier for you to learn Spanish, German, or even Korean from scratch than it would be to learn English. How many other countries do you know that have to teach their own native language throughout all the school grades (and even college!)?

In the English language there is usually more than one way to say the same thing, even by swapping just one word. These different words with the same meaning are called *synonyms.* Synonyms are different words that have the same or very similar meanings. *Funny, amusing,* and *comical* are synonyms — they all mean the same thing.

In fact, that's what the Word Knowledge subtest on the ASVAB really does. It tests your ability to select synonyms for the underlined words contained in the question stem. Look at the following example.

Perform most nearly means:

(A) eat

(B) dance

(C) execute

(D) sing

The correct answer is C. *Execute* (to carry out something) is a synonym of *perform,* which means the same thing. Although you can perform a dance or perform a song, *dance* and *sing* don't actually mean the same thing as *perform.*

When you look up a new word in the dictionary (see the "Adding words to your vocabulary" section) and add it to your word list (see the "You're on my list: Word lists" section), you should include synonyms, because you're very likely to see these on the Word Knowledge subtest.

An *antonym* is a word that has the opposite or nearly opposite meaning of another word. *Smile* and *frown* are antonyms of one another. The test makers often use antonyms as wrong answers on the Word Knowledge subtest. Knowing antonyms for words not only improves your chances of narrowing your answer choices, but it will also improve your vocabulary. For example, if you know that *fast* is an antonym of *slow,* and you know what *slow* means, you also know what *fast* means.

How can you find the synonym of a word (or the antonym, for that matter)? A good place to start is the dictionary. Many dictionary entries include the abbreviation *syn*, which means *synonym*. The words that follow this abbreviation are synonyms of the entry word. You may also see the abbreviation *ant* in an entry. This abbreviation stands for *antonym*, and the word or words that follow it mean the opposite of the entry word.

Thesauruses are special dictionaries of synonyms and antonyms. We writers use them all the time to make us look smarter. There are several thesauruses online that you can use to look up synonyms for words on your word list. Here are a few:

- **Thesaurus.com:** http://thesaurus.reference.com
- **ARTFL Project:** http://humanities.uchicago.edu/forms_unrest/ROGET.html
- **Merriam-Webster Online:** www.merriam-webster.com

Getting Homogeneous with Homonyms

Some words in the English language are spelled the same but have two or more meanings. For example, a *fluke* can mean a fish, the end parts of an anchor, the fins on a whale's tail, or a stroke of luck.

Some words are spelled the same, but have different meanings and are often pronounced differently. The word *bow*, meaning a special kind of knot, is pronounced differently from *bow*, meaning to bend at the waist. *Bow*, meaning the front of a boat is pronounced the same as *bow*, meaning to bend at the waist, but *bow*, meaning a weapon is pronounced the same as *bow*, meaning a special knot. See why foreigners trying to learn English get frustrated?

Other words are pronounced the same but are spelled differently and mean something different. *To, too, two*, and *there, their*, and *there* are examples. All these types of words are collectively known as *homonyms*.

The last type of homonym is especially important when it comes to the Word Knowledge subtest of the ASVAB. The test makers won't try to trick you by having two homonym answers for words that are spelled the same but have multiple possible answers, but they will use homonyms that are spelled differently *and* have different meanings.

Flue most nearly means:

(A) sickness

(B) fly

(C) chimney

(D) None of the above

You may be tempted to choose A, but that would be correct if *flu* were the test word. The past tense of fly is *flew*. The word *flue* means a chimney pipe.

Table 4-5 shows you a few more examples of common homonyms.

Table 4-5		Common Homonyms
Word	**Definition**	**Example Sentence**
Allowed	Permitted	He <u>allowed</u> the audience to participate.
Aloud	Normal volume of speaking	They could not speak <u>aloud</u> in the library.
Cent	A bronze coin	I couldn't believe I got the comic for just one <u>cent</u>.
Scent	Aroma	The <u>scent</u> coming from the kitchen made my mouth water.
Sent	Past tense of *send*	He <u>sent</u> the letter Monday.
Cue	Stimulus to action	A door slamming was his <u>cue</u> to exit the stage.
Queue	Line	There was a large <u>queue</u> of cars waiting to park.
Die	To cease living	I'll <u>die</u> if my parents find out!
Dye	To color or stain	She wants to <u>dye</u> her hair red.
Elicit	To draw or bring out	He vowed to <u>elicit</u> the truth from his friend.
Illicit	Unlawful	He used <u>illicit</u> means to avoid paying taxes.
Fairy	Supernatural being	The <u>fairy</u> was dancing in the night.
Ferry	A boat for crossing rivers or other small bodies of water	The <u>ferry</u> took us quickly across the river.
Gorilla	Large ape	I threw the <u>gorilla</u> a banana.
Guerrilla	Irregular soldier	The band of <u>guerrillas</u> attacked the convoy.
Hangar	Building for airplanes	Jack pulled the aircraft into the <u>hangar</u>.
Hanger	A device for hanging things	Mom said to put the shirt on a <u>hanger</u>.
It's	Contraction of *it is*	<u>It's</u> a very hot day.
Its	Possessive pronoun	The bank said <u>its</u> savings accounts were the best.
Know	To possess knowledge	I <u>know</u> you went to the store.
No	Zero or negative	I told John there was <u>no</u> way we would travel together.
Lessen	To make less	We gave him medicine so his pain would <u>lessen</u>.
Lesson	Something to be learned	We must never forget the <u>lessons</u> of the past.
Mail	Postal delivery	I expected the check to be in the <u>mail</u>.
Male	A sex	The teacher asked all <u>males</u> to go to one room and all females go to another.
Naval	Pertaining to ships	He wanted to become a <u>naval</u> officer.

(continued)

Table 4-5 *(continued)*

Word	Definition	Example Sentence
Navel	Belly button	Mom always said not to play with my <u>navel</u>.
Ordinance	Decree or local law	Spitting on the sidewalk was against the town <u>ordinance</u>.
Ordnance	Military ammunition	We were running low, so we asked the sergeant for more <u>ordnance</u>.
Patience	The ability to suppress restlessness	I couldn't believe her <u>patience</u> with the students.
Patients	People under medical care	The nurse treated all her <u>patients</u> with respect.
Reek	Bad smell	The <u>reek</u> of the skunk invaded the living room.
Wreak	Inflict	Jack continued to <u>wreak</u> havoc every time he got upset.
Sleight	Dexterity	The magician's <u>sleight</u> of hand was amazing.
Slight	Small amount	There was only a <u>slight</u> increase in salaries this year.
Threw	Propelled by hand	He <u>threw</u> the ball to first base.
Through	In one side and out the other	Dad drove <u>through</u> the tunnel.
Vary	Change	The interest rate continues to <u>vary</u> up and down.
Very	Extreme	I am <u>very</u> happy with *ASVAB AFQT For Dummies*.
Weak	Not strong	After his illness, Paul was very <u>weak</u>.
Week	Seven days	It'll take at least a <u>week</u> to finish this report.
Your	Belongs to you	<u>Your</u> new car is really cool.
You're	Contraction of *you are*	<u>You're</u> going to be in trouble when Dad gets home.

You can see an extensive list of homonyms on Alan Cooper's Homonym Page at www.cooper.com/alan/homonym_list.html.

Chapter 5

The Word Knowledge Subtest

In This Chapter
▶ Looking at typical question types
▶ Guessing for the best score
▶ Testing your word knowledge

A decent vocabulary is essential in the military if you want to get ahead. The military operates on paperwork, and whether you're trying to get more supplies (submit necessary logistical requisitions) or get the assignment you want (application for personnel career-enhancement programs), you need to develop a good vocabulary.

Word Knowledge is what the military calls the vocabulary subtest on the ASVAB. Because a strong vocabulary is essential to success in the military, the Department of Defense has made this vocabulary test a part of the all-important AFQT score — the score that determines whether you're qualified to join the military service of your choice (see Chapter 2).

The Word Knowledge subtest is different from the other subtests that make up the AFQT in that, in general, either you know the answer at first glance, or you don't. People with larger vocabularies will score better on this subtest than those who have a limited knowledge of English words and what they mean.

Word knowledge isn't part of the AFQT score just because the military likes to use big words. It's included because words stand for ideas, and the more words you understand, the more ideas you can understand (and the better you can communicate with others). So, society (including people in the military) often equates a large vocabulary with intelligence and success.

Getting Acquainted with the Test Format

The Word Knowledge portion of the ASVAB measures your vocabulary knowledge. It consists of 35 questions, which usually come in one of two flavors. The first type of question asks for a straight definition. Your task is to choose the answer closest in meaning to the underlined word. Look at the following example:

<u>Abatement</u> most nearly means:

   (A) encourage

   (B) relax

   (C) obstruct

   (D) terminate

In this case, the correct answer is D, because abatement means putting and end to something or subsiding.

In the second type of question, you see an underlined word used in the context of a sentence. Again, your goal is to choose the answer closest in meaning to the underlined word as it is used in the sentence. For example:

His house was <u>derelict</u>.

(A) solid

(B) run-down

(C) clean

(D) inexpensive

Closest in meaning doesn't mean the exact same thing. You're looking for words most similar in meaning.

In case you're wondering, the answer is B.

Bumping Up Your Test Score

Usually, on the Word Knowledge subtest, you know the answer or you don't. Even with that restriction, however, you can learn a few tricks to get the best score possible.

Keeping an eye on the clock

Like all the ASVAB subtests, the Word Knowledge subtest is timed. You have 11 minutes to answer the 35 questions on this subtest, which means that you have slightly less than 20 seconds to answer each question. This is plenty of time, as long as you stay focused and don't waste time thinking about last night's date (sorry, I mean "social encounter").

If you're taking the computerized version of the ASVAB, your remaining time will be displayed on the computer screen. If you're taking the paper version of the test, a clock will be clearly visible in the room, and the test proctor will post the start and stop time for the subtest on a blackboard or whiteboard.

Watching out for the evil homonym

A *homonym* is a word with more than one meaning (see Chapter 4). The word may be spelled the same or it may be spelled differently, but either way it's pronounced the same.

There aren't any trick questions on the ASVAB. In other words, the test won't present you two legitimate answers and ask you to try to decide which one is the "best." However, homonyms can still trip you up if you don't pay attention. Look at the following example:

<u>Bate</u> most nearly means:

(A) tease

(B) lessen

(C) treasure

(D) pregnant

Bate and *bait* are homonyms. They are two words that sound the same, but they are spelled differently and mean different things. *Bait* means to torment or tease (it's also used to entice fish), and *bate* means to make less.

Some homonyms are spelled the same but have different meanings. You won't see multiple correct definitions on the Word Knowledge subtest when you're doing a direct definition problem, but you may see such multiple, correct definitions when the word is used in the context of a sentence. For example:

Jack tied a <u>bow</u> around his neck.

(A) knot

(B) weapon

(C) ship front

(D) respect

All the answer choices are proper definitions for the word *bow*. However, only one choice makes sense for bow in the context of the sentence. It just wouldn't make sense for Jack to tie a weapon, front of a ship, or respect around his neck.

When in doubt, guess

Sometimes on the Word Knowledge subtest, you just don't know the answer. In that case, don't leave it blank. (You can't leave answers blank on the computerized version of the test — just the paper version.) There are no penalties for wrong answers on the ASVAB. If you leave the answer blank, you have a 0 percent chance of getting it right. But if you make a wild guess, you have a 25 percent chance of stumbling upon the right answer.

Keep in mind that, although you may know the word in the question, you may not know one or more of the words in the multiple-choice answers. If this is the case, use process of elimination to narrow your choices. Eliminate the words you know *aren't* correct, and guess which of the remaining words is most *likely* correct.

Before making a wild guess, take a few seconds and look at the word from a different perspective. You may find that you know the word after all — just in a different form. In English, one root word can be changed slightly to perform all sorts of roles — it can act as a noun, a verb, an adjective, or an adverb with just a little modification. So, if you know what the root word *attach* means, you can figure out what the word *attachment* means. If you know *adherent,* you can deduce what *adherence* means. (You can find much more information on this topic in Chapter 4.)

You can use root word clues to identify unfamiliar words on the ASVAB. Say you run across the word *beneficent* on the Word Knowledge test:

<u>Beneficent</u> most nearly means:

(A) kind

(B) beautiful

(C) unhappy

(D) troubled

If you don't have a clue what the word *beneficent* means, all is not lost. Take a closer look. What other word starting with the letters *benefi* do you know? How about the word *benefit*? A benefit is something that helps or aids, so it would be a good bet that the word *beneficent* is related to helping or aiding. So when you look over the possible choices, you can choose the one that has something to do with helping.

But wait. None of the answers say *help* or *aid*. Now what? Just use process of elimination. If something is helpful (beneficent), it probably isn't troubled or unhappy. It may be beautiful, but more likely, it's kind. So the best answer would be A — and it just so happens that that's correct!

Trying On Some Sample Questions

Now you're ready to pit your skills against the Word Knowledge section of the ASVAB. Try these sample questions to see how you do. They're similar to what you'll see on the ASVAB.

1. <u>Bestial</u> most nearly means:

   (A) playful

   (B) animal-like

   (C) tantalizing

   (D) pregnant

The correct answer is B. *Bestial* is an adjective that means having animal characteristics. Noting the similarity between the words *bestial* and *beast* could lead you in the right direction with this question.

2. Tim <u>bombarded</u> the school board with questions about the new program.

   (A) asked

   (B) pleaded with

   (C) assailed

   (D) scheduled

The correct answer is C. Used as a verb, *bombard* means to overwhelm or assail. Observing that the root word is *bomb* should give you a clue as to the meaning of *bombarded*.

3. <u>Malignant</u> most nearly means:

   (A) tumor

   (B) angry

   (C) kind

   (D) evil

The correct answer is D. *Malignant* is an adjective that means evil or harmful. You may have been tempted to select A, because you may have heard of a malignant tumor, but *tumor* and *malignant* don't mean the same thing.

4. Bernard wanted to ask a lawyer if his friend's investment idea was *licit*.

    (A) legal

    (B) profitable

    (C) illegal

    (D) sensible

    The correct answer is A. *Licit* is an adjective that means lawful. Although you may not have been familiar with the word *licit,* chances are good that you've come across the opposite-meaning word, *illicit,* and you probably know that it means illegal. So, you can deduce that *licit* means the opposite of illegal, or legal.

5. Achromatic most nearly means:

    (A) automatic

    (B) tasty

    (C) colorless

    (D) manual

    The correct answer is C. *Achromatic* is an adjective that means having no color. If you knew that the word root *chrom* refers to color and that the prefix *a-* means without, you could figure out that *achromatic* means without color.

6. Peggy was angry over the umbrage she received from her brother.

    (A) gift

    (B) argument

    (C) hurt

    (D) dead flowers

    The correct answer is C. Used as a noun, *umbrage* means insult or feeling of hurt. Although the connection here is a bit out there, both *umbrage* and the more familiar word *umbrella* share the root meaning of shadow. Offended umbrage is a shadowy feeling. Umbrellas create shadows. Really, that's the connection.

7. Wry most nearly means:

    (A) smile

    (B) distorted

    (C) angry

    (D) happy

    The correct answer is B. *Wry* is an adjective that means crooked or twisted.

8. Melissa was justifiably proud of her recent abstinence.

    (A) grades

    (B) sobriety

    (C) trustworthiness

    (D) awards

    The correct answer is B. *Abstinence* is a noun that means the willful avoidance of a substance such as alcohol or drugs.

9. <u>Voluble</u> most nearly means:

    (A) fluent

    (B) taciturn

    (C) funny

    (D) religious

The correct answer is A. *Voluble* is an adjective that means fluent or glib.

10. Lyle's landlord instructed him to <u>vacate</u> the apartment.

    (A) paint

    (B) leave

    (C) clean

    (D) sell

The correct answer is B. *Vacate* is a verb that means to give up occupancy of a location. Word roots are key here. A *vac*ation involves leaving your normal place of residence. When people e*vac*uate an area, they leave that area. A *vac*uum is created when matter leaves a given area.

Chapter 6

Reading for Comprehension

The military services want their members not only to be able to read, but also to understand what they're reading. This is known as "reading comprehension," but the military being the military, calls its version "paragraph comprehension" and includes it as one of the ASVAB subtests that comprise your AFQT score.

Why does the military place so much importance on reading comprehension? Quite simple: Miscommunication has been the leading cause of almost every major military accident or battlefield disaster in history.

The military runs on paperwork. A former Air Force vice chief of staff once commented that he had looked at 13,000 pieces of paper in a five-day period. Granted, you won't see quite so much correspondence as a newly enlisted member, but you will have to read and understand your share of memos, policy letters, regulations, manuals, and forms. In fact, as an enlisted member, your promotions are based, in part, on how well you can read, comprehend, and retain information from written material. And, the higher you get in rank, the more paperwork you'll see.

Reading comprehension involves several skills that anyone can develop with practice. To thoroughly understand what you read, you must develop the ability to recognize the main idea, recall details, and make inferences about what you've read. The information in this chapter will help you improve your reading comprehension skills, making it possible for you to ace the Paragraph Comprehension subtest of the ASVAB.

Pointers about Points

When someone writes something, he almost always is trying to make a point. This message is called the *main point* or *principal idea* of the writing. The paragraph or passage may also contain information that supports or reinforces the main point; these little gems are called *subpoints*.

Picking out the main point

The main point is the most important part of a paragraph or passage. It's the primary theme that the writer wants you to understand. In many cases, the main point is stated simply. In other cases, it may be implied by the writer, rather than stated directly.

Quite often, the main point of the paragraph or passage is contained in the first sentence. You may recall from school that your English teacher referred to this sentence as the *topic sentence.* Sometimes the main point is rephrased or summarized in the last sentence of the passage. For example, in the following passage, the main idea is stated in the first sentence:

> U.S. Military forces will increasingly be called upon in the immediate future for peaceful military-to-military contacts, humanitarian intervention, peace support, and other nontraditional roles. The end of the Cold War transformed U.S. national security. The United States entered the 21st century with unprecedented prosperity and opportunities threatened by complex dangers. Problems associated with fostering a stable global system require the U.S. military to play an essential role in building coalitions and shaping the international environment in ways that protect and promote U.S. interests.

The main point is stated clearly in the very first sentence: "U.S. Military forces will increasingly be called upon in the immediate future for peaceful military-to-military contacts, humanitarian intervention, peace support, and other nontraditional roles." The sentences that follow are subpoints that help to clarify and emphasize the main point of the paragraph.

Sometimes the main point isn't found in the first sentence. Look at the passage again, slightly reworded:

> The end of the Cold War transformed U.S. national security. The United States entered the 21st century with unprecedented prosperity and opportunities threatened by complex dangers. Problems associated with fostering a stable global system require the U.S. military to play an essential role in building coalitions and shaping the international environment in ways that protect and promote U.S. interests. A key assumption is that U.S. Military forces will increasingly be called upon in peaceful military-to-military contacts, humanitarian intervention, peace support, and other nontraditional roles.

The main point of the paragraph remains the same, but it isn't stated until the last sentence.

Sometimes the main point isn't clearly stated but rather implied. Take a look at the following paragraph:

> The plane landed at 9 p.m. The children were disappointed that new security rules prevented them from meeting their father at the gate. They waited with their mother in the car outside the airport doors, amidst dozens of other people in vehicles, there for similar purposes. With each passing moment, their excitement grew. Finally, the automatic doors opened, and he walked out. "Dad! Hey, Dad!", the excited children yelled.

Though it's not directly stated, the main point of this paragraph is obviously that the children's father is coming home.

Take another look at the previous passage. When trying to determine the main point of a paragraph, ask yourself the following:

- ✔ **Who or what is this paragraph about?** A father returning to his family.

- ✔ **What aspect of this subject is the author talking about?** The moments before and the moment of the father's appearing at the airport doors.

- ✔ **What is the author trying to get across about this aspect of the subject?** The drama of the father's reunion with his family.

Simplifying subpoints

Most writers don't stick to just one point. If they did, most paragraphs could be reduced to just one sentence. But it doesn't work that way. Writers usually try to reinforce their main points by providing details. These details, or *subpoints,* may include facts or statistics, or they may be descriptions that support the main point of the passage. Subpoints help you see what the author is saying. Take, for instance, the following passage:

> For the purpose of drill, Air Force organizations are divided into elements, flights, squadrons, groups, and wings. The "rule of two" applies (that is, an element must consist of at least two people, a flight must consist of at least two elements, and so on). Usually, an element consists of between eight and ten people, and a flight has six or eight elements. Drill consists of certain movements by which the flight or squadron is moved in an orderly manner from one formation to another or from one place to another.

Notice how the writer uses the second, third, and fourth sentences to explain in detail how Air Force organizations are divided for the purposes of drill. These supporting details are subpoints.

In addition, look for signal words in the passage — words like *again, also, as well as, furthermore, moreover,* and *significantly.* These signal words may call your attention to supporting facts.

Analyzing What You've Read

Understanding what you read involves more than just picking out main points and subpoints. To analyze a paragraph, you need to examine a passage carefully and in detail, so as to identify causes, key factors, and possible results. Analyzing a passage requires you to draw conclusions from what you've read and understand relationships between the ideas presented in the text.

Say what? What does that passage mean?

By drawing conclusions about the meaning of a passage, you reach new ideas that the author implies but doesn't come right out and state. You must analyze the information the author presents in order to make inferences from what you've read. What conclusions can you infer from the following paragraph?

> The local school district is facing a serious budgetary crisis. The state, suffering a revenue shortfall of more than $600 million, has cut funding to the district by $18.7 million. Already, 65 teachers have been laid off, and more layoffs are expected.

Can you conclude that the local school district really stinks? Possibly, but that's not the point I'm trying to make. Although the author doesn't come straight out and say so, you can draw the conclusion that if the state revenue shortfall could somehow be corrected — by increasing state sales tax or income tax, for example — the local school district's budgetary crisis could be resolved. The author never actually makes this point in the paragraph. But by using reason and logic, you can draw this conclusion from the facts presented.

When analyzing a passage, leave your baggage at the door. For example, you may not like the current governor, but nothing in the passage suggests that the writer supports electing a new governor to solve the budget problem.

Say it again, Sam: Paraphrasing

Paraphrasing means to rewrite the passage using your own words. This strategy is often useful when you're trying to understand a complex idea. Putting it in your own words can help you understand the main idea, which can, in turn, help you discover information that may not be stated directly. It can also be helpful in making inferences and drawing conclusions from the information provided. Look at the following short passage:

> On-the-job training (OJT) is often the most effective method of training, because the employer tailors the training to meet the specific job requirements. OJT can be as casual as giving a few pointers to a new worker or as formal as a fully structured training program with timetables and specified subjects.

How would you paraphrase this passage? If you wrote something like the following, you'd be on the right track:

> Some OJT programs involve a formal lesson plan, while others are simply telling a new employee what to do and how to do it. OJT works well because new employees can be taught what they need to do the specific job.

Paraphrasing is just saying the same thing using different words. In basic training, your drill instructor may say, "You really need to work on your running time," or he may say "Get the %$@* lead out of your pants and run faster!" Both mean the same thing.

Improving Your Reading Comprehension Skills

Some people read and comprehend better than others, but one thing is for certain: You're not born with the ability to read — it's something you learn. Like almost anything that is learned, you can use proven techniques to help you learn to do it better:

- ✔ Read more, and watch TV less.
- ✔ Practice skimming and scanning.
- ✔ Learn to identify the main ideas and the all-important subpoints.
- ✔ Work on the meanings of strange or difficult words.
- ✔ Practice paraphrasing.
- ✔ Reflect on what you've read.

Taking the time to read

Joseph Addison once noted that "Reading is to the mind what exercise is to the body." My first tae kwon do instructor has been practicing his art for 52 years. He is very, very good at it. I have a good friend who has spent every day of his working life for the past 30 years working on air-conditioning systems. He can take your air conditioner apart and put it back together blindfolded in less time than it takes you to say, "I'm hot."

The point is that anything gets better with practice. If you don't read well, the chances are good that you don't read much. You don't need a $4-million government-funded study (although I'm sure there are a few) to know that people who read a lot are more likely to be better readers than people who don't read so much.

If you learn to read for fun, you'll automatically read more, and I guarantee that your reading skills will improve immeasurably after a relatively short time. So, how do you learn to read for fun? Simple: Choose reading material in subject areas that interest you.

You don't have to pick up *A Tale of Two Cities* or *War and Peace*. You can start with the newspaper, a biography of a person you admire, or magazines you find at the library. Personally, I like *For Dummies* books. If you devote at least one hour a day to improving your reading comprehension, you'll see results fast — maybe within a month or so.

Skimming and scanning

There are different styles of reading for different situations. The technique you choose will depend on the purpose for reading. For example, you may be reading for enjoyment, to find information, or to complete a task. If you're reading for enjoyment, you usually read and savor every word. However, in other situations — such as when you're just trying to find the main ideas or looking up specific information — you may not want to read every single word.

Skimming

You can skim to quickly identify the main ideas of a text. For example, most people don't read a newspaper word for word. Instead, they skim through the text to see if the article may be something they want to read in more depth. Most people can skim at a speed three to four times faster than normal reading. Skimming is especially useful if you have lots of material to read in a limited amount of time.

Here are some points to keep in mind when you practice skimming:

- ✒ If the article or passage has a title, read it. It's often the shortest possible summary of the content.
- ✒ Read the first sentence or paragraph. This introductory text often consists of the main point(s).
- ✒ If there are subheadings, read each one, looking for relationships among them.
- ✒ Look for clue words that answer who, where, how, why, and when.
- ✒ Pay attention to qualifying adjectives, such as *best, worst, most,* and so on.
- ✒ Look for typographical clues such as boldface, italics, underlining, or asterisks.

Scanning

Scanning involves moving your eyes quickly down the page seeking specific words and phrases. When you scan, you must be willing to skip over several lines of text without actually reading and understanding them.

Scanning is a useful technique when looking for keywords or specific ideas. For example, when you look up a name in a phonebook, you're probably using the scanning technique. In most cases, you know what you're looking for, so you're concentrating on finding a particular answer.

When scanning a document:

- ✒ **Keep in mind what you're scanning for.** If you keep a picture in your mind, the information is much more likely to jump out at you from among all the other printed words.
- ✒ **Anticipate what form the information is likely to appear in.** Will it be numbers? Proper nouns?

✔ Let your eyes run over several lines of print at a time.

✔ When you find the information that you're looking for, read the entire sentence.

Skimming and scanning are useful techniques for many of the Paragraph Comprehension problems. I talk more about this in Chapter 7.

Looking for the main ideas and subpoints

There wouldn't be much purpose to reading if you just let your eyes wander over the words without walking away with some sense of what the author was talking about. The author's ideas are included in the main point and subpoints of the writing. You need to practice extracting this information from your reading material. See the "Pointers about Points" section, earlier in this chapter.

Building your vocabulary

It's hard to understand what you're reading if you don't understand the individual words. Effective reading comprehension involves developing a solid vocabulary. Use the techniques in Chapter 4 to strengthen your vocabulary, and you'll simultaneously improve your reading comprehension skills. The two skills go hand in hand.

When practicing reading, try not to look up new words in a dictionary right away. Stopping to look up words often impairs your concentration and lessens your ability to comprehend what you've read.

Instead, start by trying to puzzle out the meaning of a new word by looking at the context in which the word is used in the sentence or phrase. For example, take the following passage:

> It had been three days since the shipwreck, and Tammy was unable to find food or much drinkable water. At that point, she would have done anything to get off that wretched island.

You can derive several important clues about the meaning of the word *wretched* based on its context in the passage. Obviously, Tammy is not having a very good time, nor does she find the island to be a very pleasant environment. Therefore, you can surmise that *wretched* has something to do with unpleasantness.

Paraphrasing

Putting the text in your own words can help you understand what the writer is talking about. I talk more extensively about this in the "Say it again, Sam: Paraphrasing" section, earlier in this chapter.

You probably won't have time on the Paragraph Comprehension subtest of the ASVAB to rewrite passages on your scratch paper. But, by practicing the technique while you're practicing your reading comprehension skills, you'll develop the ability to paraphrase in your mind.

Remembering by reflecting

Reflecting simply means thinking about what you've read. If you take a few minutes to think about it, you're much more likely to remember it. Did you enjoy the passage or article? Did you find it interesting? Do you agree or disagree with the author's views?

Thinking about what you've read may cause you to learn something.

Speaking about Speed

There are dozens of speed-reading courses, software, and online programs that absolutely guarantee, without qualification, to turn you into a reading speed demon. However, if your goal is to score well on the Paragraph Comprehension subtest of the ASVAB, I recommend you save your money.

The Paragraph Comprehension subtest is not a speed-reading test. You have 13 minutes to read between eight and ten short paragraphs and answer 15 questions. This is plenty of time for most people. There are no extra points on this test for finishing early. If you blaze through the test in six minutes, and get all the questions right, your score will be the same as if you took the entire allotted time. Instead, concentrate on improving your comprehension skills. That's what this subtest is all about: How well do you understand what you've read?

If you're still worried about your reading speed, just remember: The more you read, the better (and faster) you'll get at it. Read to comprehend by using the information in this chapter, and your speed will automatically get faster as you practice.

Chapter 7

The Paragraph Comprehension Subtest

- -

In This Chapter

▶ Trying out types of questions

▶ Looking at proven techniques for a better score

▶ Getting a handle on practice questions

- -

There are only 15 questions on the Paragraph Comprehension subtest — the fewest of any of the ASVAB subtests. However, it's one of the most important subtests of the ASVAB, because the military uses this test (along with the Word Knowledge subtest; see Chapters 4 and 5) to compute your verbal expression (VE) score, which, in turn, is an important part of your AFQT score. (If you want to see how these scores combine, turn to Chapter 2.)

This subtest is nothing more than a reading comprehension test, much like many of the reading tests you took in school. You're asked to read a short passage (a paragraph), and then answer one to four questions about information contained in that paragraph. Unfortunately, you probably won't find the reading to be very interesting. No passages from Harry Potter or spacemen shooting ray guns here. You're more likely to read about the corn crop harvest rates in Nebraska or the principles of time management. The key is to stay focused. There are, after all, only 15 questions, and the paragraphs aren't that long.

In addition to being an important part of your AFQT score, a large percentage of military jobs require a solid score on this subtest. If you're interested in which military jobs require you to score well on the Paragraph Comprehension subtest, might I humbly recommend you trot down to your neighborhood bookstore and ask for a copy of my best-selling *ASVAB For Dummies* (Wiley)? You'll be glad you did.

The Test Format: Types of Questions

The Paragraph Comprehension subtest requires you to read a short paragraph, and then answer one or more multiple-choice questions about what you've read. These questions can generally be broken down into one of four types, which I like to call the treasure hunt, getting the point, dictionary, and deep thinking.

The treasure hunt

Treasure hunt questions require you to find specific information within the paragraph. The good thing about this type of question is that, by employing the scanning techniques in Chapter 6, you can often find the answer without having to read the entire paragraph. Try the following example:

A new study has found that 21 percent of people arrested in the United States for driving under the influence were arrested again for the same crime within five years. The study, commissioned by the U.S. Department of Justice, analyzed recidivism rates for DUI between 2002 and 2007. During this period, there were more than 930,000 arrests for DUI. Of these, 195,300, or 21 percent, were arrested again for violating DUI laws a second time within the established timeframe. The study found that 34 percent of the repeat offenses occurred within six months of the original arrest.

How many people were arrested for DUI more than once between 2002 and 2007?

(A) 930,000

(B) 195,300

(C) 210,000

(D) None of the above

By using the scanning technique and letting your eyes quickly scan through the paragraph, you'll notice that all the large numbers are contained in the middle. If you stop and read the two sentences that include large numbers, you'll quickly find the answer to the question: B.

Sometimes the answer isn't so obvious, and you have to dig a little deeper to find the treasure. Take the following question, for example:

George Armstrong Custer (December 5, 1839–June 25, 1876) was a U.S. Army officer and cavalry commander in the Civil War and the American Indian Wars. At the start of the Civil War, Custer was a cadet at the U.S. Military Academy at West Point, and his class's graduation was accelerated so that they could enter the war. Early in the Gettysburg Campaign, Custer's association with cavalry commander Major General Alfred Pleasonton earned him a promotion ate the age of 23 from first lieutenant to brigadier general of volunteers. By the end of the Civil War (April 9, 1865), Custer had achieved the rank of major general of volunteers but was reduced to his permanent grade of captain in the regular army when the troops were sent home.

How old was George Custer at the end of the Civil War?

(A) 24

(B) 25

(C) 26

(D) 34

The answer is still right there in the paragraph, but you have to use a little judgment (and math) to find it. General Custer was born on December 5, 1839 (which you can find in the first sentence) and the Civil War ended on April 9, 1865 (which the last sentence tells you). Therefore, Custer was 25 years old at the end of the war. (He didn't turn 26 until December of that year.)

Getting the point

This type of question asks you to discern the main topic or main point of the paragraph (see Chapter 6 for more information). When you look for the main point, skimming the paragraph, rather than reading it in its entirety, is often helpful (again, see Chapter 6). Try this one on for size:

The farmers' market reopened the second weekend of May. Amid the asparagus and flowers, shoppers chatted about the return of temperatures in the seventies. Across the street, children (and their dogs) were playing Frisbee in the park. Finally, spring had come to town.

What is the main point of the passage?

(A) The farmers' market has reopened.

(B) Children like playing Frisbee.

(C) Spring had come to town.

(D) Shoppers were chatting.

In this paragraph, you may think that the farmers' market reopening is the main point, but the other information about the temperature and the kids playing Frisbee tells you that the main idea is something a bit broader than the market opening. The main idea is stated in the last sentence: "Finally, spring had come to town."

When skimming for the main point of a paragraph, start with the first sentence, and then read the last sentence. The main idea is often contained in one of these sentences.

Dictionary

Much like the Word Knowledge subtest (covered in Chapters 4 and 5), this type of question requires you to define a word as used in the context of the passage. The correct definition that the question is looking for can be the most common meaning of the word, or it can be a less well-known meaning of the word.

In either case, you have to read the passage, make sure you understand how the word is being used, and select the answer option that is closest in meaning to the word as it's used in the passage. Consider this example:

In the 18th century, it was common for sailors to be pressed into service in Britain. Young men found near seaports could be kidnapped, drugged, or otherwise hauled aboard a ship and made to work doing menial chores. They were not paid for their service, and they were given just enough food to keep them alive.

In this passage, *pressed* means:

(A) hired

(B) ironed

(C) enticed

(D) forced

The correct answer is D. The descriptions of the conditions these sailors found themselves in should help you decide that they weren't hired or enticed; ironed is one meaning of the word *pressed*, but it isn't correct in this context.

Deep thinking

If the paragraph comprehension questions on the ASVAB simply asked you to scan a passage and find the main point or supporting details, it would be a pretty simple test. But the subtest goes beyond that. In order to properly answer some of the questions on the test, you'll be required to analyze what you've read and draw conclusions.

The *conclusion* — which may be called an *inference* or *implication* — must be reasonably based on what the passage says. You have to use good judgment when deciding what conclusions can be logically drawn from what you've read.

Try this example:

One of the main reasons motorcyclists are killed in crashes is that the motorcycle itself provides virtually no protection in a crash. For example, approximately 80 percent of reported motorcycle crashes result in injury or death; a comparable figure for automobiles is about 20 percent.

Safe motorcycle riding means:

(A) always wearing a helmet

(B) using premium gas

(C) selecting the most expensive motorcycle

(D) always riding with a buddy

The correct answer is A. The author didn't specifically state in the passage that wearing a helmet is important, but you can infer the correct answer because the author gives the reason for fatalities: Motorcycles themselves offer virtually no protection in a crash. Based on the information provided in the passage, you can logically conclude that even the small degree of protection offered by a helmet increases the safety of riding motorcycles. None of the other choices is as closely connected to the idea of safety.

Planning Your Attack

The best way to score well on the Paragraph Comprehension subtest is to improve your reading comprehension skills by following the advice I give in Chapter 6. However, there are also a few things you can do on test day to make sure you score as high as possible:

- **Watch the time.** As with all the ASVAB subtests, this is a timed test. You have 13 minutes to read through approximately 9 paragraphs and answer 15 questions. This is plenty of time, so you shouldn't feel rushed. But still, you don't have time for daydreaming either.

- **If you don't know the answer or you run out of time, guess.** Guessing is always better than not guessing. You have a chance of getting the correct answer if you guess. So, if you're running out of time on the test, or you're not sure if you can identify the main idea of a passage, take a guess.

- **Question first, read later.** In *ASVAB For Dummies,* I recommend reading the entire paragraph first, before looking at the question. Many reading comprehension test experts now recommend the opposite. If the question asks you to find specific information or discern the main idea of the paragraph, skimming or scanning (see Chapter 6) can save loads of time. Read the question first, so that you can best decide what reading technique to use.

✔ **Take it one question at a time.** Some passages have more than one question associated with them, but look at only one question at a time.

✔ **Understand each question.** What is the question asking you to do? Are you supposed to find the main point? Draw a conclusion? Find a word that is nearest in meaning? Make sure you know what the question is asking before you choose among the answer options. This tip may seem obvious, but when you're in a hurry, you can make mistakes by misunderstanding the questions.

✔ **Read each answer option carefully.** Don't just select the first answer that seems right. *Remember:* On the Paragraph Comprehension subtest, one answer is often "most right" while others are "almost right." You want to choose the "most right" answer, not the "almost right" answer. And to do that, you have to read *all* the answers.

✔ **Check your baggage at the door.** Answer each question based on the passage, not your own opinions or views on the topic.

✔ **Don't choose ambiguous answer options.** They're incorrect 99.99 times out of 100. (Oh, heck, call it 100 times out of 100.) If an answer strikes you as not quite true but not totally false, that answer is incorrect. Those nasty ASVAB test makers have put it there to throw you off. Don't give them the satisfaction of falling for their trap!

Sample Test Questions

Time for you to put all the great advice I provide in this chapter and Chapter 6 to good use. (You can see that I'm not usually accused of being too modest.) Quiz yourself on the following sample test questions to see if your reading comprehension is up to speed.

"First, stick to one excuse. Thus, if a tradesman, with whom your social relations are slight, should chance to find you taking coppers from his till, you may possibly explain that you are interested in Numismatics and are a Collector of Coins; and he may possibly believe you. But if you tell him afterwards that you pitied him for being overloaded with unwieldy copper discs, and were in the act of replacing them by a silver sixpence of your own, this further explanation, so far from increasing his confidence in your motives, will (strangely enough) actually decrease it. And if you are so unwise as to be struck by yet another brilliant idea, and tell him that the pennies were all bad pennies, which you were concealing to save him from a police prosecution for coining, the tradesman may even be so wayward as to institute a police prosecution himself."

—G. K. Chesterton

1. The author is giving the reader advice about:

(A) collecting coins

(B) stealing

(C) dealing with tradesmen

(D) becoming a police officer

The correct answer is B. Mr. Chesterton is expounding on how sticking to one excuse may help you if you're caught taking coins from the tradesman's till.

Ethics are standards by which one should act based on values. Values are core beliefs such as duty, honor, and integrity that motivate attitudes and actions. Not all values are ethical values (integrity is — happiness is not). Ethical values relate to what is right and wrong and, thus, take precedence over nonethical values when making ethical decisions.

2. According to the paragraph, values can best be defined as:

   (A) ethics

   (B) stealing

   (C) core beliefs

   (D) right and wrong

The correct answer is C. The second sentence defines the word *values*.

Although the average consumer replaces the tires on his or her automobile every 50,000 miles, steel-belted radials can last for 60,000 miles. However, they must be properly maintained. The tires must be inflated to the correct air pressure at all times, and tires must be rotated and balanced according to a routine maintenance schedule. The tread should be checked for correct depth regularly.

3. How long can steel-belted radials last?

   (A) 25,000 miles

   (B) 50,000 miles

   (C) 60,000 miles

   (D) No one knows.

The correct answer is C. If you used the scanning technique explained in Chapter 6, you would have found this answer quickly.

4. According to the passage, proper tire maintenance does *not* include:

   (A) keeping tires properly inflated

   (B) balancing and rotating tires

   (C) checking the tread

   (D) checking the lug nuts

The correct answer is D. This is a negative question that requires extra care in answering. A *negative question* asks you for something that is not true, or not included in the paragraph. If you're rushed or in a hurry, you can easily misread the question.

Some people argue that baking is an art, but Chef Debra Dearhorn says that baking is a science. She says that if you follow a recipe carefully, assembling the ingredients accurately, cooking at the specified temperature for the specified period of time, your cookies will always turn out right. Chef Dearborn says the best baking is like the best experiment — anyone can duplicate it.

5. In this passage, the word *assembling* most nearly means:

   (A) measuring

   (B) putting together

   (C) buying

   (D) storing

The correct answer is B. Although measuring is something you do when baking, it doesn't "most nearly" mean the same thing as *assembling*. Putting together does.

6. According to the passage, a person who can't make a decent batch of cookies:

   (A) should get out of the kitchen

   (B) is an artist

   (C) isn't following the recipe carefully

   (D) is Chef Dearborn

The correct answer is C. The passage states that if you follow a recipe carefully, your cookies will always turn out right.

> Boiler technicians operate main and auxiliary boilers. They maintain and repair all parts, including pressure fittings, valves, pumps, and forced-air blowers. Technicians may have to lift or move heavy equipment. They may have to stoop and kneel and work in awkward positions.

7. According to this job description, a good candidate for this job would be

   (A) a person with management experience

   (B) an individual with keen eyesight

   (C) a person who is not mechanically minded

   (D) a person who is physically fit

The correct answer is D. Although the passage doesn't say, "This job requires a physically fit person," the duties listed imply that this is so. A person with management experience or keen eyesight may make a good candidate, but the passage doesn't list these traits as requirements for the job. A person who is not mechanically minded may not have the knowledge necessary to maintain and repair boilers and all their parts. This leaves D, and it's true that a person who is physically fit would be a good choice for the job.

> In June 2004, the city council passed a resolution requiring all residents to paint their address numbers on their homes using a bright color. This was done to assist firemen, police, and paramedics in finding an address during an emergency. In August, 300 residences were randomly sampled and it was found that 150 had complied with the new ordinance.

8. According to the above passage, what percentage of the randomly sampled residences had complied with the new ordinance?

   (A) 10 percent

   (B) 20 percent

   (C) 50 percent

   (D) 60 percent

The correct answer is C. The author didn't specifically say that 50 percent had not complied, but she included enough information in the passage so that you can calculate it on your own.

> The younger the child, the trickier using medicine is. Children under 2 years shouldn't be given any over-the-counter (OTC) drug without a doctor's approval. Your pediatrician can tell you how much of a common drug, like acetaminophen (Tylenol), is safe for babies. Prescription drugs also can work differently in children than adults. Some barbiturates, for example, which make adults feel sluggish, will make a child hyperactive.

Amphetamines, which stimulate adults, can calm children. When giving any drug to a child, watch closely for side effects. If you're not happy with what's happening with your child, don't assume that everything's okay. Always be suspicious. It's better to make the extra calls to the doctor or nurse practitioner than to have a bad reaction to a drug. And before parents dole out OTC drugs, they should consider whether they're truly necessary. Americans love to medicate—perhaps too much. A study published in the October 1994 issue of the *Journal of the American Medical Association* found that more than half of all mothers surveyed had given their 3-year-olds an OTC medication in the previous month. Not every cold needs medicine. Common viruses run their course in seven to ten days with or without medication. Although some OTC medications can sometimes make children more comfortable and help them eat and rest better, others may trigger allergic reactions or changes for the worse in sleeping, eating, and behavior. Antibiotics, available by prescription, don't work at all on cold viruses.

9. A common problem in America is:

   (A) over-medication

   (B) parents not heeding the advice of their doctors

   (C) OTC drugs not requiring a prescription

   (D) the cost of prescription medication

The correct answer is A. The 11th and 12th sentences in the passage suggest that Americans probably medicate too much.

10. When a parent is in doubt about giving a child medication, it's best to:

   (A) speak with a pharmacist

   (B) call a doctor or nurse practitioner

   (C) read the label closely

   (D) research the side effects

The correct answer is B. The passage states that it's better to make the extra calls than to have a bad reaction to a drug. While the other choices may be good advice, they are not stated or implied in the paragraph.

Part III
Calculating Better Math Knowledge

The 5th Wave   By Rich Tennant

"The math portion of that test was so easy. I figure I've got a 7 in 5 chance of acing it."

In this part . . .

Performing math equations and solving math word problems indicates a strong aptitude in problem solving, and the armed services want recruits who can solve problems. You'll find *that* out at boot camp. Basic training is a place where drill instructors like to throw problems at you over and over to see how well you handle them.

Part III gives you a chance to brush up on your numbers knowledge. It includes all kinds of information that can help you do well on the two math-related subtests that the AFQT throws at you. I also give you a ton of tips on everything from how to guess on questions if you're running out of time to what to do if you forget the quadratic equation.

Chapter 8

Know Your Math

*L*azarus Long, a fictional character created by Robert A. Heinlein, once said, "Anyone who cannot cope with mathematics is not fully human. At best, he is a tolerable subhuman who has learned to wear shoes, bathe, and not make messes in the house."

Perhaps Mr. Heinlein's observation is a little harsh. Some people seem to be born mathematicians, while others struggle with it. The fact remains, however, that the military seems to agree with Robert. You can't join the military without proving that you know the fundamentals of math.

Fully 50 percent of your AFQT score is based on your ability to solve math problems. And if you read Chapter 2, you know that your AFQT score determines whether you can join the military.

The good news is that, although the military wants you well grounded in math, they're not looking for rocket scientists. That's NASA's job. The two math subtests of the AFQT test your math ability only at the high school level — there's no advanced calculus or plotting the orbit of subatomic particles going on here.

While I was deciding what to cover in this chapter, I quickly realized that I can't give you an entire high school math education in one chapter. Heck, I couldn't do that in one whole book. Then I realized that I don't have to try to cram all the math you learned in 13 years of school into one chapter. If you're reading this book, you're obviously interested in joining the military. And in order to join the military, you must be either a high school graduate or a GED holder, or you must have at least 15 college credits. That means you've already learned this stuff. All I need to do is provide you a bit of a refresher — remind you of all those rules of math you may have forgotten or put into the back of your mind. And that's what you find here — a refresher course, designed to draw out all the math you already know!

So look at it this way: You already know what you need to know in order to ace the AFQT — your job is just to remind yourself of what you know. In this chapter, I help you do exactly that.

Math Terminology

Some people are intimidated by math, in part, because it has its own language. In Chapter 10, I explain how to use keywords in math word problems to translate English into mathematical equations. But that's not enough. You need to know basic math terminology in order to solve many of the problems you'll see on the two math subtests that make up the AFQT.

For example, a question may ask you to define a *prime number*. If you'd read this chapter, you'd know that a prime number is any positive number, evenly divisible by only itself and the number one. Another question may ask, "What is the sum of 52 and 31?" *Sum* means addition, so the answer would be 83.

I just looked in my handy-dandy pocket math dictionary. There are over 700 mathematical terms listed there. Wait a minute! Sit back down. You don't need to memorize 700 terms. You won't see the math term *brachistochrone* on any of the subtests, for example. **Remember:** The military isn't looking for physicists or mathematical theorists.

Brachistochrone is a term from Greek meaning "shortest time." The special property of a brachistochrone is the fact that a bead sliding down a brachistochrone-shaped frictionless wire will take a shorter time to reach the bottom than with a wire curved into any other shape. Just in case you were curious.

You should commit to memory a few math terms, because you're likely to see them used, in one way or another, on the Mathematics Knowledge subtest or the Arithmetic Reasoning subtest. Here's some of what you need to know:

- **Average:** The average usually refers to the *arithmetic mean* or just the *mean average*. To find the mean of a set of n numbers, add the numbers in the set and divide the sum by n. For example, the average (or arithmetic mean) of 3, 7, 10, and 12 is: $\frac{3 + 7 + 10 + 12}{4}$.

    You may have seen the term *geometric mean* and wondered how it differs from the arithmetic mean. To solve for the geometric mean, you multiply the numbers and then take the nth root of the product. The geometric mean of 4, 6, and 8 is $\sqrt[3]{4 \times 6 \times 8}$. You won't be asked to solve geometric mean problems on either of the math subtests contained in the ASVAB, though.

- **Coefficient:** The number multiplied times a variable or a product of variables or powers of variables in a term. For example, 123 is the coefficient in the term $123x^3y$.

- **Evaluate:** This means to figure out or calculate. If you're asked to evaluate 5 + 3, that means to simplify the term to 8.

- **Pi:** In mathematic equations and terms, pi is usually expressed by its Greek letter, π. Pi represents the ratio of the circumference of a circle to its diameter, and it's used in several formulas, especially formulas involving geometry. Pi's value is 3.141592653589793 . . . (on and on forever), but it's traditional in common math problems to use the value 3.14 or $\frac{22}{7}$.

- **Prime number:** A positive integer that can only be divided evenly by itself and 1. For example, 2, 3, 5, 7, 11, 13, and so on are all primes. One afternoon, all the famous mathematicians got together over a beer and agreed among themselves that 1 is not a prime number.

    Positive numbers that have factors other than themselves and 1 as factors are called *composite numbers*. Again, by convention, 1 is not considered a composite number.

- **Product:** The result of multiplication. The product of 2 and 9 is 18.

- **Quotient:** The result of division. 40 divided by 5 has a quotient of 8.

    43 divided by 5 has a quotient of 8 and a *remainder* of 3.

- **Reciprocal:** A fraction flipped upside down. The reciprocal of x is $\frac{1}{x}$. The reciprocal of $\frac{1}{x}$ is x, and $x = 0$.

- **Sum:** The result of addition. The sum of 3 and 6 is 9.

You're not done with math vocabulary yet. There are many more math words and terms you need to know. I explain them in the following sections.

Expressions and Equations: The Heart of Math

Math without expressions and equations is like a fire hydrant without a dog — they just go together. So, what's the difference between a mathematical *expression* and an *equation?*

- An **expression** is any mathematical calculation or formula combining numbers and/or variables. Expressions do not include equal signs (=). For example, 3 + 2 is an expression, and so is $x(x + 2) - 3$.

- An **equation,** on the other hand, is a mathematical sentence built from expressions using one or more equal signs (=). For example, 3 + 2 = 5 is an equation, and $x(x + 2) - 3 = 30$ is also an equation.

Order of operations

In math, you must solve equations by following steps in a proper order. If you don't, you won't get the right answer. Many of the most frequent errors that people make occur when they don't follow the order of operations when solving mathematical problems.

Keep in mind the following order of operations:

1. **Start with calculations in brackets or parentheses.**

   When you have nested parentheses or brackets (parentheses or brackets inside other parentheses or brackets), do the inner ones first and work your way outward.

2. **Then do terms with exponents and roots.**

3. **Move on to multiplication and division next, in order from left to right.**

4. **Do the addition and subtraction, also in order from left to right.**

An easy way to remember this is to think of the phrase, "**P**lease **E**xcuse **M**y **D**ear **A**unt **S**ally" (**P**arentheses, **E**xponents, **M**ultiply, **D**ivide, **A**dd, **S**ubtract).

Take the following equation out for a ride.

Solve: $3 \times (5 + 2) + 5^2 \div 2$.

Do the calculations in the parentheses first:

$3 \times (5 + 2) + 5^2 \div 2 = 3 \times 7 + 5^2 \div 2$

Next, simplify the exponents:

$3 \times 7 + 25 \div 2$

Do multiplication and division from left to right:

$21 + 12.5$

Finally, perform addition and subtraction from left to right:

33.5

Keeping equations balanced

One of the coolest things about equations is that you can do almost anything you want to them, as long as you remember to do the exact same thing to both sides of the equation. This is called *keeping the equation balanced*. For example, if you have the equation $4 + 1 = 3 + 2$, you can add 3 to both sides of the equation and it will still balance out: $4 + 1 + 3 = 3 + 2 + 3$. You can divide both sides by 3 and it will still balance: $(4 + 1) \div 3 = (3 + 2) \div 3$.

You'll come to appreciate how handy equation balancing can be when you review algebra later in this chapter (see the "Alphabet Soup: Algebra Review" section).

Mental Math: The Distributive Property

Have you ever envied those people who can perform calculations on large numbers in their heads? What if I told you that you could be one of those people? That's right. All you have to do is practice the distributive property of math.

The *distributive property*, often referred to as the *distributive law* of math, makes it possible to separate or break larger numbers into parts for simpler arithmetic. It basically says that $a(b + c)$ is the same as $(a \times b) + (a \times c)$.

Suppose you wanted to mentally multiply 4 by 53.

4×53 is the same as $(4 \times 50) + (4 \times 3)$. Four times 50 is easy — it's 200. Four times 3 is also easy. It's 12. Two hundred plus 12 is 212.

Try another one with a bit of a twist.

Mentally perform the calculation, 12×19.

12×19 is equivalent to $12x(20 - 1) = (12 \times 20) - (12 \times 1)$.

You can quickly mentally calculate that 12 times 20 is 240, and that 12 times 1 is 12. Subtract 12 from 240, and you have 228.

Figure 8-1 illustrates how this works.

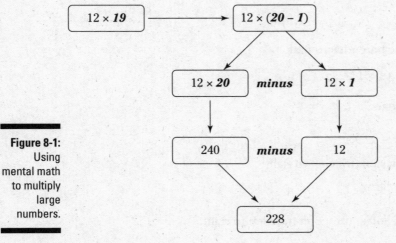

Figure 8-1:
Using mental math to multiply large numbers.

If 12 × 20 is still too large for mental calculation, you can break it down to (12 × 10) + (12 × 10), or 120 + 120.

The distributive property can be used for division, as well, although that takes a bit more practice: 340 ÷ 4 is the same as (340 ÷ 2) ÷ 2. You can quickly calculate that 340 divided by 2 is 170, and 170 divided by 2 is 85.

And 340 ÷ 4 can also be expressed as (100 ÷ 4) + (100 ÷ 4) + (100 ÷ 4) + (40 ÷ 4).

You can mentally calculate 100 divided by 4 as 25. Forty divided by 4 is also easy — it's 10. So, 25 + 25 + 25 + 10 = 85. Keep practicing, and you'll be known as the neighborhood lightning calculator.

You're not allowed to use calculators on the math subtests of the ASVAB, so practicing the distributive property can be a big timesaver.

Fun with Factors

A *factor* is simply a number that is multiplied to get a product. *Factoring* a number means taking the number apart. It's kind of like multiplying in reverse. For example, the factors of 12 are 1, 2, 3, 4, 6, and 12, because all these numbers can be divided evenly into 12.

Here are some other factors:

- **2:** 1, 2
- **3:** 1, 3
- **4:** 1, 2, 4
- **5:** 1, 5
- **6:** 1, 2, 3, 6
- **16:** 1, 2, 4, 8, 16
- **20:** 1, 2, 4, 5, 10, 20
- **45:** 1, 3, 5, 9, 15, 45

Types of factors

A factor can be either a prime number or a composite number (except that 1 and 0 are neither prime nor composite). As I mention in the "Math Terminology" section, earlier in this chapter, prime numbers have only themselves and 1 as a factor, while composite numbers can be divided evenly by other numbers.

The prime numbers up to 100 are: 2, 3, 5, 7, 11, 13, 17, 19, 23, 29, 31, 37, 41, 43, 47, 53, 59, 61, 67, 71, 73, 79, 83, 89, and 97.

Finding prime factors

Any composite number can be written as a product of prime factors. Mathematicians call this *prime factorization*. To find the prime factors of a number, you divide the number by the smallest possible prime number and work up the list of prime numbers until the result is itself a prime number.

Say you wanted to find the prime factors of 240. Because 240 is even, start by dividing it by the smallest prime number, which is 2 — 240 ÷ 2 = 120. The number 120 is also even, so it can be divided by 2 — 120 ÷ 2 = 60. Then 60 ÷ 2 = 30 and 30 ÷ 2 = 15. Now, 15 is not even, so check to see if it can be divided by 3 (the next highest prime number) — 15 ÷ 3 = 5, which itself is a prime number, so 240 is now fully factored. Now, simply list the divisors to write the prime factors of 240:

$$240 \div 2 = 120$$
$$120 \div 2 = 60$$
$$60 \div 2 = 30$$
$$30 \div 2 = 15$$
$$15 \div 3 = 5$$

The prime factors of 240 are $2 \times 2 \times 2 \times 2 \times 3 \times 5$.

Least Common Multiples

A *common multiple* is a number that is a multiple of two or more numbers. For example, 20, 30, and 40, are common multiples of the numbers 5 and 10.

The *least common multiple* (LCM) of two or more numbers is the smallest number (not zero) that is a multiple of both or all of the numbers. The LCM is number that's useful in solving many math problems — especially those involving fractions (see "Conquering the Fear of Fractions," later in this chapter).

One way to find the LCM is to list the multiples of each number, one at a time, until you find the smallest multiple that is common to all the numbers.

Find the LCM of 45 and 50.

- **Multiples of 45:** 45, 90, 135, 180, 225, 270, 315, 360, 405, 450
- **Multiples of 50:** 50, 100, 150, 200, 250, 300, 350, 400, 450

The LCM of 45 and 50 is 450.

That was rather cumbersome, wasn't it? Wouldn't it be great if there were an easier way? There is, and I'm here to let you in on the secret: The easiest way to find the LCM is first to list the prime factors of each number (see the "Finding prime factors" section, earlier in this chapter):

- The prime factors for 45 are $3 \times 3 \times 5$.
- The prime factors for 50 are $2 \times 5 \times 5$.

Then multiply each factor the greatest number of times it occurs in either number. If the same factor occurs more than once in both numbers, you multiply the factor the greatest number of times it occurs. For example, 5 occurs as a prime factor of both 45 (where it occurs *once*) and 50 (where it occurs *twice*); the two occurrences in factorization of 50 trump the single occurrence in the factorization of 45. The number 3 occurs two times, 5 occurs two times, and 2 occurs once, so you have $3 \times 3 \times 5 \times 5 \times 2 = 450$

It's always a great idea to check your answer to see if 45 and 50 both divide evenly into 450.

That was so much fun, I bet you want to try another one:

What is the least common multiple of 5, 27, and 30?

List the prime factors of each number (see the "Finding prime factors" section):

- ✔ **Prime factors of 5:** 5
- ✔ **Prime factors of 27:** $3 \times 3 \times 3$
- ✔ **Prime factors of 30:** $2 \times 3 \times 5$

The number 3 occurs a maximum of three times, 5 occurs a maximum of one time, and 2 occurs a maximum of one time: $3 \times 3 \times 3 \times 5 \times 2 = 270$. Check your answer by seeing if 5, 27, and 30 can all divide evenly into 270.

Conquering the Fear of Fractions

I don't know why, but most people I know don't like to do math with fractions. Maybe it's because, in school, teachers always used pies as an example, and that just makes you hungry. The pies were all imaginary, too, so you didn't even get a piece after all the figuring was done.

I'm going to break convention and use squares of cardboard instead. Sure, they're harder to cut than pies, but they don't smell as enticing.

A fraction is nothing more than part of a whole. Take a look at Figure 8-2.

Figure 8-2: Fractions are part of a whole.

Each shaded area represents part of a whole, or a *fraction* of the whole. It doesn't have to be fourths. If I had divided the cardboard into two equal pieces, each shaded area would represent one-half. If the cardboard were cut into three equal pieces, each piece would be one-third of the whole.

Fractions aren't difficult to work into your mathematical skills, as long as you remember a few rules and techniques.

Parts and types of fractions

The top number of a fraction is called the *numerator*. The bottom number is known as the *denominator*. For example, in the fraction $\frac{7}{16}$, 7 is the numerator and 16 is the denominator.

You may also see numerators and denominators separated by a / sign instead of one on top of the other. ¼ is the same as $\frac{1}{4}$.

If the numerator is smaller than the denominator, that means the fraction is less than a whole (smaller than 1). This is called a proper fraction. The fraction $\frac{3}{16}$ is a *proper fraction,* as is $\frac{1}{3}$.

If the numerator is larger than the denominator, the fraction is larger than a whole (larger than one), and the fraction is called an *improper fraction*. The fraction $\frac{17}{16}$ is an improper fraction.

It is customary in math to convert improper fractions to mixed numbers, especially after all mathematical operations are complete. A *mixed number* is a whole number plus a fraction. The easiest way to convert an improper fraction to a mixed number is to divide the numerator by the denominator. $\frac{17}{16}$ is converted to a mixed number by dividing 17 by 16 — $17 \div 16 = 1$, with a remainder of 1, so the improper fraction converts to $1\frac{1}{16}$.

Simplifying fractions

Simplifying (or reducing) fractions means to make the fraction as simple as possible. You're usually required to do this on the ASVAB math subtests before you can select the correct answer. For example, if you worked out a problem and the answer was $\frac{4}{8}$, the correct answer choice on the math subtest would probably be $\frac{1}{2}$, which is the simplest equivalent to $\frac{4}{8}$.

There are many methods of simplifying fractions. In this section, I give you the two that I think are the easiest — you can decide which is best for you.

Method 1: Dividing by the lowest prime numbers

Try dividing the numerator and denominator by the lowest prime numbers (see the "Types of factors" section), until you can't go any further.

Simplify $\frac{24}{108}$.

Both the numerator and denominator are even numbers, so they can be divided by the lowest prime number, which is 2. Then $24 \div 2 = 12$, and $108 \div 2 = 54$. The result is $\frac{12}{54}$.

The numerator and denominator are both still even numbers, so divide by 2 again — $12 \div 2 = 6$ and $54 \div 2 = 27$. The result is $\frac{6}{27}$.

This time the denominator is an odd number, so you know it can't be divided by 2. Try the next highest prime number, which is 3 — $6 \div 3 = 2$, and $27 \div 3 = 9$. The result is $\frac{2}{9}$.

Because no common prime numbers will divide evenly into both 2 and 9, the fraction is fully simplified.

Method 2: Listing prime factors

This method of simplification is my favorite. Simply list the prime factors of both the numerator and the denominator (see the "Finding prime factors" section), and then see if any cancel out (are the same).

Try this method using the same fraction, $\frac{24}{108}$.

The prime factors of 24 are $2 \times 2 \times 2 \times 3$.

The prime factors of 108 are $2 \times 2 \times 3 \times 3 \times 3$

The fraction can now be written as $\frac{2 \times 2 \times 2 \times 3}{2 \times 2 \times 3 \times 3 \times 3}$.

Two of the twos and one of the threes cancel out, and can be removed from both the numerator and the denominator. What's left is $\frac{2}{3 \times 3}$, or $\frac{2}{9}$.

Multiplying fractions

Multiplying fractions is very easy. All you have to do is multiply the numerators by each other, multiply the denominators by each other, and then simplify the result.

$$\frac{4}{5} \times \frac{3}{7} \times \frac{9}{15} = \frac{4 \times 3 \times 9}{5 \times 7 \times 15} = \frac{108}{525}$$

The fraction $\frac{108}{525}$ can be simplified to $\frac{36}{175}$ (see the "Simplifying fractions" section).

Before multiplying mixed numbers, change them to improper fractions.

Dividing fractions

Dividing fractions is almost the same as multiplying, with one important difference: You have to convert the second fraction (the *divisor*) to the reciprocal, and then multiply. As I explain in the "Math Terminology" section at the beginning of this chapter, the reciprocal is simply a fraction flipped over.

Solve: $\frac{3}{5} \div \frac{2}{5}$.

Take the reciprocal of the second fraction and multiply it with the other fraction:

$$\frac{3}{5} \div \frac{2}{5} = \frac{3}{5} \times \frac{5}{2} = \frac{3 \times 5}{2 \times 5} = \frac{15}{10}$$

The fraction $\frac{15}{10}$ is an improper fraction, which can be converted to $1\frac{5}{10}$ (see the "Parts and types of fraction" section). Then $1\frac{5}{10}$ can be simplified to $1\frac{1}{2}$ (see the "Simplifying fractions" section).

Adding and subtracting fractions

Adding and subtracting fractions can be as simple as multiplying and dividing them, or it can be more difficult. It all depends on whether or not the fractions have the same denominator.

Adding and subtracting fractions with like denominators

To add or subtract two fractions with the same denominator, add (or subtract) the numerators, and place that sum (or difference) over the common denominator:

$$\frac{2}{9} + \frac{3}{9} = \frac{2+3}{9} = \frac{5}{9}$$

$$\frac{3}{9} - \frac{2}{9} = \frac{3-2}{9} = \frac{1}{9}$$

Adding and subtracting fractions with different denominators

You can't add or subtract fractions with different denominators. So, what do you do? You have to convert the fractions so that they all have the same denominator, and then perform addition or subtraction as I explain in the preceding section.

Converting fractions so that they share the same denominator involves finding a *common denominator*. A common denominator is nothing more than a common multiple of all the denominators (see the "Least Common Multiples" section, earlier in this chapter).

Find a common denominator for the fractions $\frac{3}{5}$ and $\frac{1}{8}$.

The multiples of 5 are 5, 10, 15, 20, 25, 30, 35, and 40.

The multiples of 8 are 8, 16, 24, 32, and 40.

A common denominator for the fractions $\frac{3}{5}$ and $\frac{1}{8}$ is 40.

The next step in the addition/subtraction process is to convert the fractions so they share the common denominator. In order to do this, divide the original denominator into the new common denominator, and then multiply the result by the original numerator.

Start with $\frac{3}{5}$. Divide the original denominator (5) into the new common denominator (40): $40 \div 5 = 8$. Next multiply the result (8) by the original numerator (3): $8 \times 3 = 24$. The equivalent fraction is $\frac{24}{40}$.

Perform the same operation with the second fraction, . Divide the original denominator (8) into the new common denominator (40): $40 \div 8 = 5$. Next multiply this (5) by the original numerator (1): $5 \times 1 = 5$. The equivalent fraction is $\frac{5}{40}$.

Now that the fractions have the same denominator, you can add or subtract them as shown in the previous section:

$$\frac{3}{5} + \frac{1}{8} = \frac{24}{40} + \frac{5}{40} = \frac{29}{40}$$

Performing multiple operations

By now you're probably anxious to test your newfound ability to work with fractions. Give this one a try:

$$\frac{\left(\frac{1}{8}+\frac{3}{4}\right)}{\left(\frac{3}{5}-\frac{2}{10}\right)}\times\frac{4}{5}$$

On the surface, this looks like a complicated problem. But, if you remember the *order of operations* (see the "Order of Operations" section) and take the problem one step at a time, it's really easy.

Under the order of operations, you do the work in the parentheses first:

$$\frac{1}{8}+\frac{3}{4}=\frac{1}{8}+\frac{6}{8}=\frac{7}{8} \text{ and } \frac{3}{5}-\frac{2}{10}=\frac{6}{10}-\frac{2}{10}=\frac{4}{10}=\frac{2}{5}$$

The problem now reads $\left(\frac{7}{8}\div\frac{2}{5}\right)\times\frac{4}{5}$.

Continue by performing the next operation in the parentheses:

$$\frac{7}{8}\div\frac{2}{5}=\frac{7}{8}\times\frac{5}{2}=\frac{35}{16}$$

The problem is now much simpler: $\frac{35}{16}\times\frac{4}{5}$.

$$\frac{35}{16}\times\frac{4}{5}=\frac{35\times4}{16\times5}=\frac{140}{80}=\frac{70}{40}=\frac{35}{20}=1\frac{15}{20}=1\frac{3}{4}$$

Converting fractions to decimals

Some math problems will require you to perform operations on both decimal numbers (see the "Dealing with Decimals" section) and fractions. To properly perform such calculations, you must either convert the fraction to a decimal number or convert the decimal to a fraction.

Converting a fraction to a decimal number is easy. You simply divide the numerator by the denominator:

$$\frac{3}{4}=3\div4=0.75$$

What could be easier than that? Try the following:

Solve: $\frac{1}{2}+0.34$.

Convert the fraction to a decimal by dividing the numerator by the denominator:

$$\frac{1}{2}=1\div2=0.5$$

Now you can easily perform the operation: 0.5 + 0.34 = 0.84.

Comparing fractions

The two math subtests of the ASVAB will often ask you to compare fractions to determine which one is the largest or which one is the smallest. If the fractions all have the same denominator, it's easy. The fraction with the largest numerator is the largest, and the one with the smallest numerator is the smallest.

But how do you compare fractions that have different denominators? There are two proven methods. I'll leave it up to you to determine which one you like the best.

Method 1: Finding a common denominator

The first method is to convert the fractions so that they all have a common denominator (see the "Adding and subtracting fractions with different denominators" section). After conversion, the fraction with the largest numerator is the largest fraction, and the one with the smallest numerator is the smallest. This is the method you probably learned in school.

Which of the following fractions is the largest: $\frac{5}{12}$, $\frac{3}{4}$, $\frac{9}{15}$, or $\frac{13}{16}$?

First, find a common multiple for each denominator:

- ✔ **The multiples of 12 are:** 12, 24, 36, 48, 60, 72, 84, 96, 108, 120, 132, 144, 156, 168, 180, 192, 204, 216, 228, 240.
- ✔ **The multiples of 4 are:** 4, 8, 12, 16, 20, 24, 28, 32, 36, 40, 44, 48, 52, 56, 60, 64, 68, 72, 76, 80, 84, 88, 92, 100, 104, 108, 112, 116, 122 . . . 240.
- ✔ **The multiples of 15 are:** 15, 30, 45, 60, 75, 90, 105, 120, 135, 150, 165, 180, 195, 210, 225, 240.
- ✔ **The multiples of 16 are:** 16, 32, 48, 64, 80, 96, 112, 128, 144, 160, 176, 192, 208, 224, 240.

The lowest common denominator for all four fractions is 240.

Next, convert all the fractions so that they have a denominator of 240. Do this by dividing the new common denominator by the original denominator of the fraction, and then multiplying the result by the original numerator:

- ✔ $\frac{5}{12} = \frac{100}{240}$
- ✔ $\frac{3}{4} = \frac{180}{240}$
- ✔ $\frac{9}{15} = \frac{144}{240}$
- ✔ $\frac{13}{16} = \frac{195}{240}$

The largest fraction is the one with the largest numerator, or $\frac{195}{240}$ or $\frac{13}{16}$.

Method 2: The cross-product method

You may have found Method 1 to be a bit time-consuming. If so, I think you'll enjoy this method. I certainly wish my teachers had heard of it when I was in high school. Maybe they explained it and I was sleeping that day.

The second method is called the *cross-product method*. To use it, you compare the cross-product of two fractions. The first cross-product is the product of the first numerator and the second denominator. The second cross-product is the product of the second numerator and the first denominator. If the cross-products are equal, the fractions are equivalent. If the first cross-product is larger, the first fraction is larger. If the second cross-product is larger, the second fraction is larger.

Compare the same fractions again:

Which of the following fractions is the largest: $\frac{5}{12}$, $\frac{3}{4}$, $\frac{9}{15}$, or $\frac{13}{16}$?

Compare the first two fractions, $\frac{5}{12}$ and $\frac{3}{4}$: $5 \times 4 = 20$ and $12 \times 3 = 36$. The second fraction is larger.

Compare the largest fraction, $\frac{3}{4}$, with the next fraction, $\frac{9}{15}$: $3 \times 15 = 45$ and $4 \times 9 = 36$, so $\frac{3}{4}$ is still the largest fraction.

Take the largest fraction, $\frac{3}{4}$, and compare it to the final fraction, $\frac{13}{16}$: $3 \times 16 = 48$, and $4 \times 13 = 52$. The final fraction, $\frac{13}{16}$, is the largest.

Getting rational about ratios

Ratios represent how one quantity is related to another quantity. A ratio may be written as $A{:}B$ or $\frac{A}{B}$ or by the phrase "*A* to *B*."

A ratio of 1:3 says that the second quantity is three times as large as the first. A ratio of 2:3 means that the second quantity is three times larger than one-half of the first quantity. A ratio of 5:4 means the second quantity is four times larger than one-fifth of the first quantity.

A ratio is actually a fraction. For example, the fraction $\frac{3}{4}$ is also a ratio of 3 to 4. Solve problems including ratios the same way you solve problems that include fractions.

Dealing with Decimals

Decimals are a method of writing fractional numbers without writing a fraction having a numerator and denominator. The fraction $\frac{7}{10}$ could be written as the decimal 0.7. The period or decimal point indicates that this is a decimal. The decimal 0.7 could be pronounced as "seven-tenths" or as "zero point seven."

There are other decimals such as hundredths or thousandths. They're all based on the number ten, just like our number system:

- 0.7: Seven-tenths ($\frac{7}{10}$)

- 0.07: Seven-hundredths ($\frac{7}{100}$)

- 0.007: Seven-thousandths ($\frac{7}{1,000}$)

- 0.0007: Seven-ten-thousandths ($\frac{7}{10,000}$)

- 0.00007: Seven-hundred-thousandths ($\frac{7}{100,000}$)

If a decimal is less than 1, it's traditional in mathematics to place a zero before the decimal point. Write "0.7" not ".7"

A decimal may be greater than one. The decimal 3.7 would be pronounced as "three and seven-tenths" ($3\frac{7}{10}$).

Converting decimals to fractions

Remember, a decimal is just another way of expressing a fraction — 0.7 is actually $\frac{7}{10}$, 0.07 is $\frac{7}{100}$, and so on. To convert a decimal to a fraction, write all the digits following the decimal point in the numerator. If there are zeros before any nonzero digits, they can be ignored.

The denominator is always a one followed by zeros. The number of zeros in the denominator is determined by the total number of digits to the right of the decimal point (including the leading zeros):

- ✔ **One digit:** Denominator = 10. Example: $0.7 = \frac{7}{100}$

- ✔ **Two digits:** Denominator = 100. Example: $0.25 = \frac{25}{100}$

- ✔ **Three digits:** Denominator = 1,000. Example: $0.351 = \frac{351}{1,000}$

- ✔ **Four digits:** Denominator = 10,000. Example: $0.0041 = \frac{41}{10,000}$

Of course, fractions can also be converted to decimals (see the "Converting fractions to decimals" section, earlier in this chapter).

Adding and subtracting decimals

You add and subtract decimals just as you do regular numbers (integers), except that, before you perform your operation, you arrange the numbers in a column with the decimals lined up one over the other.

Add the numbers 3.147, 148.392, and 0.074.

Put the numbers in an addition column with the decimals lined up, and perform the addition:

$$
\begin{array}{r}
3.147 \\
148.392 \\
+0.074 \\
\hline
151.613
\end{array}
$$

Multiplying decimals

There are three steps to multiplying decimals:

1. **Convert the decimals to whole numbers by moving the decimal points to the right, remembering to count how many spaces you move each decimal point.**

2. **Multiply the whole numbers just as you would perform any other multiplication.**

3. **Place the decimal point in the sum by moving the decimal point to the left the same number of (total) spaces you moved them to the right at the beginning.**

Multiply: $3.724 \times 0.0004 \times 9.42$.

First convert the decimals to whole numbers by moving the decimal points to the right (remember to count).

> 3.724 becomes 3,724 (decimal moved three spaces).
>
> 0.0004 becomes 4 (decimal moved four spaces).
>
> 9.42 becomes 942 (decimal moved two spaces).

Next, perform the multiplication on the whole numbers:

> $3{,}724 \times 4 \times 942 = 14{,}032{,}032$

Finally, replace the decimal point in the correct position by moving it to the left the same number of places you moved them to the right. You moved the decimal points a total of nine spaces to the right at the beginning, so now place the decimal point nine spaces to the left:

> 14,032,032 becomes 0.014032032

Dividing decimals

Dividing decimals can be a challenge. You have to use both subtraction and multiplication. You also need to be pretty good at rounding (see the "Rounding" section) and estimating numbers.

You're not allowed to use a calculator on the ASVAB math subtests.

There are two ways to divide decimals: long division and conversion.

Long division

To do long division with decimals, follow these steps:

1. **If the divisor is not a whole number, move the decimal point in the divisor all the way to the right (to make it a whole number), and move the decimal point in the dividend the same number of places to the right.**

2. **Position the decimal point in the result directly above the decimal point in the dividend.**

3. **Divide as usual.**

    If the divisor doesn't go into the dividend evenly, add zeroes to the right of the last digit in the dividend and keep dividing until it comes out evenly or a repeating pattern shows up.

Try the following division problem:

$7.42 \div 0.7$.

Write the problem on your scratch paper in long-division form:

> $0.7\overline{)7.42}$

Now move the decimal point one place to the right, which makes the divisor a whole number. Also move the decimal point in the dividend one place to the right:

> $7\overline{)74.2}$

Position the decimal point in the result directly above the decimal point in the dividend:

$$7\overline{)74.2}$$

Divide as usual. 7 goes into 70, ten times:

$$
\begin{array}{r}
10. \\
7\overline{)74.2} \\
\underline{70} \\
04.2
\end{array}
$$

7 goes into 42 six times:

$$
\begin{array}{r}
10.6 \\
7\overline{)74.2} \\
\underline{70} \\
042 \\
\underline{42} \\
0
\end{array}
$$

Conversion method

Decimals are just another way to display fractions. The other way to divide decimals is to convert the decimals to fractions (see the "Converting decimals to fractions" section), and then divide the fractions (see "Dividing fractions").

Try the same problem using the conversion method.

$7.42 \div 0.7$.

First, convert the decimals to fractions:

$$7.42 = 7\frac{42}{100} = \frac{742}{100}$$

$$0.7 = \frac{7}{10}$$

$$7.42 \div 0.7 = \frac{742}{100} \div \frac{7}{10}$$

Take the reciprocal of the divisor (flip the second fraction upside down), and then multiply:

$$\frac{742}{100} \times \frac{10}{7} = \frac{742 \times 10}{100 \times 7} = \frac{7,420}{700}$$

The fraction $\frac{7,420}{700}$ can be simplified (see "Simplifying fractions") to $10\frac{3}{5}$. Convert $\frac{3}{5}$ to a decimal (see "Converting fractions to decimals"), and the answer is 10.6.

Rounding

Rounding a number means limiting a number to a few (or no) decimal places. For example, if you have a $1.97 in change in your pocket, you may say, "I have about two dollars." The rounding process simplifies mathematical operations.

Often, numbers are rounded to the nearest tenth. The math subtests that make up the AFQT may ask you to do this. For any number five and over, round the digit to the left up; for any number under five, round the digit to the left down. Thus, 1.55 can be rounded up to 1.6, and 1.34 can be rounded down to 1.3.

Other numbers, such as whole numbers, can also be rounded. For example, rounded to the nearest 100, 1,427 can be rounded to 1,400. However, most of the rounding operations you'll encounter on the Mathematics Knowledge subtest will involve rounding decimals to the nearest tenth or nearest hundredth.

Percents

Percent literally means "part of 100." That means, for example, that 25 percent is equal to $\frac{25}{100}$, which is equal to 0.25.

If a problem asks you to find 25 percent of 250, it's asking you to multiply 250 by 0.25.

To convert a percent to a decimal number, remove the percentage sign, and move the decimal point two places to the left: 15 percent is 0.15 and 15.32 percent is 0.1532. Conversely, to change a decimal number to percent, add the percentage sign, and move the decimal point two places to the right: 4.321 is equal to 432.1 percent.

Playing with Positive and Negative Numbers

Numbers can be positive or negative. A positive number is any number greater than zero. So, 4, 3.2, 793, $\frac{3}{4}$, $\frac{1}{2}$, and 430,932,843,784 are all positive numbers.

Numbers smaller than zero are negative numbers. For every positive number, there is a negative number equivalent. Negative numbers are expressed by putting a minus sign (–) in front of the number. –7, –18, $-\frac{3}{4}$, and –743.42 are all negative numbers.

In the math subtests of the ASVAB, you'll often be asked to perform mathematical operations on positive and negative numbers. Just remember the following rules:

- ✔ **Adding two positive numbers always results in a positive number:** 3 + 3 = 6
- ✔ **Adding two negative numbers always results in a negative number:** –3 + –3 = –6
- ✔ **Adding a negative number is the same as subtracting a positive number:** 3 + (–3) = 3 – 3 = 0
- ✔ **Subtracting a negative number is the same as adding a positive number:** 3 – (–3) = 3 + 3 = 6
- ✔ **Multiplying or dividing two positive numbers always results in a positive number:** 3 ÷ 3 = 1
- ✔ **Multiplying or dividing two negative numbers always results in a positive number:** –3 × –3 = 9
- ✔ **Multiplying or dividing a negative number with a positive number always results in a negative number:** –3 × 3 = –9

When you multiply a series of positive and negative numbers, count the number of negative numbers. If the number is even, the result will be positive. If the number is odd, the result will be negative.

Everyone knows that 10 is larger than 5 and that 20 is larger than 15. With negative numbers, however, it works just the opposite: –10 is smaller than –5, and –20 is smaller than –15.

As you'll recall from your math in school, any number multiplied by zero is zero.

Teachers used to teach that numbers could not be divided by zero, but then those Einstein think-a-likes in advanced calculus showed that was not quite true. The answer to a division-by-zero operation is known as "indeterminate" because the answer depends on what the situation is.

Rooting for Roots and Powers

Many of the problems you'll see on the ASVAB math subtests require you to perform calculation involving roots, such as square roots and cube roots, and numbers raised by exponents. If that sounds confusing, don't worry — it's really not. Read on.

Advice about exponents

Exponents are an easy way to show that a number is to be multiplied by itself a certain number of times. For example, 5^2 is the same as 5×5, and 4^3 is the same as $4 \times 4 \times 4$. The number or variable that is to be multiplied by itself is called the *base,* and the number or variable showing how many times it is to be multiplied by itself is called the *exponent*.

Here are important rules when working with exponents:

✔ **Any base raised to the power of one equals itself.** For example, $6^1 = 6$.

✔ **Any base raised to the zero power (except 0) equals 1.** For example, $3^0 = 1$.

In case you were wondering, according to most calculus textbooks, 0^0 is an "indeterminate form." What mathematicians mean by "indeterminate form" is that, in some cases, it has one value, and in other cases it has another. This is advanced calculus, however, and you won't have to worry about it on the ASVAB math subtests.

✔ **To multiply terms with the same base, you add the exponents.** For example, $7^2 \times 7^3 = 7^5$.

✔ **To divide terms with the same base, you subtract the exponents.** For example, $4^5 \div 4^3 = 4^2$.

✔ **If a base has a negative exponent, it is equal to its reciprocal with a positive exponent.** For example, $3^{-4} = \left(\frac{1}{3}\right) = \frac{1}{3^4}$.

✔ **When a product has an exponent, each factor is raised to that power.** For example, $(5 \times 3)^3 = 5^3 \times 3^3$.

Regarding roots

A root is the opposite of a power or an exponent. There are infinite kinds of roots. First, there is the *square root,* which means "undoing" a base to the second power; the cube root, which means "undoing" a base raised to the third power; a fourth root, for numbers raised to the fourth power; and so on.

However, on the ASVAB math subtests, the only questions you're likely to see will involve square roots, and possibly a couple of cube roots.

Getting square with square roots

A math operation requiring you to find a square root is designated by the *radical symbol* $\left(\sqrt{} \right)$. The number underneath the radical line is called the *radicand*. For example, in the operation $\sqrt{36}$, the number 36 is the radicand.

A square root is a number that, when multiplied by itself, produces the radicand. Take the square root of 36 — $\sqrt{36}$ — for example. If you multiply 6 by itself (6×6), you come up with 36, so 6 is the square root of 36.

However, as I mention in the "Playing with Positive and Negative Numbers" section, when you multiply two negative numbers together, it results in a positive number. For example, -6×-6 also equals 36, so -6 is also the square root of 36.

That brings me to an important rule: When you take a square root, there will be two square roots — one positive and one negative.

It's also possible to compute the square roots of negative numbers, such as $\sqrt{-36}$, but this involves concepts such as imaginary numbers, and that's college-level math, or advanced math classes in high school, so you won't be asked to do that on the ASVAB.

Square roots come in two flavors:

- **Perfect squares:** Only a few numbers, called *perfect squares,* have exact square roots.

- **Irrational numbers:** All the rest of the numbers have square roots that include decimals that go on forever and have no pattern that repeats (non-repeating, non-terminating decimals), so they're called *irrational numbers.*

Perfect squares

Finding a square root can be difficult to find without a calculator, but because you can't use a calculator during the test, you're going to have to use your mind and some guessing methods. To find the square root of a number without a calculator, make an educated guess and then verify your results.

The radical symbol indicates that you're to find the principal square root of the number under the radical. The principal square root is a positive number. But if you're solving an equation such as $x^2 = 36$, then you give both the positive and negative roots: 6 and -6.

To use the educated-guess method, you have to know the square roots of a few perfect squares. One good way to do this is to study the squares of the square roots 1 through 12:

- 1 and -1 are both square roots of 1.

- 2 and -2 are both square roots of 4.

- 3 and -3 are both square roots of 9.

- 4 and -4 are both square roots of 16.

- 5 and -5 are both square roots of 25.

- 6 and -6 are both square roots of 36.

- 7 and -7 are both square roots of 49.

- 8 and -8 are both square roots of 64.

- 9 and –9 are both square roots of 81.
- 10 and –10 are both square roots of 100.
- 11 and –11 are both square roots of 121.
- 12 and –12 are both square roots of 144.

Irrational numbers

When the ASVAB asks you to figure square roots of numbers that don't have perfect squares, the task gets a bit more difficult. If you have to find the square root of a number that isn't a perfect square, the ASVAB usually asks you to find the square root to the nearest tenth.

Suppose you run across this problem:

$\sqrt{54} =$

Think about what you know:

- You know from the preceding section that the square root of 49 is 7, and 54 is slightly greater than 49.
- You also know that the square root of 64 is 8, and 54 is slightly less than 64.
- So, if the number 54 is somewhere between 49 and 64, the square root of 54 is somewhere between 7 and 8.
- Because 54 is closer to 49 than to 64, the square root will be closer to 7 than to 8, so you can try 7.3 as the square root of 54:

  1. Multiply 7.3 by itself.

     $7.3 \times 7.3 = 53.29$, which is very close to 54.

  2. Try multiplying 7.4 by itself to see if it's any closer to 54.

     $7.4 \times 7.4 = 54.76$, which isn't as close to 54 as 53.29.

  3. So 7.3 is the square root of 54 to the nearest tenth.

Cube roots

A *cube root* is a number that when multiplied by itself three times equals the number under the radical line. For example, the cube root of 27 is 3 because $3 \times 3 \times 3 = 27$. A cube root is expressed by the radical sign with a 3 written on the left of the radical line. For example, the cube root of 27 would be expressed as $\sqrt[3]{27}$.

You may see one or two cube-root problems on the math subtests of the ASVAB, but probably not more than that. Plus, the problems you'll encounter will be perfect cubes and won't involve irrational numbers.

Unlike square roots, numbers only have one possible cube root. If the radicand is positive, the cube root will be a positive number.

Also, unlike square roots, it's possible to find the cube root of a negative number, without involving advanced mathematics. If the radicand is negative, the cube root will also be negative. For example, $\sqrt[3]{-27} = -3$.

Just like square roots, you should memorize a few common cube roots:

- 1 is the cube root of 1 and –1 is the cube root of –1.
- 2 is the cube root of 8 and –2 is the cube root of –8.

✔ 3 is the cube root of 27 and –3 is the cube root of –27.

✔ 4 is the cube root of 64 and –4 is the cube root of –64.

✔ 5 is the cube root of 125 and –5 is the cube root of –125.

✔ 6 is the cube root of 216 and –6 is the cube root of –216.

✔ 7 is the cube root of 343 and –7 is the cube root of –343.

✔ 8 is the cube root of 512 and –8 is the cube root of –512.

✔ 9 is the cube root of 729 and –9 is the cube root of –729.

✔ 10 is the cube root of 1,000 and –10 is the cube root of –1,000.

Scientific notation

Scientific notation is a compact format for writing very large or very small numbers. Although it's most often used in scientific fields, you may find a question or two on the Mathematics Knowledge subtest of the ASVAB asking you to covert a number to scientific notation, or vice versa.

Scientific notation separates a number into two parts: a *characteristic,* always greater than or equal to 1 and less than 10, and a *power of ten.* Thus 1.25×10^4 means 1.25 times 10 to the fourth power or 12,500; 5.79×10^{-8} means 5.79 divided by 10 to the eighth power or 0.0000000579.

Alphabet Soup: Algebra Review

Algebra problems are equations, which means that the quantities on both sides of the equal sign are equal — they're the same: 2 = 2, 1 + 1 = 2, and 3 – 1 = 2. In all these cases, the quantities are the same on both sides of the equal sign. So, if $x = 2$, then x *is* 2 because the equal sign says so.

Visiting variables

Most algebraic equations involve the use of one or more variables. A *variable* is a symbol that represents a number. Usually, algebra problems use letters such as n, t, or x for variables. In most algebra problems, your goal is to find the value of the variable. For example, in the equation, $x + 4 = 60$, you would try to find the value of x by making use of several different useful rules of algebra.

Rules of algebra

Algebra has several rules or properties, which — when combined — allow you to simplify equations. Some (not all) equations can be simplified to a complete solution:

✔ **You may combine like terms.** This means adding or subtracting terms with variables of the same kind. The expression $4x + 4x$ simplifies to $8x$. $2y + y$ is equal to $3y$. The expression 13 – 7 + 3 simplifies to 9.

✔ **You may use the distributive property to remove parentheses around unlike terms (see "Mental Math: The Distributive Property," earlier in this chapter).**

✔ You may add or subtract any value, as long as you do it to both sides of the equation.

✔ You may multiply or divide by any number (except 0), as long as you do it to both sides of the equation.

Combining like terms

One of the most common ways to simplify an expression is to combine like terms. Numeric terms may be combined, and any terms with the same variable part may be combined.

Take, for instance, the expression $5x + 3 + 3x - 6y + 4 + 7y$.

In algebra, when two or more variables are multiplied, it's traditional to place the variables next to each other, and omit the multiplication sign ($\times$): $a \times b = ab$. The same rule applies to variables multiplied by numbers: $4 \times y = 4y$.

$5x$ and $3x$ are like terms. So are $-6y$ and $7y$. 3 and 4 are also like terms, because they are numbers without variables. So, combining the like terms, you have

$5x + 3x = 8x$

$-6y + 7y = 1y$ (or just y)

$3 + 4 = 7$

By combining the like terms, the expression $5x + 3 + 3x - 6y + 4 + 7y$ simplifies to $8x + y + 7$.

Using the distributive property

I know what you're thinking: You're thinking that combining like terms is pretty cool, but what if you have unlike terms contained within parentheses? Doesn't the order of operations require you to deal with terms in parentheses first? Indeed, it does, and that's where the distributive property comes in.

Recall from the "Mental Math: The Distributive Property" section, $a(b + c) = ab + ac$. For example, $6(4 + 3)$ is the same, mathematically, as $(6 \times 4) + (6 \times 3)$.

Applying the same principle to algebra, the distributive property can be pretty darn useful in getting rid of those pesky parentheses:

$4(x + y) = 4x + 4y$

Using addition and subtraction

You can use addition and subtraction to get all the terms with variables on one side of an equation, and all the numeric terms on the other. That's an important step in finding the value for the variable.

The equation $3x = 21$ has only the variable on one side and only a number on the other. The equation $3x + 4 = 25$ does not.

You can add and subtract any number, as long as you do it to both sides of the equation. In this case, you want to get rid of the number 4 on the left side of the equation. How do you make the 4 disappear? Simply subtract 4 from it:

$3x + 4 - 4 = 25 - 4$

The equation simplifies to $3x = 21$.

Using multiplication and division

The rules of algebra also allow you to multiply and divide both sides of an equation by any number except zero. From the last section, you have an equation that reads $3x = 21$, or 3 times x equals 21. However, you want to find the value of x, not three times x.

What happens if you divide a number by itself? The result is 1. Therefore, to change $3x$ to $1x$ (or x), divide both sides of the equation by 3:

$$3x = 21$$

$$\frac{3x}{3} = \frac{21}{3}$$

$$1x = 7$$

$$x = 7$$

But what if the equation was $\frac{2}{3}x = 21$? What would you do then?

I'll give you a hint: If you multiply any fraction by its reciprocal, the result is 1. Remember, a reciprocal is a fraction flipped upside-down.

$$\frac{2}{3}x = 21$$

$$\frac{3}{2} \times \frac{2}{3}x = 21 \times \frac{3}{2}$$

Remember to multiply both sides of the equation by $\frac{3}{2}$.

$$1x = \frac{21}{1} \times \frac{3}{2}$$

$$x = \frac{21 \times 3}{2}$$

$$x = \frac{63}{2}$$

$$x = 31\frac{1}{2}$$

All Is Not Equal: Inequalities

Remember when I said that all equations include one or more equal signs (=)? I stand by that statement. After all, I wouldn't lie to you. However, some math problems look very much like equations, but they use signs other than the equal sign.

These problems are called *inequalities*. An equation states that each side of the equation separated by the equal sign is equal to the other. An inequality, on the other hand, says that the two sides, separated by an inequality sign, are *not* equal to each other.

Just as with equations, the solution to an inequality is all the values that make the inequality true. For the most part, you solve inequalities the same as you would solve a normal equation. There are some facts of inequality life you need to keep in mind, however. Short and sweet, here they are:

- ✔ **Negative numbers** are less than zero and less than positive numbers.
- ✔ **Zero** is less than positive numbers but greater than negative numbers.
- ✔ **Positive numbers** are greater than negative numbers and greater than zero.

Although there is only one equal sign (=), there are several signs associated with inequalities:

- ✔ ≠ means *does not equal* in the way that 3 *does not equal* 4 or 3 ≠ 4.

- ✔ > means *greater than* in the way that 4 *is greater than* 3 or 4 > 3.

- ✔ < means *less than* in the way the 3 *is less than* 4, or 3 < 4.

- ✔ ≤ means *less than or equal to* in the way that x may be *less than or equal to* 4 or $x ≤ 4$.

- ✔ ≥ means *greater than or equal to* in the way that x may be *greater than or equal to* 3 or $x ≥ 3$.

You solve inequalities using the same principles of algebra used to solve equations, with the exception of multiplying or dividing each side by a negative number (see the "Rules of algebra" section). Take the following example:

Solve: $3x + 4 < 25$

You'll note that the preceding inequality is very similar to the equation I used as an example in the last section ($3x + 4 = 25$).

The equation says that $3x$ plus 4 is equal to 25. The inequality says that $3x$ plus 4 is less than 25. However, the inequality is solved in the same way as the equation:

$$3x + 4 < 25$$
$$3x + 4 - 4 < 25 - 4$$
$$3x < 21$$
$$\frac{3x}{3} < \frac{21}{3}$$
$$x < 7$$

Although you solve inequalities the same way you solve equations, there are two important rules you need to keep in mind when working with inequalities:

- ✔ In algebra, if $a = b$, then $b = a$. In other words, you can swap the data on each side of the equal sign, and the equation means the same thing. So, $2x + 4 = 18$ and $18 = 2x + 4$ are the same thing. This doesn't work with inequalities. In other words, $2x + 4 > 18$ is not the same as $18 > 2x + 4$. When you swap the data in an inequality, you have to change the inequality sign to balance the inequality (keep the inequty true). So, $2x + 4 > 18$ is the same as $18 < 2x + 4$.

- ✔ When you multiply or divide both sides of the inequality by a negative number, the inequality sign is reversed. So, if you multiply both sides of the inequality $3 < 4$ by –4, your answer is $-12 > -16$.

Solving Quadratics

Algebra questions often ask you to solve for x or solve for an unknown. These questions can be expressed, for example, as $x = 2 + 3$. You simply isolate the unknown on one side of the equation and solve the other side to learn what x equals. In this case, x equals 5. The topic of solving for unknowns is covered in more depth in the section, "Alphabet Soup: Algebra Review," earlier in this chapter.

So what's a quadratic equation? Sounds a little scary, huh? The Mathematical Knowledge subtest may ask you to solve one of these equations, but have no fear. You've come to the right place. This section can help.

Recognizing quadratics

A *quadratic equation* is an algebraic equation in which the highest exponent to which the unknown is raised is 2, as in x^2. They can be very simple, or very complex (or several degrees of difficulty in between). Here are some examples:

- ✔ $x^2 = 36$
- ✔ $x^2 + 4 = 72$
- ✔ $x^2 + 3x - 33 = 0$

The exponent in quadratics is never higher than 2 (because it would then no longer be the *square* of an unknown, but a cube or something else). An equation that includes the variable x^3 or x^4 is *not* a quadratic.

Solving quadratics

There are three primary ways to solve quadratics: the square-root method, factoring, or the quadratic formula. Which method you choose depends on the difficulty of the equation.

The square-root method

Simple quadratic equations (those that consist of just one squared term and a number) can be solved by using the *square-root rule:*

If $x^2 = k$, then $x = \pm\sqrt{k}$, as long as k isn't a negative number.

Remember to include the ± sign, which indicates that the answer is a positive or negative number. Take the following simple quadratic equation:

Solve: $3x^2 + 4 = 31$

1. **First, isolate the variable by subtracting 4 from each side.**

   The result is $3x^2 = 27$.

2. **Next, get rid of the 3 by dividing both sides of the equation by 3.**

   The result is $x^2 = 9$.

3. **You can now solve by using the square root rule.**

   $x^2 = 9$

   $x = \pm\sqrt{9}$

   $x = 3$ and $x = -3$

The factoring method

Most quadratic equations you'll encounter on the ASVAB math subtests can be solved by putting the equation into the quadratic form, and then factoring.

The *quadratic form* is $ax^2 + bx + c = 0$, where a, b, and c are just numbers. All quadratic equations can be expressed in this form. Want to see some examples?

- ✔ **$2x^2 - 4x = 32$:** This equation can be expressed in the quadratic form as $2x^2 + (-4x) + (-32) = 0$. So, $a = 2$, $b = -4$, and $c = -32$.

- ✔ **$x^2 = 36$:** You can express this as $1x^2 + 0x + (-36)$. So, $a = 1$, $b = 0$, and $c = -36$.

- ✔ **$3x^2 + 6x + 4 = -33$:** Expressed in quadratic form, this would read $3x + 6x + 37 = 0$. So, $a = 3$, $b = 6$, and $c = 37$.

Ready to factor? How about trying the following equation?

Solve: $x^2 + 5x + 6 = 0$.

Because I like you, I've already expressed the equation in quadratic form, saving you a little time.

You can use the factoring method for most quadratic equations where $a = 1$ and c is a positive number.

The first step in factoring a quadratic equation is to draw two sets of parentheses on your scratch paper, and then place an x at the front of each. As with the original quadratic, the equation should equal zero:

$$(x\ )(x\ ) = 0$$

The next step is to find two numbers that, when multiplied together, equal c, and when added together, equal b. In our example equation, $b = 5$, and $c = 6$, so you need to hunt for two numbers that multiply to 6, and when added, results in 5. For example, $2 \times 3 = 6$ and $2 + 3 = 5$. In this case, the two numbers you're seeking are positive 2 and positive 3.

Finally, put these two numbers into your set of parentheses:

$$(x + 2)(x + 3) = 0$$

This means that $x + 2 = 0$, and/or $x + 3 = 0$. The solution to this quadratic equation is $x = -2$ and/or $x = -3$.

When choosing your factors, remember that they can be either positive or negative numbers. You can use clues from the signs of b and c to help you find the numbers (factors) you need:

- ✔ If c is positive, then the factors you're looking for are either both positive or both negative:
  - If b is positive, then the factors are positive
  - If b is negative, then the factors are negative.
  - b is the sum of the two factors that give you c.

- ✔ If c is negative, then the factors you're looking for are of alternating signs; that is, one is negative and one is positive:
  - If b is positive, then the larger factor is positive.
  - If b is negative, then the larger factor is negative.
  - b is the difference between the two factors that give you c.

Try another one, just for giggles:

Solve: $x^2 - 7x + 6 = 0$

Start by writing your parentheses:

$$(x \quad)(x \quad) = 0$$

In this equation, b = –7 and c = +6. Because b is negative and c is positive, both factors will be negative.

You're looking for two negative numbers that multiply to 6 and add to –7. Those numbers are –1 and –6. Plugging the numbers into your parentheses, you get $(x - 1)(x - 6) = 0$. So, $x = 1$ and/or $x = 6$.

The quadratic formula

The square-root method can be used for simple quadratics, and the factoring method can easily be used for many other quadratics, as long as $a = 1$. But what if a doesn't equal 1, or you can't easily find two numbers that multiply to c and add up to b?

You can use the quadratic formula to solve any quadratic equation. So, why not just use the quadratic formula and forget about the square-root and factoring methods? Because the quadratic formula is kind of complex:

$$x = \frac{-b \pm \sqrt{b^2 - 4ac}}{2a}$$

The quadratic formula uses the a, b, and c from $ax^2 + bx + c = 0$, just like the factoring method.

Armed with this knowledge, you can apply your skills to a complex quadratic equation:

Solve: $2x^2 - 4x - 3 = 0$

In this equation, $a = 2$, $b = -4$, and $c = -3$. Plug the known values into the quadratic formula:

$$x = \frac{-b \pm \sqrt{b^2 - 4ac}}{2a}$$

$$x = \frac{-(-4) \pm \sqrt{(-4)^2 - 4(2)(-3)}}{2(2)}$$

$$x = \frac{4 \pm \sqrt{16 + 24}}{4}$$

$$x = \frac{4 \pm \sqrt{40}}{4}$$

$$x = \frac{4 \pm 6.32}{4}$$

$$x = \frac{4 + 6.32}{4} \text{ and } x = \frac{4 - 6.32}{4}$$

$$x = \frac{10.325553}{4} \text{ and } x = \frac{-2.32}{4}$$

$$x = 2.58 \text{ and } x = -0.58$$

Knowing All the Angles: Geometry Review

According to my handy pocket dictionary, *geometry* is "the branch of mathematics that deals with the deduction of the properties, measurement, and relationships of points, lines, angles, and figures in space from their defining conditions by means of certain assumed properties of space." Huh? Want to try that again in English?

Geometry is simply the branch of mathematics that is concerned with shapes, lines, and angles. From the perspective of the ASVAB math subtests, you should be able to identify basic geometric shapes and know certain properties about them, so you can determine their angles and measurements. You'll see a lot of geometry-related questions on both the Mathematics Knowledge and the Arithmetic Reasoning subtests of the ASVAB.

Knowing all the angles

Angles are formed when two lines intersect at a point. Many geometric shapes are formed by intersecting lines, which form angles. Angles can be measured in degrees. The greater the number of degrees, the wider the angle is:

- A *straight line* is 180°.
- A *right angle* is exactly 90°.
- An *acute angle* is more than 0° and less than 90°.
- An *obtuse angle* is more than 90° but less than 180°.
- *Complementary angles* are two angles that equal 90° when added together.
- *Supplementary angles* are two angles that equal 180° when added together.

Take a look at the different types of angles in Figure 8-3.

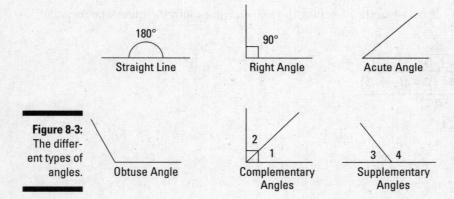

Figure 8-3: The different types of angles.

Common geometric shapes

I'm not going to explain all the possible geometric shapes for two reasons: (1) It would take this entire book and (2) You don't need to know them all to solve the math problems you'll find on the ASVAB. However, you should recognize the most common shapes associated with geometry.

Getting square with quadrilaterals

A *quadrilateral* is a geometric shape with four sides. All quadrilaterals contain interior angles totaling 360°. Here are the five most common types of quadrilaterals:

- **Squares** have four sides of equal length, and all the angles are right angles.
- **Rectangles** have all right angles.
- **Rhombuses** have four sides of equal length, but the angles don't have to be right angles.
- **Trapezoids** have at least two sides that are parallel.
- **Parallelograms** have opposite sides that are parallel, and their opposite sides and angles are equal.

Figure 8-4 gives you an idea of what these five quadrilaterals look like.

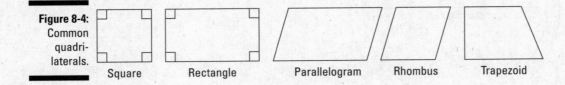

Figure 8-4: Common quadrilaterals.

Square   Rectangle   Parallelogram   Rhombus   Trapezoid

Trying out triangles

A *triangle* consists of three straight lines whose three interior angles always add up to 180°. The sides of a triangle are called *legs*. Triangles can be classified according to the relationship between their angles or the relationship between their sides or some combination of these relationships. You should know the three most common types of triangles:

- **Isosceles triangle:** Has two equal sides, and the angles opposite the equal sides are also equal.
- **Equilateral triangle:** Has three equal sides, and all the angles measure 60°.
- **Right triangle:** Has one right angle (90°; therefore, the remaining two angles are *complementary* (add up to 90°).

  The side opposite the right angle is called the *hypotenuse,* which is the longest side of a right triangle.

Check out Figure 8-5 to see what these triangles look like.

Figure 8-5: The three most common types of triangles.

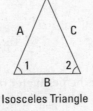

Isosceles Triangle

If sides A and C are equal, then angles 1 and 2 are equal.

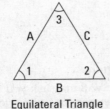

Equilateral Triangle

Sides A, B, C are equal. Angles 1, 2, 3 are equal.

Right Triangle

$A^2 + B^2 = C^2$

Settling on circles

A *circle* is formed when the points of a closed line are all located equal distances from a point called the *center* of the circle. A circle always has 360°. The closed line of a circle is called its perimeter or *circumference*. The *radius* of a circle is the measurement from the center of the circle to any point on the circumference of the circle. The *diameter* of the circle is measured as a line passing through the center of the circle, from a point on one side of the circle all the way to a point on the other side of the circle. The diameter of a circle is always twice as long as the radius. Figure 8-6 shows these relationships.

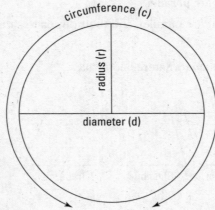

Figure 8-6: The parts of a circle.

Famous geometry formulas

The math subtests of the ASVAB will often ask you to use basic geometry formulas to calculate geometric measurements. You should commit these simple formulas to memory.

Quadrilateral formulas you should know

You may be asked to calculate the length of the perimeter, the area, or the diagonal of a square or rectangle. Use the following formulas:

- **Perimeter of a square:** $p = 4s$, where s = one side of the square
- **Area of a square:** $a = s^2$
- **Diagonal of a square:** $d = s\sqrt{2}$
- **Perimeter of a rectangle:** $p = 2l + 2w$, where l = the length and w = the width of the rectangle
- **Area of a rectangle:** $a = lw$
- **Diagonal of a rectangle:** $d = \sqrt{l^2 + w^2}$

Good-to-know triangle formulas

Some math problems on the ASVAB may ask you to calculate the perimeter or area of a triangle. The following formulas are used for these two purposes:

- **Perimeter of a triangle:** $p = s_1 + s_2 + s_3$, where s = the length of each leg of the triangle
- **Area of a triangle:** $a = \frac{1}{2}bh$, where b = the length of the triangle's base (bottom) and h = the height of the triangle

There is a special formula, called the *Pythagorean theorem,* that says if you know the length of any two sides of a triangle, you can find the length of the third side. This only works, however, on *right triangles* (see the "Trying out triangles" section). The formula is $a^2 + b^2 = c^2$, where c equals the length of the triangle's hypotenuse, and a and b equal the lengths of the remaining two sides, called *legs.*

Seizing circle formulas

Circles are a bit more complex than squares, rectangles, and triangles, and often involve invoking the value of π. In the "Math Terminology" section, earlier in this chapter, I tell you that π is approximately equal to 3.14.

- **Radius of a circle:** $r = \frac{1}{2}d$, where d = the diameter of the circle
- **Diameter of a circle:** $d = 2r$
- **Circumference of a circle:** $c = 2\pi r$
- **Area of a circle:** $a = \pi r^2$

Handy formulas for three-dimensional shapes

Sometimes the math subtests will require you to calculate measurements for solid (three-dimensional) shapes. These types of questions generally come in two flavors: calculating volume or calculating surface area.

Volume is the space a shape takes up. You can think of volume as how much a shape would hold if you poured water into it. *Surface area* is the area of the outside of the shape — for example, the amount of area you would have to cover if you were to paint the outside of the solid shape.

- **Volume of a cube:** $v = s^3$, where s = the length of one side of the cube
- **Volume of a rectangular box:** $v = lwh$, where l = the length, w = the width, and h = the height of the box
- **Volume of a cylinder:** $v = \pi r^2 h$, where r = the radius of the cylinder and h = the height of the cylinder
- **Surface area of a cube:** $SA = 6s^2$
- **Surface area of a rectangular box:** $SA = 2lw + 2wh + 2lh$

Chapter 9

The Mathematics Knowledge Subtest

Two math subtests help determine your AFQT score. I talk about the Arithmetic Reasoning subtest, which is all about math word problems, in Chapters 10 and 11. This chapter and Chapter 8 are designed to help you get ready for the other math subtest: the Mathematics Knowledge subtest.

Most of the time, the Mathematics Knowledge subtest only contains one or two questions testing each specific mathematical concept. For example, one question may ask you to multiply fractions, the next question may ask you to solve a mathematical inequality, and the question after that may ask you to find the value of an exponent. (If I've freaked you out with the last sentence, calm down. I cover all this stuff in Chapter 8.)

All this variety forces you to constantly shift your mental gears to quickly deal with different concepts. You can look at this situation from two perspectives: These mental gymnastics can be difficult and frustrating, especially if you know everything about solving for *x* but nothing about deriving a square root. But variety can also be the spice of life, as your grandma may have said. If you don't know how to solve a specific type of problem, this oversight may only cause you to get one question wrong (or maybe two — but think positive).

Taking Stock of the Test Structure

The Mathematics Knowledge subtest consists of 25 questions covering the entire array of high school math. You have 24 minutes to complete the subtest. You don't necessarily have to rush through each calculation, but the pace you need to set (a little less than a minute per question) doesn't exactly give you time to daydream about what you're having for dinner. You have to focus and concentrate to solve each problem quickly and accurately.

Like all math subtests on the ASVAB, the narrow-minded people who make up the rules have dictated you can't use a calculator. When you enter the testing room, you'll be given a pencil and a sheet of scratch paper. (I guess their thinking is that if you're in the middle of a combat zone and find a sudden need to solve for *x*, you may find your calculator full of sand and worthless.) The good news is, all the questions on the math subtests of the ASVAB are designed so that they can be solved without electronic calculation.

There are three types of questions on the Mathematics Knowledge subtest:

- **Direct math:** This type of question presents you with a mathematical equation and asks you to solve it.
- **Math law:** This type of question asks you a about a mathematical law, rule, term, or concept.
- **Combined:** This type of question asks you to use a mathematical law, rule, term, or concept to solve a problem.

Direct math questions

The direct math question is the most common type of question on the Mathematics Knowledge subtest. In a direct math question, you're presented with an equation and asked to solve it. You'll see a lot of these.

Solve for x: $2x + 4(2x + 7) = 3(2x + 4)$

(A) 0.75

(B) –4

(C) 1.25

(D) –1.25

This is an algebraic equation that you can solve using the rules of algebra (see Chapter 8):

$$2x + 4(2x + 7) = 3(2x + 4)$$
$$2x + 8x + 28 = 6x + 12$$
$$10x + 28 = 6x + 12$$
$$4x + 28 = 12$$
$$4x = -16$$
$$x = -4$$

Math law questions

Sometimes the Mathematics Knowledge subtest asks you a question that doesn't involve solving a mathematical problem. Instead, you're expected to answer a question concerning a mathematical concept, math term, rule, or law. You're not likely to see more than two or three of these kinds of questions on the test, however.

In the expression "$432xy + 124xy$," the "432" is called the:

(A) multiplier

(B) coefficient

(C) matrix

(D) prime

The answer is B, coefficient. A *coefficient* is the number multiplied times a variable or a product of variables or powers of variables in a term. (You'll find more useful math terms in Chapter 8.)

Combined questions

You may see eight or nine combined questions on the Mathematics Knowledge subtest. These questions require you to use a particular math term, rule, or concept to solve a mathematical problem.

What is the quotient of 4 and 4.

(A) 8

(B) 16

(C) 0

(D) 1

To solve this problem, you need to know that a *quotient* is the result of a division operation. When you've figured that out, you have to perform the operation:

$$4 \div 4 = 1$$

Planning Your Test Attack

For most people, scoring well on the Mathematics Knowledge subtest requires more than just showing up on time and borrowing a No. 2 pencil and piece of scratch paper. Maybe everything on the test will go perfectly, and you'll breeze through without a problem. On the other hand, maybe you'll get stuck on a question or run into other roadblocks. When this happens, having a plan of attack is helpful.

Keeping an eye on the all-important clock

Like all subtests of the ASVAB, the Mathematics Knowledge subtest is timed. You have just 24 minutes to try to correctly answer 25 questions. That's 57.6 seconds per question. (Do you like the way I used math to figure that out?)

If you're taking the computerized version of the ASVAB, your remaining time will be in the upper corner of your computer screen. If you're taking the paper version, the room will have a clock in it, and the start time and stop time will be posted somewhere in the room, easily visible to you and the other test takers.

Keep an eye on the clock. You want to try to finish the test before time runs out. Try to average about 45 or 50 seconds per question. If you get stuck on a question, try the "Playing the guessing game" techniques, later in this chapter.

Doubling your chances by double-checking

If you have time, double-check your answers. Those crafty test makers often provide wrong answer choices that work if you made a common error, so don't assume that just because your answer matches one of the possible answer choices that it's the right one. Look at the following example:

Solve: $\frac{1}{4} \div \frac{1}{2} =$

(A) $\frac{1}{8}$

(B) 2

(C) 17

(D) $\frac{1}{2}$

To correctly solve this problem, you multiply the first fraction by the reciprocal (flipped over) value of the second fraction:

$$\frac{1}{4} \div \frac{1}{2} = \frac{1}{4} \times \frac{2}{1} = \frac{2}{4} = \frac{1}{2}$$

If you multiplied the fractions instead of dividing, you would've gotten A. If you took the reciprocal of the first fraction instead of the second, you would've gotten B. If you took a wild guess, you might've gotten C.

Although double-checking your answers is always a good idea, remember to keep an eye on the clock. You don't want to run out of time with only half the questions answered, because you've spent too much time double-checking all your answers.

Using the answer choices to your advantage

If you're stuck on a particular problem, sometimes plugging the possible answer choices into the equation can help you find the right answer.

Solve: $\frac{1}{2}x - 45 = 5$

(A) 25

(B) 50

(C) 100

(D) 75

Suppose you experience a complete brain-freeze and can't remember how to handle a variable multiplied by a fraction. You don't have to jump straight to random guessing at this point. You can replace x in the equation with the known possible answer choices and see if any of them work.

The equation can be simplified to $\frac{1}{2}x = 50$.

> ✔ $x = 25$: $\frac{1}{2} \times 25 = 50 \to 12.5 = 50$. That doesn't work.

> ✔ $x = 50$: $\frac{1}{2} \times 50 = 50 \to 25 = 50$. That certainly doesn't work.

> ✔ $x = 100$: $\frac{1}{2} \times 100 = 50 \to 50 = 50$. You can stop here because C is the correct answer.

Don't forget that plugging in all the answers is time-consuming, so save this procedure until you've answered all the problems you can answer. If you're taking the computer version, you can't skip a question, so remember to budget your time wisely — if you don't have much time, just make a guess and move on. You may be able to solve the next question easily.

Playing the guessing game

Guessing wrong on any of the ASVAB subtests doesn't count against you. So scribble an answer — any answer — on your answer sheet because, if you don't, your chances of getting that answer right are zero. But, if you take a shot at it, your chances increase to 25 percent, or one in four.

If you're taking the paper version of the ASVAB, you can always skip the tough questions and come back to them after you've finished the easier ones. If you're taking the computerized version of the ASVAB, the software won't let you skip questions.

If you're taking the paper version of the test and elect to skip questions until later, make sure you mark the next answer in the correct space on the answer sheet. Otherwise you may wind up wearing out the eraser on your pencil when you discover your error at the end of the test. Or, even worse, you may not notice the error, and you may wind up getting several answers wrong because you mismarked your answer sheet.

The process of elimination

Guessing doesn't always mean "pick an answer, any answer." You can increase you chances of picking the right answer by eliminating answers that can't be right.

Solve: $\frac{1}{8} \times \frac{4}{5} =$

(A) $1\frac{1}{8}$

(B) $1\frac{1}{4}$

(C) $\frac{1}{10}$

(D) $\frac{1}{5}$

Any fraction that is less than one, multiplied by another fraction that is less than one is going to result in an answer that is less than one. That means that A and B can't be correct. Your odds of guessing the right answer have just improved from one in four to one in two, or a 50/50 chance. (By the way, the correct answer is C.)

Solving what you can and guessing the rest

Sometimes you may know how to solve part of a problem, but not all of it. If you don't know how to do all the operations, don't give up. You can still narrow your choices by doing what you can. Suppose this question confronts you:

What is the value of $(-0.4)^3$?

(A) −0.0027

(B) −0.000064

(C) 0.000064

(D) 0.0009

What if you don't remember how to multiply decimals? All is not lost! If you remember how to use exponents, you'll remember that you have to multiply $-0.04 \times -0.04 \times -0.04$. So, if you simplify the problem and just multiply $-4 \times -4 \times -4$, without worrying about those pesky zeroes, you know that your answer will be negative and will end in the digits 64. With this pearl of wisdom in mind, you can see that A, C, and D are all wrong. You logically guessed your way to the correct answer!

Practice Makes Perfect

How about putting all the knowledge you've gained about the Mathematics Knowledge subtest to the test? Here are ten questions that are very similar to those you'll likely see when you take the actual test.

1. Which of the following fractions is the smallest?

(A) $\frac{3}{4}$

(B) $\frac{14}{17}$

(C) $\frac{4}{7}$

(D) $\frac{5}{8}$

The correct answer is C. One method of comparing fractions is called the *cross-product method* (see Chapter 8).

The cross-products of the first fraction and the second fraction are $3 \times 17 = 51$ and $14 \times 4 = 56$. The first fraction is the smallest.

The cross-products of the first fraction and the third fraction are $3 \times 7 = 21$ and $4 \times 4 = 16$. The third fraction is the smallest.

The cross-products of the third fraction and the fourth fraction are $4 \times 8 = 32$ and $5 \times 7 = 35$. The third fraction, Choice C, is still the smallest.

2. What is the product of $\sqrt{36}$ and $\sqrt{49}$?

   (A) 1,764

   (B) 42

   (C) 13

   (D) 6

The correct answer is B. The square root of 36 is 6 and the square root of 49 is 7. The product of those two numbers is $6 \times 7 = 42$.

3. Solve: $2x - 3 = x + 7$

   (A) 10

   (B) 6

   (C) 21

   (D) −10

The correct answer is A:

$$2x - 3 = x + 7$$
$$2x - x = 7 + 3$$
$$x = 10$$

4. A circle has a radius of 15 feet. What is most nearly its circumference?

   (A) 30 feet

   (B) 225 feet

   (C) 94 feet

   (D) 150 feet

The correct answer is C. The circumference of a circle is $\pi \times$ diameter; the diameter equals two times the radius; and π is approximately 3.14. Therefore, $30 \times 3.14 \approx 94$.

TIP

The $\approx$ sign means *approximately equals*. It's used here because the answer, 94, is a rounded number.

5. At 3 p.m., the angle between the hands of the clock is

   (A) 90 degrees

   (B) 180 degrees

   (C) 120 degrees

   (D) 360 degrees

The correct answer is A. At 3 p.m., one hand is on the 12, and the other is on the 3. This creates a right angle — a 90-degree angle.

6. If $3 + y \geq 13$, what is the value of y?

   (A) Greater than or equal to 10

   (B) Less than or equal to 10

   (C) 10

   (D) 6

The correct answer is A. Solve the inequality the same way you would solve an algebraic equation:

$$3 + y \geq 13$$
$$y \geq 13 - 3$$
$$y \geq 10$$

7. $y^3 \times y^2 \times y^{-3} =$

   (A) y^2

   (B) y^{-18}

   (C) y^8

   (D) x^{23}

The correct answer is A. When you multiply powers with the same base, add the exponents: $y^3 - y^2 - y^{-3} = y^{3 + 2 + (-3)} = y^2$.

8. 14 yards + 14 feet =

   (A) 16 yards

   (B) 15 yards

   (C) 28 feet

   (D) 56 feet

The correct answer is D. Convert the yards to feet by multiplying by 3: $14 \times 3 = 42$ feet. Add this to 14 feet: $42 + 14 = 56$ feet.

9. What is 35 percent of 85?

   (A) 33.2

   (B) 65.32

   (C) 21.3

   (D) 29.75

The correct answer is D. Multiply 85 with the decimal equivalent of 35 percent, or 0.35: $0.35 \times 85 = 29.75$.

10. What is most nearly the average of 37, 22, 72, and 44?

   (A) 43.8

   (B) 55.2

   (C) 175

   (D) 77.1

The correct answer is A. Add the numbers, and then divide by the number of terms: $37 + 22 + 72 + 44 = 175$, and $175 \div 4 = 43.75$. Round this number up to 43.8.

Chapter 10

Working with Word Problems

Two types of mathematics tests are part of the AFQT. The first type is the Mathematics Knowledge subtest that I discussed in the last two chapters. The second type is the Arithmetic Reasoning subtest which is the topic of this chapter and Chapter 11.

In the Mathematics Knowledge subtest, you have it pretty easy. You see a mathematical equation, and you do your best to solve it. The Arithmetic Reasoning subtest is more involved. You have to set up your own equations to solve the problem. Ouch! How unfair! Those test makers are asking you not only to solve the problem, but also to write the equation in the first place!

Lots of people have difficulty with translating a math word problem into a mathematical equation that can be solved. If you feel yourself starting to sweat at the mere thought of math word problems, you're not alone. Just take a deep breath, relax, and don't worry. I'm here to guide you through the process.

Making Sense of Word Problems

The purpose of math word problems is to test your ability to use general mathematics to solve everyday, real-world problems. That's what all the textbooks say. However, in my "real world," I've never once wondered how old Anna is if she's three years older than Chuck, and in five years, her age and Chuck's age would equal 54. I'd just ask Anna how old she is. If she didn't answer, I wouldn't buy her a birthday present.

When you realize that math word problems are designed to measure your ability to use basic math to solve *fictional* problems, they can be kind of fun — sort of like solving a puzzle.

Setting Up the Problem

Word problems are nothing more than a series of expressions that fit into an equation. An equation is a combination of math expressions. (If that sounds like Greek to you, check out Chapter 8.) The expressions in math word problems are generally stated in English. Your job is to dig out the relevant facts and state them in mathematical terms. You do this by:

- Getting organized
- Understanding the problem
- Identifying the information you need
- Translating the problem into one or more solvable mathematic equations

I cover all of these tasks in greater detail in the following sections.

Getting organized

Getting organized isn't really a step as much as it is a method. You need to be organized throughout the problem-solving process. Working clearly will help you think clearly, and it'll ensure you don't get lost, while trying to define and solve the problem.

When using your scratch paper, draw and label your pictures and graphs clearly. If you go back to your notes and can't remember what you were thinking about when you drew that picture, not only will you be frustrated, but you'll have wasted valuable time — and you don't have any time to waste on the Arithmetic Reasoning subtest. (For more on pictures, see the sidebar "A picture can be worth a thousand equations.")

A picture can be worth a thousand equations

When you walk in to take the ASVAB, the kindly test proctors are going to give you a piece of blank scratch paper. If you want more, they'll gladly give you more — they'll even give you more you if you run out during the exam.

Sure, the scratch sheet is handy for figuring out equations — and writing love notes to that cute guy or gal sitting next to you — but it's also useful for drawing diagrams and pictures to help you clarify the problem in your mind.

Sometimes, drawing a simple diagram can save you loads of time when trying to get a quick grasp on how to solve a math word problem. Here's one of my favorite examples:

A ladybug walks 5 inches directly south. She then turns and walks 10 inches directly east. If she then sprouts her wings and flies directly back to her starting point, how far will she have to fly?

This problem becomes instantly clear with a quick diagram on your scratch paper, like the sketch shown here.

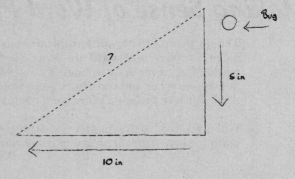

The crudely drawn diagram on your scratch paper makes it instantly clear that you need to find the length of the hypotenuse of a right triangle. If you read Chapter 8, you know that you can use the Pythagorean theorem $(a^2 + b^2 = c^2)$ to quickly figure this out. Without that sketch, you might not realize how simple this problem really is.

Understanding the problem

Make sure you read the entire problem, but be careful: Don't try too hard to understand the problem on the first read-through. I know that doesn't seem to make any sense, but bear with me.

Math word problems can be broken down into two parts:

- ✔ **The problem statement:** The problem statement is not really an object to be understood. It's simply a source of information, much like a dictionary or telephone book that has information you can look up, as needed, to solve the equation.

  The information included in the problem statement is often confusing or disorganized. Sometimes *distracters* (information that has nothing to do with solving the problem) are mixed in, leading to confusion and making the problem difficult to solve. (See the "Dealing with distracters" sidebar for more information.) A famous mathematician once said, "A problem is understood by solving it, not pondering it." Actually, he wasn't that famous. It was my Uncle Ed, who lives just down the street.

- ✔ **The problem question:** The problem question is the meat of the matter. Exactly what is the questioner asking you to find? This is the part of the problem you really need to understand.

Identifying the information you need

After you've separated the question from the statement (see the preceding section), list the facts in a clear, concise list. Figure out what you need but don't have, and name things. Pick variables to stand for the unknowns, clearly labeling these variables with what they stand for.

Be as clear as possible when you identify the information you need. You don't want to spend five minutes on a word problem solving for x, only to reach the end and forget what x is supposed to stand for. How frustrating!

Pay particular attention to include units of measure, such as feet, miles, inches, pounds, dollars, and so on. One of the fastest ways to mess up on a math word problem is by forgetting the apples-and-oranges rule. You can't perform mathematical operations on different units of measurement. Ten apples plus ten oranges equals 20 pieces of fruit; it does *not* equal 20 apples, nor does it equal 20 oranges. Look at the following example:

> A carpenter buys 44 feet of wood. If she adds the wood to the 720 inches of wood she already owns, how many feet of wood will she have?

If you add 44 to 720, you're going to get the wrong answer. Before you can add the numbers, you have to either convert 44 feet of wood to inches ($44 \times 12 = 528$ inches) or convert 720 inches to feet ($720 \div 12 = 60$ feet).

Translating the problem

Now you're at the tough part. The hardest thing about doing word problems is taking the English words and translating them into mathematics. Luckily, math word problems often contain certain *keywords* that can help.

Dealing with distracters

If math word problems were all straightforward questions, such as "What is 10 multiplied by 10?", you could skip this chapter. However, those wascally wabbits who write the questions stay awake at night to think up ways to complicate things. The use of distracters is one such way.

A distracter is any piece of information included in the problem statement that has absolutely nothing to do with solving the problem. Consider the following example:

> In November, the National Weather Service recorded 1 inch of snow and 3 inches of rain in Grand Forks, North Dakota. In December, these numbers were reversed, with 3 inches of snow, and only 1 inch of rain. How much snow did Grand Forks Receive in total?

You don't need to know how much rain fell in Grand Forks in order to solve this problem. The amount of rain has absolutely nothing to do with the problem question. It's a distracter — its purpose is to distract you from focusing on the real question. The problem mentions rain, so it has to figure into the problem in some way, doesn't it? Wrong! Be sure to read the question carefully and cross out any information that's just there to trip you up.

Addition keywords

Several words and phrases used in math word problems indicate an addition operation:

- Increased by
- More than
- Combined
- Together
- Total of
- Sum
- Added to

"The drill sergeant can do 100 pushups more than Private Jones" is equivalent to Private Jones + 100 = drill sergeant. "Together, they can do 300 pushups" can be mathematically stated as drill sergeant + Private Jones = 300.

Try the following example, just to see if you're getting the hang of things:

The drill sergeant can do 100 pushups more than Private Jones. Together, they can do 300 pushups. How many pushups can Private Jones do?

The question is asking you how many pushups Private Jones can do. You're not really interested in how many the drill sergeant can do, and the problem statement tells you that they can do 300 total pushups together. You also know that the drill sergeant can do 100 more than Private Jones.

List the important information:

- Let j = the number of pushups that Private Jones can do. This is what you really want to find out, so it's important that you define it first.
- Let d = the number of pushups that the drill sergeant can do. You don't really want to know this, but it's a necessary fact in order to solve the problem.

✔ You know another definition of *d*. The problem statement tells you that the drill sergeant can do 100 more pushups than Private Jones, which means that $d = j + 100$, which
is the same (mathematically) as saying $j = d - 100$.

✔ You know that together they can do 300 pushups, which tells you that $d + j = 300$.

All you need to do now is to solve that final equation in terms of *j*. First, use the distributive
property of math to express the equation in terms of *j*: $d + j = 300$ is the same as $j = 300 - d$.

You already have a definition for *d* from above ($d = j + 100$). Substitute this value for *d* in the
equation you're now working to solve:

$$j = 300 - d$$
$$j = 300 - (j + 100)$$
$$j = 300 - j - 100$$
$$2j = 200$$
$$j = 100$$

Private Jones can do 100 pushups.

As an alternative, you could also substitute "$j + 100$" for d in the equation $d + j = 100$. The
answer will be the same.

Because math can be a tricky thing (I've been known to believe $2 + 2 = 3$, before my morning
coffee), it's always a good idea to check your answer to make sure it makes sense. Plug your
answer into the original problem and see if it works out: The drill sergeant can do 100
pushups more than Private Jones: $100 + 100 = 200$. The drill sergeant can do 200 pushups.
Together, they can do 300 pushups: $100 + 200 = 300$. Makes sense.

Subtraction keywords

If you see any of the following words and phrases in a math word problem, it generally indicates a subtraction operation:

✔ Decreased by

✔ Minus

✔ Less

✔ Difference between/of

✔ Less than

✔ Fewer than

"Becky's pay decreased by \$10" can be stated mathematically as Becky – 10. This is also the
same as "Becky's pay minus \$10," or "Becky's pay less \$10."

"The difference between Bob's pay and Becky's pay" can be expressed as Bob – Becky.

The *less than* and *fewer than* terms work backwards in English from what they are in the
math. Although "Becky's pay minus \$10" is Becky – 10, "Becky's pay less than *x*" is *not*
Becky – *x*; It's *x* – Becky.

Multiplication keywords

The following words and phrases usually mean a mathematical multiplication operation when included in a math word problem:

- ✔ Of
- ✔ Times
- ✔ Multiplied by
- ✔ Product of
- ✔ Increased/decreased by a factor of

"15 percent of x" is mathematically expressed as $x \times 0.15$. "x times y" and "x multiplied by y" mean $x \times y$. The product of x and y is the same as $x \times y$.

Increased by a factor of and *decreased by a factor of* can involve addition and subtraction in combination with multiplication. "x increased by a factor of 10 percent" is expressed as $x + (x \times 0.10)$.

Division keywords

If you see the following words/phrases in a math word problem, "division operation" should pop into your mind.

- ✔ A
- ✔ Per
- ✔ Average
- ✔ Ratio of
- ✔ Quotient of

Per and *a* means "divided by" — for example, "I bought 2 gallons of milk at the grocery store and paid \$3, so milk was \$1.50 *a* gallon," or "Milk was \$1.50 *per* gallon."

To find the average of a group of numbers, you add the numbers, and then divide by the number of terms. "The average of a, b, and c" is $(a + b + c) \div 3$.

Mathematically, ratios are expressed as fractions. A ratio of five to three is written as $\frac{5}{3}$, which is the same as saying $5 \div 3$. Chapter 8 has more detail about how to work with ratios.

The "quotient of x and y" is the same as $x \div y$.

Although the preceding keywords *often* indicate a mathematical operation in a word problem, that's not always the case. You have to use a little common sense. "A man was walking down the street," does not mean a division operation. "Matt and Paul were working *together*" does not necessarily mean you're going to perform a math addition problem regarding Matt and Paul.

Practicing keywords

Learning how to recognize keywords is essential in translating English into mathematical expressions. Try a few examples, just to see if you're getting the hang of it:

- ✔ **Translate "the sum of 13 and y" into an equation.** This translates to $13 + y$. The keyword *sum* indicates an addition operation.

- ✔ **How would you write "the quotient of a and 6" as an equation?** The keyword *quotient* means division. This translates to $a \div 6$.

✔ **How would "7 less than y" be written as a mathematical equation?** It would be $y - 7$. If you answered $7 - y$, you forgot that "less than" is backwards in math from how it's used in English.

✔ **Translate "the ratio of x plus 6 to 8" into an equation.** "x plus 6" is an addition operation, while the keyword *ratio* indicates division. This translates to $\frac{x+6}{8}$.

Are you ready to try a couple of longer ones? I knew you were!

✔ **The length of a rectangle is 45 inches more than its width. Let the width = w, and express the length in mathematical terms.** *More than* is a keyword that means addition. Because the width = w, the length is mathematically written as $w + 45$.

✔ **Paul is three years older than Marsha, who is four times the age of Brian. Express Marsha's age as an algebraic expression.** You can express Paul's age, Marsha's age, and Brian's age using any variables you choose, but it just makes sense to use the first letters of their name. That way, there's less chance of forgetting what variable stands for what factor. "Four *times*" indicates multiplication. Marsha's age can be written as $4 \times b$, or $4b$. Paul's age can be expressed as $m + 3$, so Marsha's age can also be written as $p - 3$.

Confused? Check out Chapter 8 for the distributive properties of algebraic equations.

Trying Out Typical Word Problems

Now that you can recognize common keywords and translate them into mathematical expressions, you're ready to take on a few math word problems.

Because math word problems represent fictional real-life situations, there is an infinite number of possible problems that test writers could come up with. However, math word problem test writers must have limited imaginations, because certain types of questions seem to pop up more often than others. This is true whether you're taking the SAT or the Arithmetic Reasoning subtest of the ASVAB.

Age problems

Age problems involve figuring out how old someone is, was, or will be at some time in the future. You generally do this by comparing their ages to the ages of other people.

Sid is twice as old as Mary. In three years, the sum of their ages will be 66. How old are they now?

Sometimes an age problem can be solved by using a one-variable solution, and sometimes it takes several variables. This particular problem can be solved by using either a one-variable solution or a two-variable solution.

One-variable solution

Let Mary's age = x. Because Sid is twice as old as Mary, his age can be represented as $2x$.

In three years, Mary's age will be $x + 3$, and Sid's age will be $2x + 3$. The sum of their ages together will be 66.

You now have an equation you can work with:

$$(x + 3) + (2x + 3) = 66$$
$$3x + 6 = 66$$
$$3x = 60$$
$$x = \frac{60}{3}$$
$$x = 20$$

What did x stand for again? Was it Mary's age, or Sid's age? Be sure to clearly label variables on your scratch paper, so you don't get frustrated and tear your hair out in front of everyone else. That causes talk.

x represents Mary's age, so Mary is 20 years old. Because Sid is twice Mary's age, Sid is 40 ($2 \times 20 = 40$).

If you have time, check your answer to see that it makes sense: Sid (age 40) is twice as old as Mary (age 20). In three years, the sum of their ages will be $(40 + 3) + (20 + 3) = 43 + 23 = 66$. It fits! Isn't math fun?

Two-variable solution

Let m = Mary's age and s = Sid's age. You know that Sid is twice as old as Mary, so $s = 2m$. That gives you your first equation.

You also know that in three years, the sum of their ages will be 66. Stated mathematically:

$$(m + 3) + (s + 3) = 66$$

This equation can be simplified:

$$m + s + 6 = 66$$
$$m + s = 60$$

You now have two equations, with two variables that you can use to solve the problem:

$$s = 2m$$
$$m + s = 60$$

Replace s in the second equation with the definition of s in the first equation:

$$m + 2m = 60$$
$$3m = 60$$
$$m = \frac{60}{3}$$
$$m = 20$$

Mary is 20 years old. That's the same answer you got when using the one-variable solution.

Geometric problems

These problems require you to compute the volume, perimeter, area, circumference, diameter, and so on of various geometric shapes.

You're painting a fence that is 20 feet long and 6 feet high. How much square footage of fence will you be covering with paint?

The area formula for a rectangle is $a = lw$, so the answer to this simple problem is $A = 6 \times 20 = 120$ square feet.

Generally, the Arithmetic Reasoning test makers won't let you off so easy, though. The problem is more likely to be written something like the following.

You're painting a fence that is 20 feet long and 6 feet high. Paint cost $7.23 per gallon, and 1 gallon of paint will cover 60 square feet of fence. How much will you need to spend on paint to complete the project?

The problem now requires a couple more steps to answer. First, you have to compute the area of the fence. You already did that: 120 square feet.

Now you have to determine how many gallons of paint you need to buy to cover 120 square feet. Because 1 gallon of paint will cover 60 square feet, you'll need $120 \div 60 = 2$ gallons of paint.

Finally, you need to figure how much 2 gallons of paint will cost. Paint is $7.23 per gallon, and you need 2 gallons, so $7.23 \times 2 = \$14.46$.

You'll see quite a few geometric problems on the Arithmetic Reasoning subtest. To make sure you're ready for them, memorize the basic geometric formulas in Table 10-1. You can find more information about using these formulas in Chapter 8.

Table 10-1	Basic Geometric Formulas	
Shape	**Function**	**Formula**
Square	Area	$a = s^2$
	Perimeter	$p = 4s$
	Diagonal	$d = s\sqrt{2}$
Rectangle	Area	$a = lw$
	Perimeter	$p = 2l + 2w$
	Diagonal	$d = \sqrt{l^2 + w^2}$
Triangle	Perimeter	$p = s_1 + s_2 + s_3$
	Area	$a = \frac{1}{2}bh$
Right Triangle	Pythagorean theorem	$a^2 + b^2 = c^2$
Circle	Radius	$r = \frac{1}{2}d$
	Diameter	$d = 2r$
	Circumference	$c = 2\pi r$
	Area	$a = \pi r^2$
Cube	Volume	$v = s^3$

(continued)

Table 10-1 (continued)

Shape	Function	Formula
	Surface Area	$SA = 6s^2$
Rectangular Box	Volume	$v = lwh$
	Surface Area	$SA = 2lw + 2wh + 2lh$
Cylinder	Volume	$v = \pi r^2 h$

Coin problems

I think mathematicians must have big piggy banks. Many math word problems ask you to figure out how many coins of various types a person has.

Jeremy has 12 more nickels than quarters. How many coins does he have if the total value of his coins is $2.70?

Let q = quarters. Because Jeremy has 12 more nickels than quarters, this could be represented as $q + 12$. Jeremy has $2.70 worth of coins, which is equal to 270¢. A quarter is 25¢, and a nickel is 5¢. Jeremy's total coins together must equal 270¢. Therefore:

(25¢ × number of quarters) + (5¢ × number of nickels) = 270¢

Or, writing it another way:

$25q + 5(q + 12) = 270$

$25q + 5q + 60 = 270$

$30q = 210$

$q = \dfrac{210}{30}$

$q = 7$

Jeremy has 7 quarters. Because he has 12 more nickels than quarters, he has 7 + 12 = 19 nickels, for a total of 19 + 7 = 26 coins.

Does this answer make sense? Jeremy has 12 more nickels (19 nickels) than quarters (7 quarters). How many coins does he have if the total value of his coins is $2.70? So, 19 nickels = 95¢ and 7 quarters = 175¢, so 95¢ + 175¢ = 270¢ = $2.70. It looks good to me.

Travel problems

I wish I could travel as much as word problem test writers seem to. They come up with a lot of travel problems. They especially seem to like trains and planes. Sometimes they like cars, but not as often.

Travel problems involve using the distance formula $d = rt$, where d is the distance, r is the rate, and t is the time. Generally, the problems come in three basic flavors: traveling away from each other, traveling in the same direction, and traveling at 90-degree angles.

Traveling away from each other

When two planes (or trains or cars or people or even bugs) travel in opposite directions, they increase the distance between them in direct proportion. To solve these types of problems, you compute the distance traveled from the starting point for each plane (or train or car or person or bug).

Train A travels north at 60 mph. Train B travels south at 70 mph. If both trains leave the station at the same time, how far apart will they be at the end of two hours?

To solve this problem, you compute the distance traveled by train A, and then the distance traveled by train B, and add the results together.

The distance formula is $d = rt$. The rate of travel for train A is 60 mph, and it travels for two hours:

$$d = 60 \times 2$$
$$d = 120$$

Train A travels 120 miles during the two-hour period.

When using the distance formula, you have to pay attention to the units of measurement. Remember the apples-and-oranges rule (see the "Identifying the information you need" section, earlier in this chapter). If rate (r) is expressed in kilometers per hour, your result (d) will be kilometers. If rate (r) is expressed as miles per second, you must either convert it to mph, or you must convert time (t) to seconds.

The rate of travel for train B is 70 mph, and it also travels for two hours:

$$d = 70 \times 2$$
$$d = 140$$

Train B travels 140 miles during the two-hour period.

Train A is 120 miles from the station and train B is 140 miles from the station, in the opposite direction. The two trains are 120 + 140 = 260 miles apart.

Traveling in the same direction

If the two trains are traveling in the same direction as each other, but at different rate of speeds, one travels farther in the same time than the other travels. The distance between the two trains is the difference between the distance traveled by train A and the distance traveled by train B.

You know what they say about assuming . . .

Math word problems require you to make basic assumptions. In the train problem in the "Traveling away from each other" section, you're to assume that both trains travel at a constant rate of speed. You're supposed to ignore the fact that they may slow down for a curve, or that it will probably take them a little time to get up to cruising speed.

If a question gives you the average daily output of a factory and asks you what the output will be in a year, you're supposed to assume that the year is 365 days long.

If you're asked how high the kite is flying 300 feet away from you, you must assume that the ground is perfectly level.

If . . . well, you get the point.

Train A travels north at 60 mph. Train B also travels north, on a parallel track, at 70 mph. If both trains leave the station at the same time, how far apart will they be at the end of two hours?

From the calculations you've already done (see the preceding section), you know that train A traveled 120 miles, and train B traveled 140 miles. However, because they were traveling in the same direction, to find the distance between them, you subtract, instead of add: $140 - 120 = 20$. The two trains are 20 miles apart.

Traveling at 90-degree angles

Travel that involves two people or things moving at 90-degree angles, then stopping, then asking you what the distance is (as the crow flies) between the two people or things require the use of the distance formula and a little basic geometry.

Train A travels north at 60 mph. Train B travels east at 70 mph. Both trains travel for two hours. A bee flies from train A and lands on train B. Assuming the bee flew in a straight line, how far did the bee travel between the two trains?

Through the skull sweat you've already done (see the "Traveling away from each other" section, earlier in this chapter), you know that Train A traveled 120 miles and Train B traveled a distance of 140 miles.

Because the trains are traveling at 90-degree angles (one north and one east), the lines of travel form two sides of a right triangle. Figure 10-1 should make this easy to visualize.

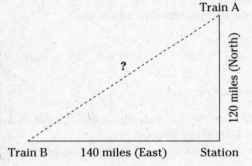

Figure 10-1:
Traveling at 90-degree angles forms a right triangle.

The Pythagorean theorem says that if you know the length of two sides of a right triangle, you can find the length of the third side by using the formula $a^2 + b^2 = c^2$:

$$120^2 + 140^2 = c^2$$
$$14,400 + 19,600 = c^2$$
$$c = \sqrt{34,000}$$
$$c = 184.39$$

The bee will have to fly 184.39 miles.

Finding the square root of a very large number can be a daunting task. When you reach this point of the equation, it's often easier just to square the possible answers to see which one works.

Investment/loan problems

These problems are primarily focused on simple interest rates for investments and loans, using the formula $I = prt$, where I is the interest, p is the principal, r is the rate of interest (in percentage), and t is the time.

The investment/loan problems you'll see on the Arithmetic Reasoning subtest are pretty simple. They're nowhere near as difficult as similar situations in real life, where interest is compounded.

To solve these problems, replace what is known in the interest formula, and then solve for anything else.

John invests $1,500 for three years at an annual interest rate of 7 percent. How much will John have at the end of the three-year period?

Plug the known information into the interest formula, $I = prt$:

$I = \$1,500 \times 0.07 \times 3$

$I = \$315$

Percent means "part of 100." To convert percentage into a decimal, divide the percentage by 100. So, 7 percent $= \frac{7}{100} = 0.07$. To convert a decimal into percentage, multiply by 100. So, $0.07 = 0.07 \times 100 = 7$ percent. (See Chapter 8 for more information about working with percentages and decimals.)

John will make $315 in interest. Added to his original investment of $1,500, John will have a total of $1,500 + $315 = $1,815.

That was pretty easy, so let me throw another one at you.

You invest $700, and after five years you receive a total of $900. What was the annual interest rate?

On the surface, this one looks a bit more complicated, but you solve it the same way: Plug what is known into the interest formula, $I = prt$, and solve for the rest.

You invested $700 and received $900. Therefore, you made $900 − $700 = $200 in interest.

$\$200 = \$700 \times r \times 5$

$\$200 = \$3,500r$

$r = \frac{\$200}{\$3,500}$

$r = 0.057$

Expressed as a percentage, this is $0.057 \times 100 = 5.7$ percent

Mixture problems

Mixture problems involve mixing different items at different costs, and determining the final cost of the mixture. They can also involve mixing various solutions and determining percentages of the solution mixture. This sounds difficult, but it's really pretty easy when you know how. Are you ready to try a couple?

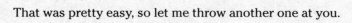

How many quarts of a 70 percent alcohol solution must be added to 50 quarts of a 40 percent alcohol solution to produce a 50 percent alcohol solution?

Let x = the number of quarts of 70 percent solution needed. The amount of alcohol contained in x quarts of the 70 percent solution is represented by $0.7x$. (Remember how to convert a percentage into a decimal?)

There are 50 quarts of the 40 percent solution, so the amount of alcohol contained in those 50 quarts is represented by $50 \times 0.4 = 20$ quarts.

The total number of quarts of solution can be represented as $50 + x$ (the number of quarts of 40 percent solution, plus the unknown number of quarts of 70 percent solution). It will contain 50 percent of the amount of total alcohol, so $0.5(50 + x)$.

Maybe the following chart will make this a bit clearer:

	Quarts of Solution	*Percent Alcohol*	*Total Quarts of Alcohol*
70 percent solution	x	0.7	$0.7x$
40 percent solution	50	0.4	$0.4 \times 50 = 20$
50 percent solution	$50 + x$	0.5	$0.5(50 + x)$

The third column of the table gives you your equation: $0.7x + 20 = 0.5(50 + x)$.

$$0.7x + 20 = 25 + 0.5x$$
$$0.7x = 5 + 0.5x$$
$$0.7x - 0.5x = 5$$
$$0.2x = 5$$
$$x = \frac{5}{0.2}$$
$$x = 25$$

The final mixture will require 25 quarts of 70 percent solution.

A grocery store wants to offer a mixture of white and dark grapes to sell for $4.20 per pound. If white grapes cost $3 per pound, and dark grapes retail for $6 per pound, how many pounds of dark grapes should the grocer add to 12 pounds of white grapes to produce the desired mixture?

Let x = the pounds of dark grapes. The total amount of grapes will be the pounds of white grapes (12), plus the unknown pounds of dark grapes (x), or $12 + x$. The total cost of white grapes at $3 per pound is $12 \times 3 = \$36$.

Dark grapes sell for $6 per pound, so their total cost is represented as $6x$.

The total cost of the mixture is to be $4.20 per pound, so this can be represented as $4.2(12 + x)$.

The table worked so well in the last problem, I want to use one again:

Type	Cost per Pound	Pounds	Total Cost
White	$3	12	$3 × 12 = $36
Dark	$6	x	$6x
Mixture	$4.20	12 + x	$4.20(12 + x)

Again, the last column gives you your equation: $36 + 6x = 4.2(12 + x)$.

$$36 + 6x = 50.4 + 4.2x$$
$$6x - 4.2x = 50.4 - 36$$
$$1.8x = 14.4$$
$$x = \frac{14.4}{1.8}$$
$$x = 8$$

The mixture will require 8 pounds of dark grapes.

Percent problems

Percent problems involve working with percentages, such as discount savings, pay raises, and such. You'll often see them on the Arithmetic Reasoning subtest. They're relatively simple to solve.

Leroy makes $8.95 per hour. He's such a good worker, his boss gives him a 25 percent raise. How much per hour does Leroy make now?

To find the dollar amount of the raise, multiply Leroy's previous salary by the decimal equivalent of 25 percent: $8.95 × 0.25 = 2.237$. Round this up to $2.24, just to make Leroy smile. Now add the raise to Leroy's original salary: $8.95 + $2.24 = $11.19.

Katie is very excited. For only $45, she bought a blouse that usually sells for $60. What percent was her discount?

Divide the new price by the original price: $45 ÷ 60 = 0.75$. The new price is 75 percent of the original price, which means Katie's discount is 25 percent.

Work problems

These problems involve two or more people or things working together. You're expected to figure out how long it will take them to complete a task together.

Patrick can build a wall in five hours. Dennis can build the same wall in seven hours. How long will it take them to build the wall together?

There's a general formula to solve such work problems. It's $\frac{a \times b}{a+b}$, where a is the time it takes the first person or thing to do the job and b is the time it takes the second person or thing to do the job.

It takes Patrick five hours to build the wall, and Dennis seven hours. Plugging the data into the work formula:

$$\frac{5 \times 7}{5+7} = \frac{35}{12} = 2\frac{11}{12}$$

It will take them $2\frac{11}{12}$ hours to build the wall together.

Wasn't that fun? I bet you're eager to try another one.

One hose can fill an aboveground pool in three hours. Another hose will fill it in six hours. How long will it take to fill the pool using both hoses?

Just plug the numbers into your handy-dandy work equation:

$$\frac{3 \times 6}{3+6} = \frac{18}{9} = 2$$

It will take two hours to fill the pool using both hoses.

Number problems

Number problems are pretty straightforward. The questions ask you to manipulate numbers using basic addition, subtraction, multiplication, or division. Most people find these types of word problems to be pretty easy.

Do you want to try a few, just to get your feet wet? Sure, you do.

Jesse is a bartender at a local pub. On Friday, he made $27.40 in tips, on Saturday he made $34.70 in tips, and on Sunday he made $7 less than he made on Friday. How much in tips did Jesse earn during the three days?

See what I mean? Pretty straightforward. Jesse made $27.40 + $34.70 + ($27.40 − $7) = $82.50 in tips.

Rob "Speedy Gonzalez" Barton ran 1.5 miles in 9:57. The next day he ran it in 10:02. On the third day, he ran it in 10:07. What is his average time for the 1.5-mile run?

First, convert all the times into seconds, just to make the math a little easier:

9:57 = (9 × 60) + 57 = 597 seconds

10:02 = (10 × 60) + 2 = 602 seconds

10:07 = (10 × 60) + 7 = 607 seconds

Add the seconds together: 597 + 602 + 607 = 1,806 seconds. Now, divide by the number of times Rob ran the 1.5-mile run (3 times) to discover that his average speed is 1,806 ÷ 3 = 602 seconds. Finally, convert the seconds to minutes by dividing by 60: 602 ÷ 60 = 10 minutes, with 2 seconds left over. Rob's average time for the 1.5-mile run is 6:02.

The sum of two consecutive odd positive numbers is 112. What are the numbers?

You may remember from the "Addition keywords" section, earlier in this chapter, that *sum* means addition. Let n = the first number. That means that $n + 2$ = the second number (because they're consecutive *odd* numbers). Here's your equation:

$$n + (n + 2) = 112$$

Solve for n:

$$2n + 2 = 112$$
$$2n = 110$$
$$n = \frac{110}{2}$$
$$n = 55$$

The first number is 55. The second number is $55 + 2 = 57$.

Chapter 11

The Arithmetic Reasoning Subtest

There are two math subtests on the ASVAB, and both of them are used when computing your AFQT score. Of the two, the Arithmetic Reasoning subtest is the more difficult for most people.

Among other things, math word problems measure your reasoning skills. That's why the military services put so much emphasis on this particular subtest. They want recruits who can figure things out — recruits who can solve problems.

If you're starting to get nervous, just remember: You've been doing arithmetic word problems since the third grade. Sure, they're a little more difficult than when Mrs. Grundy was telling you that you had three apples and gave one to Tammy, but the fact is, this is not new material for you. You've done it before. The military is just asking you to do it again, that's all.

I'm here to help you get ready. In this chapter, I tell you what you can expect on the Arithmetic Reasoning subtest, give you a few methods that may help improve your score and get you through those rough spots, and then — just for fun — toss a few practice questions at you. Don't worry — I toss them underhand.

Looking At the Test Structure

The Arithmetic Reasoning subtest is the second subtest on the ASVAB, right after the General Science subtest. Therefore, it's the first subtest you'll encounter on the ASVAB that affects your AFQT score.

The Arithmetic Reasoning subtest asks you to read a word problem, determine what the question is asking, and select the correct answer. (Then you have to repeat the process 29 more times.) Most of the problems look like this:

Jane walks 5 miles to work each morning and 5 miles home each evening. How many miles does Jane walk in a day?

(A) 6 miles

(B) 8 miles

(C) 7 miles

(D) 10 miles

You have 36 minutes to answer 30 questions, so you have to work quickly to finish, but you're not being tested on speed. You don't get extra points for finishing the subtest early.

You'll see a mixture of hard questions, medium questions, and easy questions on this subtest. The hard ones are worth more points than the medium ones, which are worth more points than the easy ones. If you're taking the computerized version of the ASVAB (see Chapter 2), and you're really good at math word problems, you may only see hard questions. The computer automatically selects the question difficulty based on how you answered the previous question.

The test administrator will supply you with scratch paper so that you can work out some of the problems on paper, if necessary.

Those dirty communists who make up the rules don't allow the use of calculators on the ASVAB. All you're allowed is your brain, your trusty No. 2 pencil, and a piece of scratch paper. If you're lucky, they may let you sneak in your thinking cap.

Developing a Test Strategy

The U.S. military doesn't win wars without a strategy, and you should have a set strategy for conquering the Arithmetic Reasoning subtest. A strategy is more than "I'll try to solve all the problems quickly and correctly." That'll work fine if everything goes right and you know how to solve the questions instantly when you see them, but it probably won't work that way. Your strategy needs to include plans to keep things going smoothly, as well as ideas of what to do if things start going wrong.

Keeping track of the time

This chapter is supposed to be about the Arithmetic Reasoning subtest, so I think it's time for a practice question. Ready?

You have to take a test consisting of 30 multiple-choice questions. You have 36 minutes to complete the test. How much time do you have for each question?

(A) 1 minute, 12 seconds

(B) 90 seconds

(C) 1 minute

(D) 1 minute 20 seconds

First, convert the minutes to seconds, so you won't have to deal with fractions or decimals: $36 \times 60 = 2,160$ seconds. Now, divide the total number of seconds by the number of test questions: $2,160 \div 30 = 72$ seconds. You have 72 seconds, or 1 minute and 12 seconds to complete each question.

That's not much time, considering that you're expected to read the question, determine what the question is asking, translate the problem into mathematical equations, solve those equations, and then answer the question — and, if you have time, check your answer.

If you're taking the paper version of the ASVAB, there will be a large clock, clearly visible somewhere on the wall. The test proctor will also post the start time and end time of the subtest where you can easily see it.

If you're taking the computerized version of the ASVAB, the time remaining for the subtest will be clicking down right there on your computer screen.

Don't spend too much time on any one question. If a question is stumping you, admit defeat, choose an answer (see the "Logical guessing" section, later in this chapter), and move on. You don't want to find yourself in a position where you only have 15 minutes left, and you're on question 3.

Choosing an answer and checking it twice

In Chapter 10, I mention that it's always a good idea to check your answer to ensure it makes sense in relation to the question, if you have time. You won't always have time on the Arithmetic Reasoning subtest, but if you find yourself running ahead of the clock, take a few seconds extra to check your answer.

Don't assume that just because the answer you got is one of the *possible* answer choices, that it's the *correct* answer. Those crafty test makers often use common mistakes as possible answer choices.

If you're taking the paper version of the ASVAB, you should also leave enough time at the end of the subtest to check and make sure you've marked your answer sheet correctly. Make sure the answer blocks are completely filled in, and make sure you didn't make the rookie mistake of answering the wrong question with the right answer.

Using the answer choices: There's more than one way to skin an equation

If you're stumped and just can't seem to write equations to solve the problem, you can often answer the question by seeing which of the answer choices work. Look at the following example:

The product of two consecutive negative even integers is 24. Find the smallest number.

(A) –2

(B) –4

(C) –6

(D) –7

Correctly solving this problem involves factoring a quadratic equation (see the end of this section, in case you're interested). Perhaps quadratic equations aren't your cup of tea, and you get stuck at $n^2 + 2n - 24 = 0$. (If so, Chapter 8 may be of some help.) But, before giving up and making a wild guess, try seeing which of the answer choices work.

> ✔ **–2:** There is no negative even integer larger than –2, so that choice won't work.
>
> ✔ **–4:** $-4 \times -2 = 8$, so that choice doesn't work.
>
> ✔ **–6:** $-6 \times -4 = 24$. It works!

Don't use this method unless you're absolutely stuck. It uses up a lot of time. In essence, you're computing the problem (up to) four times.

Thought I forgot about the original problem? Here's the proper way to solve it:

$$(n)(n + 2) = 24$$
$$n^2 + 2n = 24$$
$$n^2 + 2n - 24 = 0$$
$$(n + 6)(n - 4) = 0$$
$$n = -6 \text{ and } n = 4$$

The answer can't be 4, because the problem asks for a negative number. The first number (the smallest) is –6, which means the second number ($n + 2$) is –4.

Logical guessing

Sometimes nothing else works, and you just have to guess. If you're taking the paper version of the ASVAB, you can always skip the hard questions and go back to them when you finish the other questions. If you choose to do so, remember to leave enough time to go back and answer, even if your answer is "eeny, meeny, minee, mo." There is no penalty for wrong answers on the ASVAB. If you get the question wrong, you get zero points. If you leave the answer blank, you also get zero points. If you make a wild guess, you have at least a one in four chance of getting the answer right and getting points. If you leave it blank, you have a 0 percent chance of getting any points for that question.

If you're taking the computerized version of the ASVAB, you can't leave the answer blank. The computer won't present you with the next question until you answer the current one with A, B, C, or D. Unfortunately, that means you don't have the option of going back and giving the question another try when you finish the rest of the subtest. You have to decide whether to use more of your precious time to figure it out, or guess and move on.

Keep an eye on the clock. (See the "Keeping track of time" section, earlier in this chapter.)

Guessing doesn't have to be wild, however. Sometimes you can improve your chances by eliminating obviously wrong answers. Take another look at one of my previous brain stumpers:

The product of two consecutive negative even integers is 24. Find the smallest number.

(A) –2

(B) –4

(C) –6

(D) –7

A is obviously incorrect, because there is no number larger than –2 that would be both negative and even. You can quickly see that D is wrong, because it's an odd number, and the question is asking for a negative *even* number. Now, if you have to guess, you've just changed the odds from a one in four chance to a 50/50 chance.

Taking Arithmetic Reasoning out for a Spin

I promised you a chance to practice, and here it is. In this section, I give you ten fairly simple math word problems, similar to what you'll see on the Arithmetic Reasoning subtest.

Don't worry about time — use these questions to get used to the general test structure and to practice some of the things you learned in this chapter and Chapter 10. When you're ready, you can move on to the full-blown AFQT practice tests in the following chapters.

1. If apples are on sale at 15 for $3, what is the cost of each apple?

   (A) 50¢

   (B) 25¢

   (C) 20¢

   (D) 30¢

   The correct answer is C. Divide $3 by 15.

2. A noncommissioned officer challenged her platoon of 11 enlisted women to beat her record of performing a 26-mile training run in four hours. If all the enlisted women match her record, how many miles will they have run?

   (A) 71.5 miles

   (B) 6.5 miles

   (C) 286 miles

   (D) 312 miles

   The correct answer is C. Multiply 26 × 11. The other information in the question is irrelevant — it's there to throw you off.

3. Margaret gets her hair cut and colored at an expensive salon in town. She is expected to leave a 15 percent tip for services. If a haircut is $45 and a color treatment is $150, how much of a tip should Margaret leave?

   (A) $22.50

   (B) $29.25

   (C) $20.00

   (D) $195.00

   The correct answer is B. Add $45 and $150 and multiply the answer by 15 percent, or 0.15.

4. A bag of sand holds 1 cubic foot of sand. How many bags of sand are needed to fill a square sandbox measuring 5 feet long and 1 foot high?

   (A) 5 bags

   (B) 10 bags

   (C) 15 bags

   (D) 25 bags

   The correct answer is D. The volume formula for a square or rectangular box is $v = lwh$, so $v = 5 \times 5 \times 1 = 25$ cubic feet. Each bag holds 1 cubic foot of sand.

5. The day Samantha arrived at boot camp, the temperature reached a high of 90 degrees in the shade and a low of –20 at night in the barracks. What is the average between the high and low temperatures for the day?

    (A) 35 degrees

    (B) 45 degrees

    (C) 70 degrees

    (D) 62 degrees

The correct answer is A. Add the two temperatures given — 90 + –20 — and then divide by the number of terms, 2: (90 + –20) ÷ 2 = 70 ÷ 2 = 35.

6. Farmer Beth has received an offer to sell her 320-acre farm for $3,000 per acre. She agrees to give the buyer $96,000 worth of land. What fraction of Farmer Beth's land is the buyer getting?

    (A) $\frac{1}{4}$

    (B) $\frac{1}{10}$

    (C) $\frac{1}{5}$

    (D) $\frac{2}{3}$

The correct answer is B. $96,000 divided by $3,000 (the price per acre) equals 32 acres, and 32 acres divided by 320 acres (the total size of the farm) equals 10 percent, or $\frac{1}{10}$ of the land.

7. A map is drawn so that 1 inch equals 3 miles. On the map, the distance from Kansas City to Denver is 192.5 inches. How far is the roundtrip from Kansas City to Denver in miles?

    (A) 192.5 miles

    (B) 577.5 miles

    (C) 385 miles

    (D) 1,155 miles

The correct answer is D. Multiply 192.5 × 3 to get the distance in miles and then double the answer to account for both legs of the trip.

8. Margaret and Julie can sell their tattoo parlor for $150,000. They plan to divide the proceeds according to the ratio of the money they each invested in the business. Margaret put in the most money, at a 3:2 ratio to Julie. How much money should Julie get from the sale?

    (A) $50,000

    (B) $30,000

    (C) $60,000

    (D) $90,000

The correct answer is C. According to the ratio, Margaret should get $\frac{3}{5}$ of the money and Julie should get $\frac{2}{5}$ of the money. The fractions are calculated by adding both sides of the ratio together (3 + 2 = 5) to determine the denominator. Each side of the ratio then becomes a numerator, so that Margaret's investment can be shown to be $\frac{3}{5}$ of the total investment, and

Julie's is $\frac{2}{5}$ of the total investment. (You can check these fractions by adding $\frac{3}{5}$ and $\frac{2}{5}$ to get $\frac{5}{5}$ or 1, which is all the money.) Divide $150,000 by 5, and then multiply the answer by 2 to determine Julie's share of the money.

9. In the military, $\frac{1}{4}$ of an enlisted person's time is spent sleeping and eating, $\frac{1}{12}$ is spent standing at attention, $\frac{1}{6}$ is spent staying fit, and $\frac{2}{5}$ is spent working. The rest of the time is spent at the enlisted person's own discretion. How many hours per day does this discretionary time amount to?

   (A) 6 hours

   (B) 1.6 hours

   (C) 2.4 hours

   (D) 3.2 hours

   The correct answer is C. Calculate this answer by first assigning a common denominator of 60 to all the fractions and adjusting the numerators accordingly: $\frac{15}{60}$, $\frac{5}{60}$, $\frac{10}{60}$, and $\frac{24}{60}$. Add the fractions to find out how much time is allotted to all these tasks. The total is $\frac{54}{60}$, which leaves $\frac{6}{60}$ or $\frac{1}{10}$ of the day to the enlisted person's discretion. $\frac{1}{10}$ of 24 hours is 2.4 hours.

10. Train A is headed east at 55 mph. Train B is also heading east on an adjacent track at 70 mph. At the end of four hours, how much farther will train B have traveled than train A?

   (A) 40 miles

   (B) 50 miles

   (C) 60 miles

   (D) 70 miles

   The correct answer is C. The distance formula is $d = rt$. Plug in the known values:

   ✔ Train A: $d = 55 \times 4 = 220$ miles
   ✔ Train B: $d = 70 \times 4 = 280$ miles

   Train B traveled $280 - 220 = 60$ miles farther than train A.

Part IV
AFQT Practice Exams

The 5th Wave   By Rich Tennant

Brad felt foolish letting a fly on the wall distract him from his ASVAB.

In this part . . .

Scoring high on the AFQT requires an effective study plan. You want to concentrate your study time on subject areas that you may be having problems with. The practice exams in this part are great tools to use in order to map out your study program. Take the first test in this part to determine your strengths and weaknesses. Concentrate most of your study efforts on the subject areas that are hard for you. When you think you've got it down, take the second and third tests to measure your improvement. Take the last test right before you're ready to take the actual ASVAB, to brush up on your test-taking skills.

Because I like you, I also include four practice answer score sheets. If you want, you can cut them out of the book and use them to record your answers. Of course, if you got this book from the library, you probably shouldn't cut out the answer sheets, or even mark on them. Librarians hate it when that happens.

Taking the sample tests helps you understand where you need to study, but it also gets you into the test-taking mindset. By taking the tests, you get used to the format of each subtest. Trust me — these sample tests give you confidence on test day.

Chapter 12

Practice Exam 1

• •

The Armed Forces Qualification Test (AFQT) consists of four of the nine subtests given on the Armed Services Vocational Aptitude Battery (ASVAB). The four subtests used to determine your AFQT score are: Arithmetic Reasoning, Word Knowledge, Paragraph Comprehension, and Mathematics Knowledge.

The AFQT score is very important. Although all the ASVAB subtests are used to determine which military jobs you may qualify for, the AFQT score determines whether you're even qualified to join the military. All the military service branches have established minimum AFQT scores, according to their needs (see Chapter 2 for more information).

The AFQT is not a stand-alone test (it's part of the ASVAB), but, in this chapter, I present the subtests applicable to the AFQT in the same order in which you'll encounter them when you take the actual ASVAB.

After you complete the entire practice test, check your answers against the answer key in Chapter 13.

The test is scored by comparing your raw score to the scores of other people, which produces a scaled score. So just because you missed a total of 20 questions doesn't mean that your score is 80. (That would be too simple.) Turn to Chapter 2 to find out how the AFQT score is derived from these four subtests.

Your goal in taking this practice test is to determine which areas you may still need to study. If you miss only one question on the Word Knowledge subtest, but you miss 15 questions on Arithmetic Reasoning, you probably want to devote some extra study time to developing your math skills before you take the ASVAB.

Practice Exam 1 Answer Sheet

Part 1: Arithmetic Reasoning

1. (A) (B) (C) (D)   8. (A) (B) (C) (D)   15. (A) (B) (C) (D)   22. (A) (B) (C) (D)   29. (A) (B) (C) (D)
2. (A) (B) (C) (D)   9. (A) (B) (C) (D)   16. (A) (B) (C) (D)   23. (A) (B) (C) (D)   30. (A) (B) (C) (D)
3. (A) (B) (C) (D)   10. (A) (B) (C) (D)   17. (A) (B) (C) (D)   24. (A) (B) (C) (D)
4. (A) (B) (C) (D)   11. (A) (B) (C) (D)   18. (A) (B) (C) (D)   25. (A) (B) (C) (D)
5. (A) (B) (C)   12. (A) (B) (C) (D)   19. (A) (B) (C) (D)   26. (A) (B) (C) (D)
6. (A) (B) (C) (D)   13. (A) (B) (C) (D)   20. (A) (B) (C) (D)   27. (A) (B) (C) (D)
7. (A) (B) (C) (D)   14. (A) (B) (C) (D)   21. (A) (B) (C) (D)   28. (A) (B) (C) (D)

Part 2: Word Knowledge

1. (A) (B) (C) (D)   8. (A) (B) (C) (D)   15. (A) (B) (C) (D)   22. (A) (B) (C) (D)   29. (A) (B) (C) (D)
2. (A) (B) (C) (D)   9. (A) (B) (C) (D)   16. (A) (B) (C) (D)   23. (A) (B) (C) (D)   30. (A) (B) (C) (D)
3. (A) (B) (C) (D)   10. (A) (B) (C) (D)   17. (A) (B) (C) (D)   24. (A) (B) (C) (D)   31. (A) (B) (C) (D)
4. (A) (B) (C) (D)   11. (A) (B) (C) (D)   18. (A) (B) (C) (D)   25. (A) (B) (C) (D)   32. (A) (B) (C) (D)
5. (A) (B) (C) (D)   12. (A) (B) (C) (D)   19. (A) (B) (C) (D)   26. (A) (B) (C) (D)   33. (A) (B) (C) (D)
6. (A) (B) (C) (D)   13. (A) (B) (C) (D)   20. (A) (B) (C) (D)   27. (A) (B) (C) (D)   34. (A) (B) (C) (D)
7. (A) (B) (C) (D)   14. (A) (B) (C) (D)   21. (A) (B) (C) (D)   28. (A) (B) (C) (D)   35. (A) (B) (C) (D)

Part 3: Paragraph Comprehension

1. (A) (B) (C) (D)   8. (A) (B) (C) (D)   15. (A) (B) (C) (D)
2. (A) (B) (C) (D)   9. (A) (B) (C) (D)
3. (A) (B)   10. (A) (B) (C) (D)
4. (A) (B) (C) (D)   11. (A) (B) (C) (D)
5. (A) (B) (C) (D)   12. (A) (B) (C) (D)
6. (A) (B) (C) (D)   13. (A) (B) (C) (D)
7. (A) (B) (C) (D)   14. (A) (B)

Part 4: Mathematics Knowledge

1. (A) (B) (C) (D)   8. (A) (B) (C) (D)   15. (A) (B) (C) (D)   22. (A) (B) (C) (D)
2. (A) (B) (C) (D)   9. (A) (B) (C) (D)   16. (A) (B) (C) (D)   23. (A) (B) (C) (D)
3. (A) (B) (C) (D)   10. (A) (B) (C) (D)   17. (A) (B) (C) (D)   24. (A) (B) (C) (D)
4. (A) (B) (C) (D)   11. (A) (B) (C) (D)   18. (A) (B) (C) (D)   25. (A) (B) (C) (D)
5. (A) (B)   12. (A) (B) (C) (D)   19. (A) (B) (C) (D)
6. (A) (B) (C) (D)   13. (A) (B) (C) (D)   20. (A) (B) (C) (D)
7. (A) (B) (C) (D)   14. (A) (B) (C) (D)   21. (A) (B) (C) (D)

Part 1: Arithmetic Reasoning

Time: 36 minutes

30 questions

Directions: Arithmetic Reasoning is the second subtest of the ASVAB. These questions are designed to test your ability to use mathematics to solve various problems that may be found in real life — in other words, math word problems.

Each question is followed by four possible answers. Decide which answer is correct, and then mark the corresponding space on your answer sheet. Use your scratch paper for any figuring you want to do. You may not use a calculator.

1. In the town of RodPowersville, all the license plates have four characters. The first character is always an R or a P. The second and third characters are digits between 0 and 9. The fourth character is a single letter of the alphabet from A to Z. How many possible license plates are there?

   (A) 52

   (B) 520

   (C) 5,200

   (D) 52,000

2. Patty is 45 years old. She is 15 years older than twice her daughter's age. How old is Patty's daughter?

   (A) 15

   (B) 18

   (C) 20

   (D) 22

3. John wants to buy a new computer that costs $3,280. He decides to use his own car and hire out as a taxi during the four months of summer. It costs him $693 to insure his car for those four months. He spends $452 per month on gas. Assuming no other expenses, how many fares will he have to get before he earns enough money for the computer, if he charges an average of $7 per fare?

   (A) 450

   (B) 583

   (C) 826

   (D) 927

4. Jeanie has twice as many quarters as nickels. She has a total of $8.25. How many quarters does she have?

   (A) 15

   (B) 20

   (C) 25

   (D) 30

Go on to next page

5. Patrick was going to buy a car for $5,800. The car dealer offered him two options for buying the car: He could pay the full amount in cash, plus 10 percent for tax and license, or he could pay $1,000 down and $230 a month for 24 months, and the dealer would pick up the tax and license costs. Which is the better deal?

   (A) The cash plan.

   (B) The payment plan.

   (C) Neither — the plans are the same.

6. Pop's House of Nuts offers a mixture of walnuts and almonds that sells for $6 per pound. If walnuts sell for $4.50 per pound and almonds sell for $7 per pound, what should be the weight of the walnuts in a 1-pound mix?

   (A) 0.2 pound

   (B) 0.4 pound

   (C) 0.6 pound

   (D) 0.7 pound

7. A rectangle with an area of 60 square inches is 4 inches longer than it is wide. What is the width of the rectangle?

   (A) 4 inches

   (B) 6 inches

   (C) 8 inches

   (D) 10 inches

8. Rod is a very fast runner. One day he ran 100 meters in 40 seconds, 200 meters in 1 minute and 10 seconds, and 200 meters over low hurdles in one and a half minutes. How many more seconds did it take him to run the 200 meters over low hurdles than it did to run the 200-meter dash?

   (A) 10

   (B) 12

   (C) 18

   (D) 20

Go on to next page

9. A triangle with a perimeter of 60 inches has one side that's twice as long as the shortest side, and a third side that's 8 inches longer than the shortest side. What is the length of the shortest side?

(A) 5 inches

(B) 10 inches

(C) 13 inches

(D) 15 inches

11. There is a pile of 12 marbles. Three of the marbles are yellow. You select a marble without looking. If you do this 12 times, what is the best prediction possible for the number of times that you will pick a marble that is *not* yellow?

(A) 3

(B) 5

(C) 7

(D) 9

10. Timothy bought a new car after the dealer promised that it averaged 36 miles per gallon on the highway. The very next week, Timothy took a highway trip. On the first leg of the trip, Timothy traveled 321 miles and used 9.3 gallons of fuel. On the second leg of the trip, he traveled 290 miles and used 7.6 gallons. On the last leg of the trip, Timothy used 8.3 gallons of gas to travel 303 miles. What was Timothy's average gas mileage during the trip?

(A) 36 miles per gallon

(B) 25 miles per gallon

(C) 24 miles per gallon

(D) 23 miles per gallon

12. Pete had 27 baseball cards. He bought 21 more cards from a nearby collector's store and got 24 more cards for his birthday. Then he lost 6 of the cards to his friend Tom on a bet and gave 21 of the cards to his brother Steven. If the cards are valued at $11 each, what is the value of the baseball cards Pete has left?

(A) $355

(B) $495

(C) $525

(D) $575

Go on to next page

13. Your commander orders you to fly a weather balloon at the end of a 500-foot string. Your first sergeant comes out of a nearby building and stands directly under the balloon 300 feet away from you, and yells, "How high is that balloon?" Assuming the ground is level, what is the correct answer?

    (A) 200 feet

    (B) 300 feet

    (C) 400 feet

    (D) 500 feet

14. Patricia is twice as old as Laura. In three years, the sum of their ages will be 42. How old is Patricia?

    (A) 12

    (B) 18

    (C) 24

    (D) 28

15. Your boss tells you to neatly stack a pile of boards behind a building. Each board is 8 feet long, 6 inches wide, and 4 inches thick. She tells you to place four boards side-by-side, then four more boards on top of those, then four more boards on top of those, and so on, to create your stack. When you're finished, the stack is 10 feet high. How many pieces of lumber are in the entire stack?

    (A) 120

    (B) 130

    (C) 140

    (D) 150

16. Rod took his girlfriend, Jackie, out to dinner. Dinner cost $18.45 and Rod tipped 15 percent. If Rod gave the waitress $40, how much change should he get back?

    (A) $15.32

    (B) $17.91

    (C) $18.13

    (D) $18.78

Go on to next page

17. Christina's salary of $320 per week is increased to $360. What percentage pay raise did she receive?

    (A) 12.5

    (B) 14.3

    (C) 9.2

    (D) 8.4

18. Bailey loaned Robin $1,500 at a simple annual interest rate of 7 percent. If she repays the loan after two years, how much would she have to pay?

    (A) $1,810

    (B) $1,710

    (C) $1,765

    (D) $1,832

19. What is the best probability that two people will have the same birthday? (Disregard leap years — assume that each year is 365 days long.)

    (A) 0.14 percent

    (B) 0.27 percent

    (C) 0.39 percent

    (D) 0 percent

20. There are 8 pints in a gallon. A half-pint of milk is what part of a gallon?

    (A) $\frac{1}{8}$

    (B) $\frac{1}{4}$

    (C) $\frac{1}{16}$

    (D) $\frac{1}{3}$

Go on to next page

21. Train A is heading west, and train B is heading east at 4 p.m. They are 260 miles apart. If train A is traveling at 70 mph and train B is traveling at 60 mph, what time will they meet?

    (A) 5 p.m.

    (B) 6 p.m.

    (C) 7 p.m.

    (D) 8 p.m.

23. A store manager makes $35,000 per year. Of this, 28 percent is withheld for federal and state taxes, but he receives 52 percent of his withholdings back at the end of the year when he files his taxes. What is his net income for the year?

    (A) $28,413

    (B) $30,296

    (C) $31,422

    (D) $32,041

22. NASA decides that it's a fine day to launch a rocket. The rocket blasts off at 3:52 p.m. At 3:55 p.m., the rocket has reached point A, 35 miles above ground level (AGL). At 4:10 p.m., the rocket reaches point B, 232 miles AGL. Assuming a constant rate of speed, how fast is the rocket traveling between point A and point B?

    (A) 558 mph

    (B) 652 mph

    (C) 683 mph

    (D) 788 mph

24. You have to carpet a room that measures 8 feet by 14 feet. How many square feet of carpet should you buy?

    (A) 112

    (B) 23

    (C) 224

    (D) 46

Go on to next page

25. In a two-child family, one child is a boy. What is the probability that the other child is a girl?

    (A) 100 percent

    (B) 50 percent

    (C) 2 out of 3

    (D) 1 out of 4

26. A computer depreciates by 25 percent each year. If a computer costs $2,350 new, how much will it be worth in two years?

    (A) $972.80

    (B) $1,321.87

    (C) $1,421.40

    (D) $1, 821.62

27. Igor wants to paint his back patio and front porch. The patio measures 14 feet by 12 feet and the porch measures 10 feet by 8 feet. If each can of paint covers 48 square feet, how many cans of paint should Igor buy to completely paint the porch and patio?

    (A) 5

    (B) 6

    (C) 7

    (D) 8

28. A tuneup increases a car's fuel efficiency by 5 percent. If a car averaged 20 miles per gallon before the tuneup, how many miles per gallon will it average after the tuneup?

    (A) 25

    (B) 22

    (C) 20.5

    (D) 21

Go on to next page

29. Two trains leave two towns that are 50 miles apart. They travel toward each other at rates of 30 mph and 20 mph, respectively. A bumblebee flying at the rate of 50 mph starts out just as the faster train departs the train station and flies to the slower train. The bee then turns around and goes back to meet the faster train. Then the bee turns around again. It keeps flying back and forth between the trains until the trains meet. How far does the tired bumblebee fly?

(A) 25 miles

(B) 30 miles

(C) 40 miles

(D) 50 miles

30. Find the missing length in a right triangle where the lengths of the two known legs are 10 inches and 24 inches.

(A) 20 inches

(B) 26 inches

(C) 28 inches

(D) 30 inches

STOP DO NOT TURN THE PAGE UNTIL TOLD TO DO SO.
DO NOT RETURN TO A PREVIOUS TEST.

Part 2: Word Knowledge

Time: 11 minutes

35 questions

Directions: The Word Knowledge subtest is the third subtest of the ASVAB. The questions are designed to measure your vocabulary knowledge. You'll see two types of questions on this subtest. The first type simply asks you to choose a word or words that most nearly mean the same as the underlined word in the question. The second type includes an underlined word used in a sentence, and you are to choose the word or words that most nearly mean the same as the underlined word, as used in the context of the sentence. Each question is followed by four possible answers. Decide which answer is correct, and then mark the corresponding space on your answer sheet.

1. <u>Nexus</u> most nearly means:
   (A) solar system
   (B) series
   (C) ice cream
   (D) Star Trek

2. <u>Dissolution</u> most nearly means:
   (A) breakup
   (B) money
   (C) disinfect
   (D) transfer

3. <u>Opulent</u> most nearly means:
   (A) rich
   (B) shiny
   (C) tasty
   (D) plentiful

4. <u>Dross</u> most nearly means
   (A) boring
   (B) resentful
   (C) garbage
   (D) picky

5. We found him living in the <u>dregs</u> of society
   (A) downtown
   (B) suburbs
   (C) slums
   (D) outskirts

6. <u>Implicit</u> most nearly means:
   (A) timed
   (B) implied
   (C) direct
   (D) relied upon

7. The important matters were left to the <u>codicil</u> of the will.
   (A) addendum
   (B) lawyer
   (C) executor
   (D) small print

8. He was asked to <u>elaborate</u> on his excellent speech.
   (A) rewrite
   (B) translate
   (C) shorten
   (D) expand

9. <u>Incendiary</u> most nearly means:
   (A) perishable
   (B) fast
   (C) tangible
   (D) flammable

10. Although we liked his plan, many felt it to be too <u>unorthodox</u>.
    (A) sketchy
    (B) unusual
    (C) practical
    (D) dangerous

Go on to next page

11. Becky <u>implored</u> Bill not to go to the fight.

    (A) forbade

    (B) asked

    (C) told

    (D) begged

12. In <u>retrospect</u>, going to the fight wasn't such a bright idea.

    (A) hindsight

    (B) forethought

    (C) fact

    (D) town

13. He turned out to be an <u>implacable</u> enemy.

    (A) unbeatable

    (B) unchangeable

    (C) friendly

    (D) strong

14. <u>Circumvent</u> most nearly means:

    (A) deflate

    (B) trade

    (C) go around

    (D) mislead

15. If you're going to work here, you must <u>comply with</u> our requests.

    (A) agree

    (B) obey

    (C) negotiate

    (D) None of the above

16. Jim didn't <u>notice</u> Tom going around the house.

    (A) see

    (B) hear

    (C) tell

    (D) order

17. <u>Importunate</u> most nearly means

    (A) important

    (B) inopportune

    (C) annoying

    (D) practical

18. Tammy is one of the most <u>persistent</u> young ladies I know.

    (A) persevering

    (B) annoying

    (C) practical

    (D) important

19. We need a volunteer to tend to the <u>enduring</u> flame exposition.

    (A) everlasting

    (B) hot

    (C) weekend

    (D) weekly

20. <u>Amicable</u> most nearly means:

    (A) friendly

    (B) trace

    (C) temperamental

    (D) relationship

21. Our midnight encounter with Shylinn and Katie was <u>fortuitous</u>.

    (A) scary

    (B) accidental

    (C) tragic

    (D) perilous

22. I simply <u>abhor</u> ice cream on my cake.

    (A) eat

    (B) relish

    (C) love

    (D) hate

23. <u>Cascade</u> most nearly means:

    (A) stack

    (B) waterfall

    (C) movement

    (D) playful

24. <u>Deluge</u> most nearly means:

    (A) plentiful

    (B) maximum

    (C) rainfall

    (D) persistent

Go on to next page ➡

25. <u>Engulf</u> most nearly means:
    - (A) diverse
    - (B) swallow
    - (C) playful
    - (D) taxidermy

26. <u>Heresy</u> most nearly means:
    - (A) opinion
    - (B) falsehood
    - (C) religion
    - (D) testimony

27. I've told Tom a hundred times not to <u>slouch</u> in his chair.
    - (A) slump
    - (B) jump
    - (C) sit
    - (D) stand

28. Joyce used an <u>incisive</u> method of summarizing the situation.
    - (A) confusing
    - (B) humorous
    - (C) direct
    - (D) imaginative

29. The lawyer asked the judge for time to <u>confer</u> with her clients.
    - (A) eat
    - (B) play
    - (C) consult
    - (D) leave

30. No matter how hard we tried, we continued to <u>argue</u> about last night.
    - (A) negotiate
    - (B) fistfight
    - (C) discuss
    - (D) disagree

31. <u>Wrangle</u> most nearly means:
    - (A) get
    - (B) run
    - (C) work
    - (D) manage

32. Linda's speech <u>embodied</u> everything our association stands for.
    - (A) contained
    - (B) included
    - (C) pacified
    - (D) Both A and B

33. <u>Encroach</u> most nearly means:
    - (A) upset
    - (B) intrude
    - (C) movement
    - (D) trade-off

34. I hope he takes an <u>appropriate</u> approach to this problem.
    - (A) unusual
    - (B) respectful
    - (C) speedy
    - (D) suitable

35. <u>Paragon</u> most nearly means:
    - (A) excellence
    - (B) distasteful
    - (C) practical
    - (D) painful

STOP DO NOT TURN THE PAGE UNTIL TOLD TO DO SO.
DO NOT RETURN TO A PREVIOUS TEST.

Part 3: Paragraph Comprehension

Time: 13 minutes

15 questions

Directions: Paragraph Comprehension is the fourth subtest on the ASVAB. The questions are designed to measure your ability to understand what you read. This section includes one or more paragraphs of reading material, followed by incomplete statements or questions. Read the paragraph and select the choice that best completes the statement or answers the question. Then mark the corresponding space on your answer sheet.

Every American can be proud of the history of the United States Army. The American Army was created on June 14, 1775, when the Continental Congress first authorized the muster of troops to serve under its own authority. Those soldiers came from the provincial forces of the colonies, which were at that time laying siege to Boston. From its birth, the American Army has relied on the citizen soldier, exemplified by the militia and the Minutemen who fought the British at Lexington and Concord. Commanded by General George Washington and supported by our French allies, the Continental Army defeated the British at Yorktown and secured the freedoms so eloquently stated in the Declaration of Independence.

1. The backbone of the United States Army is

    (A) the soldier

    (B) tanks

    (C) rifles

    (D) strategy

2. Who helped defeat the British, resulting in American independence?

    (A) England

    (B) France

    (C) Abraham Lincoln

    (D) Rod Powers

3. According to the passage, Congress appointed General George Washington as the first President of the United States in recognition of his accomplishments at Yorktown.

    (A) True

    (B) False

Army enlisted ranks range from private to sergeant major (grades E1 through E9). Address privates (E1 and E2) and privates first class (E3) as "Private (last name)." Address specialists as "Specialist (last name)." Address sergeants, staff sergeants, sergeant's first class, and master sergeants as "Sergeant (last name)." Address higher-rank sergeants by their full ranks in conjunction with their names.

4. According to the passage, enlisted soldiers holding the rank of sergeant major should be addressed as:

    (A) "Sergeant Major (last name)"

    (B) "Sergeant (last name)"

    (C) "Sir" or "Ma'am"

    (D) "Sergeant (first and last name)"

Most airline trips are uneventful; however, airlines don't guarantee their schedules, and you should realize this when planning your trip. Many things can make it impossible for flights to arrive on time. Some of these problems, such as bad weather and resulting air-traffic delays, are beyond the airlines' control.

5. According to the passage, airline delays

    (A) are avoidable with proper planning

    (B) can be an unpleasant experience

    (C) are on the rise over recent years

    (D) are often unavoidable

Go on to next page

Front air bags saved 25,782 lives between 1987 and 2008. However, they are supplemental safety devices. Always wear your seat belt. Place all children under 13 in the rear seat. The rear seat is the safest for children. If you have an air bag on-off switch, check its position every time you enter your vehicle. One survey shows that 48 percent of these on-off switches were incorrectly left on for child passengers under age 13.

6. According to the passage, young children:

(A) should always have an airbag

(B) should not have an airbag

(C) should ride in the front seat

(D) should take their seat belts off when sleeping

In the event of a fire, remember: Time is the biggest enemy, and every second counts! Escape plans help you get out of your home quickly. In less than 30 seconds, a small flame can get completely out of control and turn into a major fire. It only takes minutes for a house to fill with thick, black smoke and become engulfed in flames.

7. The main point of the passage is that

(A) fires can get out of control quickly

(B) fires are more dangerous than earthquakes

(C) having an escape plan is important

(D) most fires get out of control

Enlisted members commissioned as temporary officers after OCS graduation perform duties and enjoy the privileges of regular commissioned officers. They serve in a probationary period of about four years to ensure a fair, accurate appraisal of their capabilities over two or more types of duty. Probation expires about the time they are considered for promotion to lieutenant, and selection under the "best qualified" system amply indicates their qualification for permanent status.

8. Enlisted members who receive a commission as a result of officer candidate school:

(A) remain enlisted until after a probationary period

(B) perform essentially the same duties as other commissioned officers

(C) remain on probation for six years

(D) return to enlisted status if they fail the probationary period

Hurricanes are severe tropical storms that form in the southern Atlantic Ocean, the Caribbean Sea, the Gulf of Mexico, and the eastern Pacific Ocean. A tornado, on the other hand, is a violent, dangerous, rotating column of air that is in contact with both the surface of the Earth and a cumulonimbus cloud or, in rare cases, the base of a cumulus cloud. Tornadoes come in many sizes but are typically in the form of a visible condensation funnel, whose narrow end touches the Earth and is often encircled by a cloud of debris and dust. Tornadoes often develop from a class of thunderstorms known as supercells. Supercells contain mesocyclones, an area of organized rotation a few miles up in the atmosphere, usually 1 to 6 miles (2 to 10 km) across. Most intense tornadoes (EF3 to EF5 on the Enhanced Fujita Scale) develop from supercells.

9. According to the passage, tornados:

(A) are invisible

(B) sound like a train

(C) are visible funnels

(D) are more dangerous than hurricanes

Go on to next page

The military services shall design, implement, supervise, and tailor physical-fitness programs to suit the particular needs and mission of the Department of Defense, and their respective service, consistent with established scientific principles of physical conditioning. Service members should exercise on a regular basis (that is, three to five times each week) and to an intensity that provides a training effect. Individuals with injuries and on medical profiles, shall be placed on a medically approved exercise program only after consultation with medical authorities. Pregnant service members will engage in physical activity to maintain cardiovascular and muscular fitness throughout the pregnancy and postpartum period, in accordance with medical guidance. Exercise regimens will consist of routines that include physical training and nutritional counseling. Military services shall extend their physical-fitness programs to incorporate occupational-specific physical-fitness requirements for those career fields where it is deemed necessary to ensure adequate skill, performance, and safety. This extension shall include identifying each specific physical capability needed by the occupational specialties. These additional physical-fitness standards will include a risk assessment for prevention of injuries and will reflect levels of physical abilities necessary to meet the duty demands of the occupation. Once the levels or desired physical capabilities are identified, physical-fitness training and testing should be linked to these capabilities. Emerging training methodologies should be considered when designing the appropriate physical-fitness training.

10. The main focus of the passage is on

    (A) pregnant service members

    (B) fitness limitations

    (C) duty hours

    (D) physical fitness for service members

11. From information in the passage, you may infer that

    (A) each military branch has a different physical-fitness program

    (B) each military branch is likely to have a different physical-fitness program

    (C) cardiovascular fitness is the most important type of fitness

    (D) pregnant women are excused from military fitness programs

12. According to this Department of Defense policy directive, which service members must consult with medical officials prior to engaging in a physical-fitness program?

    (A) Pregnant service members

    (B) Injured service members

    (C) Those with medical profiles

    (D) Both B and C

"Take the case of a person who attends to the petty occupations of his everyday life with mathematical precision. The objects around him, however, have all been tampered with by a mischievous wag, the result being that when he dips his pen into the inkstand he draws it out all covered with mud, when he fancies he is sitting down on a solid chair he finds himself sprawling on the floor, in a word his actions are all topsy-turvy or mere beating the air, while in every case the effect is invariably one of momentum. Habit has given the impulse: what was wanted was to check the movement or deflect it. He did nothing of the sort, but continued like a machine in the same straight line."

—Henri Bergson

13. The author of the passage is expounding upon:

    (A) humor

    (B) practical jokes

    (C) daily living

    (D) accidents

Go on to next page

"It is very easy to learn how to speak and write correctly, as for all purposes of ordinary conversation and communication, only about 2,000 different words are required. The mastery of just twenty hundred words, the knowing where to place them, will make us not masters of the English language, but masters of correct speaking and writing. Small number, you will say, compared with what is in the dictionary! But nobody ever uses all the words in the dictionary or could use them did he live to be the age of Methuselah, and there is no necessity for using them. There are upwards of 200,000 words in the recent editions of the large dictionaries, but the one-hundredth part of this number will suffice for all your wants. Of course, you may think not, and you may not be content to call things by their common names; you may be ambitious to show superiority over others and display your learning or, rather, your pedantry and lack of learning. For instance, you may not want to call a spade a spade. You may prefer to call it a spatulous device for abrading the surface of the soil. Better, however, to stick to the old, familiar, simple name that your grandfather called it. It has stood the test of time, and old friends are always good friends."

—Joseph Devlin

14. The author of this passage believes that everyone should develop as large a vocabulary as possible for common conversation.

    (A) True
    (B) False

There are the subordinates who are both competent and committed to their jobs. They know what to do and are enthusiastic about doing it. These are the individuals the leader tasks to develop or implement new procedures, informing the leader only of their progress. Projects may be delegated to these subordinates, and they should be allowed to make the decisions that will ensure task accomplishment. Low-supportive and low-directive behavior is appropriate because followers are both committed to and competent on the task.

15. According to the passage,

    (A) all subordinates require close supervision
    (B) most subordinates are incompetent
    (C) managers should be careful when delegating assignments
    (D) managers should identify subordinates who are committed to their jobs

STOP DO NOT TURN THE PAGE UNTIL TOLD TO DO SO. DO NOT RETURN TO A PREVIOUS TEST.

Part 4: Mathematics Knowledge

Time: 24 minutes

25 questions

Directions: Mathematics Knowledge is the fifth subtest on the ASVAB. The questions are designed to test your ability to solve general mathematical problems. Each question is followed by four possible answers. Decide which answer is correct, and then mark the corresponding space on your answer sheet. Use your scratch paper for any figuring you want to do. You may not use a calculator.

1.   If $x = 3$, then $\dfrac{6x}{2} =$
   - (A) 3
   - (B) 5
   - (C) 8
   - (D) 9

3.   The number 81 is what percent of 1,000?
   - (A) 0.81
   - (B) 8.1
   - (C) 81
   - (D) 810

2.   If $0.25y = 2$, then $y =$
   - (A) 5
   - (B) 8
   - (C) 10
   - (D) 15

4.   Find the smallest possible missing digit to make the following integer divisible by 3: 41_89
   - (A) 2
   - (B) 3
   - (C) 4
   - (D) 5

Go on to next page

5. Is the number 51 a *prime* or *composite* number?

   (A) Prime

   (B) Composite

6. Solve: $-83 = t - 7$.

   (A) -42

   (B) -76

   (C) 42

   (D) 76

7. Solve: $\frac{y}{4} = 15$.

   (A) 25

   (B) 30

   (C) 35

   (D) 60

8. Translate the following sentence into an equation or inequality: "A savings account with $50 added is now worth more than $800."

   (A) $\$50 + s = \$800$

   (B) $50 + s = 200$

   (C) $\$50 + s \geq \$800$

   (D) $\$50 + s > \$800$

Go on to next page

9. The area of the rectangle shown here is 250 cm². Find the width of the rectangle.

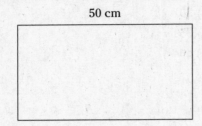

50 cm

(A) 5 cm

(B) 10 cm

(C) 25 cm

(D) 30 cm

11. Express the ratio, *5 inches to 10 feet* as a fraction.

(A) $\frac{1}{24}$

(B) $\frac{5}{10}$

(C) $\frac{10}{5}$

(D) $\frac{1}{2}$

10. A cube has a volume of 216 square inches. What is the length of one side of the cube?

(A) 4 inches

(B) 6 inches

(C) 8 inches

(D) 10 inches

12. 9 is what percent of 72?

(A) 7.8

(B) 11.4

(C) 12.5

(D) 15.3

Go on to next page

13. What is the mean of the numbers 17, 27, 52, 81, and 93?

    (A) 43

    (B) 48

    (C) 54

    (D) 59

14. What is the least positive integer value of x, if $y^{-2} = -1$ and $[(y^{-2})^5]^x = 1$?

    (A) 2

    (B) 4

    (C) 6

    (D) 8

15. What is the total volume of the shape shown here?

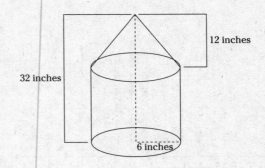

    (A) 2,638 cubic inches

    (B) 2,713 cubic inches

    (C) 2,801 cubic inches

    (D) 2,261 cubic inches

16. What is $\frac{1}{7}$ percent of 210?

    (A) 0.4

    (B) 4

    (C) 0.3

    (D) 3

Go on to next page

Use the following figure for questions 17 and 18.

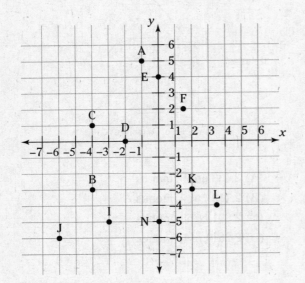

17.   What are the coordinates for point *B*?

(A) 8^0 by 4^0

(B) (–4, –3)

(C) (7, 3)

(D) (2, 6)

18.   What are the coordinates for point *K*?

(A) 3^0 by 7^0

(B) (2, –3)

(C) (–3, 2)

(D) (3, 3)

19.   In which quadrant would the coordinates (–3, –4) be located?

(A) Quadrant I

(B) Quadrant II

(C) Quadrant III

(D) Quadrant IV

20.   Simplify: 4(7 + *i*) =

(A) 17

(B) 27*i*

(C) 28 + 4*i*

(D) 32*x*

Go on to next page

21. $\dfrac{-22}{-11} =$

    (A) -2

    (B) 2

    (C) -0.2

    (D) 0.2

23. Solve the inequality using transformations: $-13 - 7 > k$.

    (A) $-20 < k$

    (B) $k < -20$

    (C) $k > -20$

    (D) $k = -20$

22. If $x^2 = 0.49$, what is the value of x?

    (A) 0.7

    (B) -0.7

    (C) -7

    (D) Both A and B

24. Write 0.0000000000000004932 using scientific notation.

    (A) 4.932×10^{-16}

    (B) 4.932×10^{16}

    (C) $4,932^{-16}$

    (D) $4,932^{16}$

Go on to next page

25. Solve for *x*:

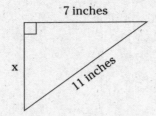

(A) 4 inches

(B) 5 inches

(C) 6.5 inches

(D) 8.5 inches

STOP DO NOT TURN THE PAGE UNTIL TOLD TO DO SO.
DO NOT RETURN TO A PREVIOUS TEST.

Chapter 13

Practice Exam 1: Answers and Explanations

• •

Did you do well on the first practice exam? I sure hope so! Use this answer key to score the practice exam in Chapter 12. If you don't do well, don't worry — there are three more full-length practice tests in this book to help you hone your English and math skills.

The AFQT isn't scored based on number correct, number wrong, or even percent of questions correct. Instead, the score is derived by comparing your raw score with the raw score of others who have taken the test before you. In determining the raw score, harder questions are worth more points than easier questions. (For more on scoring, turn to Chapter 2.)

Don't waste time trying to equate your score on this practice test with your potential score on the actual AFQT. It can't be done. Instead, use the results of this practice test to determine which areas you should devote more study time to.

Part 1: Arithmetic Reasoning

Mathematical word problems can be tough. You have to develop a skill for determining which factors are relevant to the problem and then be able to convert those factors into a mathematical formula to arrive at a correct solution. Yikes! No wonder so many math books are on the market! A few good ones that may help are *Math Word Problems For Dummies, Algebra I For Dummies,* and *Algebra II For Dummies,* all by Mary Jane Sterling; *Geometry For Dummies,* 2nd Edition, and *Calculus For Dummies,* both by Mark Ryan; and *SAT II Math For Dummies,* by Scott Hatch, JD, and Lisa Zimmer Hatch, MA — all published by Wiley.

Reviewing Chapters 8 and 10 and the additional practice questions in Chapter 11 may also help. Finally, Chapters 20 and 21 may help you improve your scores.

1. **(C)** There are two possibilities (R and P) for the first character. There are ten possible choices (0 through 9) for the second and third characters. There are 26 letters in the alphabet, so there are 26 possible choices for the last characters. Applying the multiplication principle, you get $2 \times 10 \times 10 \times 26 = 5,200$.

   I don't really have a town named after me, but it could happen.

2. **(A)** You want to find out Patty's daughter's age, so let d = daughter's age. You know that Patty is 45 and her age is 15 years more than twice the daughter's age. This can be expressed mathematically as $45 = 2d + 15$. The rest is simply skull-sweat.

$$45 - 15 = 2d$$
$$30 = 2d$$
$$\frac{30}{2} = d$$
$$d = 15$$

3. **(C)** John needs to make the cost of his expenses, plus the cost of the new computer: $3,280 + $693 + ($452 × 4) = $3,280 + $693 + $1,808 = $5,781. Each fare averages $7, so, to find the number of fares: $\frac{5,781}{7} = 825.85$. Because a fraction of a fare isn't practical, round this up to 826 fares.

4. **(D)** Let x = the number of nickels. That means $2x$ = the number of quarters. All of Jeanie's coins total $8.25 or 825 cents. Mathematically, this can be expressed as:

$$5(x) + 25(2x) = 825$$
$$5x + 50x = 825$$
$$55x = 825$$
$$x = \frac{825}{55}$$
$$x = 15$$

Jeanie has 15 nickels.

Because she has twice as many quarters, she has 30 quarters.

5. **(A)** First, compute the total cost of the cash plan: $5,800 + 10 percent = $5,800 + $580 = $6,380.

The total cost of the payment plan would be $1,000 + ($230 × 24) = $6,520.

The cash plan is the better deal.

6. **(B)** Let x = the amount of walnuts in a pound. That means $1 - x$ = the pounds of almonds. In a pound of the mixture, walnuts cost $4.50x$ and almonds cost $7(1 - x)$. Together a pound of the mixture costs $6. So:

$$4.5x + 7(1 - x) = 6$$
$$4.5x + 7 - 7x = 6$$
$$-2.5x + 7 = 6$$
$$-2.5x = 6 - 7$$
$$-2.5x = -1$$
$$x = \frac{-1}{-2.5}$$
$$x = 0.4$$

7. **(B)** Let w = the width of the rectangle. That means the length = $w + 4$. The area formula for a rectangle is $a = lw$. Substitute the known values:

$$60 = (w + 4)w$$
$$60 = w^2 + 4w$$
$$0 = w^2 + 4w - 60$$

Guess what? This is a quadratic equation, which can be factored as follows:

$$0 = (w - 6)(w + 10)$$
$$w = 6, -10$$

Because a rectangle with a negative width isn't much use, the width of this rectangle is 6 inches.

8. **(D)** Converting to seconds, it took Rod 60 + 10 = 70 seconds to run the 200-meter dash, and 60 + 30 = 90 seconds to run the hurdles. Then, 90 – 70 = 20 seconds.

Rod really can run faster than a speeding bullet.

9. **(C)** Let s = the length of the shortest side. That means that the two other sides are $2s$ and $s + 8$. The perimeter formula for a triangle is $p = s_1 + s_2 + s_3$. Substitute the known values:

$$60 = s + 2s + s + 8$$
$$60 = 4s + 8$$
$$52 = 4s$$
$$\frac{52}{4} = s$$
$$s = 13$$

10. **(A)** First, total the number of miles that Timothy drove: 321 + 290 + 303 = 914. Next, find the sum of the amount of gas he used: 9.3 + 7.6 + 8.3 = 25.2. Finally, divide the total miles driven by the amount of gas used:

$$\frac{914}{25.2} = 36.26$$

How about that? Timothy found an honest car salesman.

11. **(D)** There are 12 marbles, which means there are 12 possible outcomes. Nine of the marbles are not yellow, which means there are 9 favorable outcomes. This can be shown as a ratio: 9:12, or chances of 9 in 12.

12. **(B)** This is a relatively simple problem, just to see if you're still paying attention. The problem can be solved in a few simple steps.

    First, total the number of cards Pete had originally: 27 + 21 + 24 = 72.

    Next, find the number of cards he gave away: 6 + 21 = 27.

    Subtract the number of cards given away from the total number of cards: 72 – 27 = 45.

    Pete has 45 cards left, each worth $11: 45 × $11 = $495.

13. **(C)** This problem actually makes up the parts of a right triangle. Take a look at the following figure.

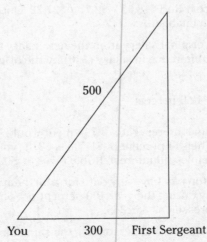

The Pythagorean theorem says that if you know the length of two sides of a right triangle, you can figure out the length of the third by using the formula, $a^2 + b^2 = c^2$.

The 500-foot string forms the hypotenuse, so the equation reads $300^2 + x^2 = 500^2$. Solve for x:

$$90,000 + x^2 = 250,000$$
$$x^2 = 250,000 - 90,000$$
$$x^2 = 160,000$$
$$x = \pm\sqrt{160,000}$$
$$x = 400, -400$$

It wouldn't be possible to have a weather balloon flying 400 feet under the ground, so use the positive solution.

14. **(C)** Let x = Laura's age. Since Patricia is twice as old as Laura, her age can be expressed as $2x$. In three years, Laura will be $x + 3$, and Patricia will be $2x + 3$. In three years, the sum of their ages will be 42. You can now set up the equation:

$$x + 3 + 2x + 3 = 42$$
$$3x + 6 = 42$$
$$3x = 36$$
$$x = \frac{36}{3}$$
$$x = 12$$

Since Laura is 12, and Patricia is twice as old as Laura, Patricia is 24 years old.

15. **(A)** First, multiply the height of the stack by 12 to convert the feet into inches: $10 \times 12 = 120$ inches.

Next, divide the height (in inches) by the thickness of each piece of lumber: $\frac{120}{4} = 30$.

The stack is 30 pieces of lumber high, but there are 4 pieces of lumber in each layer, so: $30 \times 4 = 120$.

16. **(D)** First, 15 percent of $18.45 is $2.77 (you get that by multiplying $18.45 × 0.15 = $2.77). Dinner plus tip cost Rod $18.45 + $2.77 = $21.22. Out of $40, Rod should get back $40.00 – $21.56 = $18.78 in change.

17. **(A)** Subtract the original salary from the new salary to get the difference: $360 – $320 = $40. Then divide the difference in salary ($40) by the original salary ($320) to determine the percent increase:

$$\frac{40}{320} = 0.125 = 12.5 \text{ percent}$$

18. **(B)** A simple annual interest rate of 7 percent would be 14 percent for two years: 7 percent × 2 = 14 percent. Then 14 percent of $1,500 is $210 (you get that by multiplying $1,500 × 0.14 = $210). With principle and interest, Robin owes $1,500 + $210 = $1,710.

19. **(B)** The first person can have any date for a birthday. That makes the probability of him having a birthday during the year 100 percent or 365 chances out of 365 possibilities. As a radio, this is expressed as 365:365.

The chance that the second person has the same birthday is 1 out of 365 or 1:365.

To find the probability that both people have the same birthday, express the ratios as fractions and multiply them together:

$$\frac{365}{365} \times \frac{1}{365} = \frac{1}{365} \text{ or about } 0.27 \text{ percent}$$

20. **(C)** 8 pints make up a gallon, so a gallon contains 16 half-pints. One half-pint equals $\frac{1}{16}$ of a gallon.

21. **(B)** The distance formula is $d = rt$, where d is the distance, r is the rate, and t is the time. In this case, you want to find out the time, so the formula can be restated as $t = \dfrac{d}{r}$.

The trains are 260 miles away (distance) and their combined rate of speed is 70 mph + 60 mph = 130 mph.

You can now plug the known values into the distance formula:

$$t = \frac{260}{130}$$
$$t = 2 \text{ hours}$$

Because the trains were 260 mph apart at 4 p.m., they will meet at 6 p.m.

22. **(D)** The distance formula is $d = rt$. You want to find the rate of speed, so the formula can be expressed as $r = \dfrac{d}{t}$.

The time between point A and point B is 15 minutes (4:10 – 3:55 = 15 minutes). Between these points, the rocket traveled 232 – 35 = 197 miles. You now have enough information to plug into the formula:

$$r = \frac{197 \text{ miles}}{15 \text{ minutes}}$$
$$r = 13.1333 \text{ miles per minute}$$

There are 60 minutes in an hour, so to express the speed as mph, multiply by 60: 13.1333 × 60 = 787.998. Round this up to 788.

23. **(B)** Twenty-eight percent of $35,000 is $9,800 (you get this by multiplying $35,000 × 0.28 = $9,800). After deductions, the store manager's take-home salary is $25,200. The store keeper gets 52 percent of his deductions back at the end of the year: $9,800 × 0.52 = $5,096. Adding what he gets back to his remaining take-home salary, $25,200 + $5,096 = $30,296.

24. **(A)** The area of a rectangle is determined from the formula $a = lw$. Substitute the known values:

$$a = 8 \times 14$$
$$a = 112$$

25. **(C)** In a two-child family, there are only four possible combinations: BB, BG, GB, or GG. You already know that one child is a boy, so there can't be two girls. That leaves the following possibilities: BB, BG, GB. Two of those probabilities include girls, so the probability that the second child is a girl is $\dfrac{2}{3}$.

26. **(B)** The computer depreciates by $587.50 the first year: $2,350 × 0.25 = $587.50. Thus, at the end of the first year it's worth $2,350 – $587.50 = $1,762.50. The next year it depreciates by another $440.63: $1,762.50 × 0.25 = $440.63. The computer is now worth $1,762.50 – $440.63 = $1,321.87.

27. **(B)** To find the area of a rectangle, the formula is $a = lw$.

The area of the patio is 12 × 14 = 168 square feet. The area of the porch is 8 × 10 = 80 square feet.

The total area to be painted is 80 + 168 = 248 square feet.

Since one can of paint will cover 48 square feet, divide the total area by the number of square feet each can will cover: $\dfrac{248}{48} = 5.16$. Because five cans won't complete the job, Igor needs to buy six cans.

28. **(D)** Five percent of 20 is 1 (you get that by multiplying 20 × 0.05 = 1). Add that to the original miles per gallon and the result is 20 + 1 = 21.

29. **(D)** This problem sounds a lot more complicated than it really is. In fact, it's a very, very old word problem, designed to confuse. However, you can solve it relatively easily.

    The distance formula is $d = rt$. This can also be expressed as $t = \dfrac{d}{r}$.

    Forget about the bee for a moment, and find out how long until the trains meet by plugging the known values into the distance formula:

    $$t = \frac{50}{50}$$
    $$t = 1 \text{ hour}$$

    Because the trains are traveling for one hour, and the bee is moving at 50 mph, the bee covers 50 miles in this time.

30. **(B)** The Pythagorean theorem states that you can find the length of any side of a right triangle by using the formula $a^2 + b^2 = c^2$. Plug in the known values:

    $$10^2 + 24^2 = c^2$$
    $$100 + 576 = c^2$$
    $$676 = c^2$$
    $$c = \pm\sqrt{676}$$
    $$c = 26, -26$$

    Only the positive answer makes sense.

Part 2: Word Knowledge

I hope you did well on this subtest. (I was crossing my fingers the whole time!) If not, you may want to take another gander at Chapter 4 and the practice questions in Chapter 5. Chapters 20 and 21 may also help.

If you need additional study references to improve your vocabulary ability, you may want to consider *Vocabulary For Dummies,* by Laurie E. Rozakis, PhD, and *SAT Vocabulary For Dummies,* by Suzee Vlk (both published by Wiley).

1. **(B)** *Nexus* is a noun that means a series of connections.

2. **(A)** *Dissolution* is a noun that means the undoing or breaking of a bond, tie, union, partnership, and so on.

3. **(A)** *Opulent* is an adjective that means wealthy, rich, or affluent.

4. **(C)** As a noun, *dross* means waste matter or refuse.

5. **(C)** *Dregs* is a noun that means the least desirable portion.

6. **(B)** *Implicit* is an adjective that means implied rather than directly stated.

7. **(A)** *Codicil* is a noun that means an addition or addendum to a will.

8. **(D)** *Elaborate,* when used as a verb, means to explain in great detail.

9. **(D)** As an adjective, *incendiary* means used or adapted for setting property on fire.

10. **(B)** *Unorthodox* is an adjective that means breaking with convention or tradition.

11. **(D)** *Implore* is a verb that means to beg urgently or piteously.

12. **(A)** *Retrospect,* when used as a verb, means to look back in time.

13. **(B)** *Implacable* is an adjective that means unable to be appeased, mollified, or pacified. In other words, it proved impossible to change this enemy.

14. **(C)** *Circumvent* is a verb that means to bypass, or to avoid by using deception.

15. **(B)** *Comply* is a verb that means to yield or obey. Agree (B) is close, but a person can obey without agreeing.

16. **(A)** Used as a verb, *notice* means to see or perceive.

17. **(C)** *Importunate* is an adjective that means troublesome or annoying.

18. **(A)** *Persistent* is an adjective that means unending or enduring.

19. **(A)** *Enduring* is an adjective that means lasting forever.

20. **(A)** *Amicable* is an adjective that means done in a friendly spirit.

21. **(B)** Used as an adjective, *fortuitous* means happening or produced by chance.

22. **(D)** *Abhor* is a verb that means to have a strong, extreme aversion to or to dislike.

23. **(B)** Used as a noun, *cascade* means anything resembling a waterfall.

24. **(C)** *Deluge,* when used as a noun, means a great flood of water or a drenching rain.

25. **(B)** Used as a verb, *engulf* means to swallow up.

26. **(A)** *Heresy* is a noun that means opinion at variance with the orthodox or accepted doctrine.

27. **(A)** *Slouch,* when used as a verb, means to sit or stand with an awkward, drooping posture.

28. **(C)** *Incisive* is an adjective that means remarkably clear and direct.

29. **(C)** *Confer* is a verb that means to consult or discuss.

30. **(D)** *Argue,* when used as a verb, means to contend in oral disagreement.

31. **(A)** Used as a verb, *wrangle* means to obtain, often by contrivance or scheming.

32. **(D)** *Embody* is a verb that means to organize and incorporate.

33. **(B)** *Encroach* is a verb that means to advance beyond proper, established, or usual limits.

34. **(D)** *Appropriate,* when used as an adjective, means suitable or fitting for a specific purpose.

35. **(A)** Used as a noun, *paragon* means model or pattern of excellence.

Part 3: Paragraph Comprehension

So, how did you do? I certainly hope you did very well on this subtest. If not, you may want to engage in some more reading practice. Improving your vocabulary can also help improve your reading comprehension skills — see Chapter 6 for some tips. You may also want to try a few of the practice questions in Chapter 7.

1. **(A)** According to the passage, the American Army has relied on citizen-soldiers from its very birth. Tanks, rifles, and strategy aren't mentioned in the passage.

2. **(B)** The last sentence of the passage clearly states that the French allies supported the Continental Army during their defeat of the British at Yorktown.

3. **(B)** The passage does not address the presidency of George Washington.

4. **(A)** The first sentence makes it clear that those in the rank of sergeant major hold the highest enlisted rank. The final sentence of the passage instructs on the proper address of those who hold this high rank.

5. **(D)** Although B and C may be true, these issues are not addressed by the passage.

6. **(B)** The last sentence states that automatic airbag switches should be in the off position for young children, which indicates that airbags are unsafe for small children.

7. **(C)** The main point of the passage is to have an escape plan to help you get out of the house quickly. The information concerning how quickly fires can get out of control is a subpoint, designed to support the main point.

8. **(B)** The first sentence makes this clear.

9. **(C)** This is pointed out in the third sentence of the passage.

10. **(D)** The passage tells the reader that the service branches must establish physical-fitness programs and directs some of the requirements of those programs.

11. **(A)** The passage makes it clear that each service branch will tailor fitness programs to meet its own individual needs.

12. **(D)** According to the passage, service members who are injured or have a medical profile must consult with medical authorities, prior to engaging in a fitness program. Pregnant women are required to participate in a "medically approved" program for pregnant service members, but the policy does not direct them to actually consult with medical personnel.

13. **(B)** The author is discussing practical jokes. Although A is close, B is the more precise response.

14. **(B)** The author specifically states that a vocabulary of only 2,000 words is sufficient for normal conversation.

15. **(D)** When you analyze the passage, it's apparent that the author suggests identifying subordinates who are competent, so the manager can delegate responsibility to those who can be trusted.

Part 4: Mathematics Knowledge

This subtest would have been much easier if the ASVAB folks allowed you to use a calculator, wouldn't it? I mean, what are these folks, electronically challenged or something? Even so, the problems on this subtest are designed so that they can be solved using only scratch paper, the ol' no. 2 pencil, and a little brain sweat.

If you're still having difficulty, give Chapter 8 another gander. *Algebra I For Dummies* and *Algebra II For Dummies,* both by Mary Jane Sterling; *Geometry For Dummies,* 2nd Edition, and *Calculus For Dummies,* both by Mark Ryan; and *SAT II Math For Dummies,* by Scott Hatch, JD, and Lisa Zimmer Hatch, MA (all published by Wiley) can also help you improve your math knowledge score. You can find additional practice questions in Chapter 9.

1. **(D)** Insert the known value, 6, for x: $\frac{6(3)}{3} = \frac{18}{3} = 9$.

2. **(B)** Isolate the y by dividing both sides of the equation by 0.25:

$$\frac{25y}{25} = \frac{2}{0.25}$$
$$y = \frac{2}{0.25}$$
$$y = 8$$

3. **(B)** Begin by putting the problem into a fraction: $\dfrac{81}{1,000}$. Now convert the fraction to a decimal: 0.081. Because *percent* means part of 100, move the decimal place two spaces to the right to get the number expressed as a percent: 8.1 percent.

4. **(A)** An integer is divisible by a number if the sum of its digits is divisible by the same number.

   Add the known digits: $4 + 1 + 8 + 9 = 22$

   The next nearest multiple of 3 closest to 22 is 24: $3 \times 8 = 24$.

   To find the missing digit, subtract 22 from 24: $24 - 22 = 2$.

   The missing digit is 2.

5. **(B)** A natural number is prime if it has exactly two factors: itself and 1. A natural number is composite if it has three or more factors. The number 51 can be factored 2 ways: 51×1 and 17×3. Therefore, the factors of 51 are 51, 17, 3, and 1.

6. **(B)** Isolate the variable on one side of the equation by adding 7 to each side: $7 - 83 = t$ and $t = -76$.

7. **(D)** Isolate the variable on one side of the equation by multiplying both sides by 4:

   $$4\left(\frac{y}{4}\right) = 15 \times 4$$
   $$y = 15 \times 4$$
   $$y = 60$$

8. **(D)** The sentence translates into an inequality.

9. **(A)** The area of a rectangle is determined by multiplying its length times its width. Set up an equation as follows:

   $$250 = 50w$$
   $$w = \frac{250}{50}$$
   $$w = 5$$

10. **(B)** Volume equals length $\times$ width $\times$ height. Because a cube has equal dimensions, find the cube root of 216: $6 \times 6 \times 6 = 216$.

11. **(A)** Convert the ratio into common units of measurement (you can't compare apples to oranges): 5 inches to 10 feet = 5 inches to 120 inches (there are 12 inches in 1 foot).

    Express the ratio as a fraction: $\dfrac{5}{120}$. Simplify: $\dfrac{5}{120} = \dfrac{1}{24}$.

12. **(C)** Begin by putting the problem into a fraction: $\dfrac{9}{72}$. Now convert the fraction to a decimal: 0.125. Because *percent* means part of 100, move the decimal place two spaces to the right to get the number expressed as a percent: 12.5 percent.

13. **(C)** *Mean* is another word for *average*. To find the mean of a series of numbers, add the numbers together, then divide the sum by the number of items: $17 + 27 + 52 + 81 + 93 = 270$.

    There are a total of five numbers, so divide 270 by 5: $\dfrac{270}{5} = 54$.

14. **(A)** Substitute the value of y^2 in the first equation, -1, into the second equation: $[(-1)^5]^x = 1$. Simplify to: $-1^x = 1$. To make -1 a positive number, the value of its exponent, x, has to be even. The least positive even integer is 2.

15. **(B)** The figure shown is a cylinder and a cone. Therefore, compute the volume of each separately, then add them together.

The formula for the volume of a cylinder is $V = \pi r^2 h$. Substitute the known values:

$V = \pi 6^2 \times 20$

$V = 3.14 \times 36 \times 20$

$V = 2{,}260.8$

The formula for the volume of a cone is $V = \frac{1}{3}\pi r^2 h$. Substitute the known values:

$V = \frac{1}{3}\pi 36 \times 12$

$V = 12\pi \times 12$

$V = 144\pi$

$V = 452.16$

Add the volume of the cylinder and cone: $2{,}260.8 + 452.16 = 2{,}712.96$. Because the possible answer choices do not include decimals, round up.

16. **(C)** The first step is to convert the $\frac{1}{7}$ percent to a fractional number by dividing it by 100:

$\frac{\frac{1}{7} \text{ percent}}{100} = \frac{1}{700}$. To find the percentage, use the formula, $p = br$. In this case, p is unknown,

$b = \frac{1}{7}$ percent or $\frac{1}{700}$, and $r = 210$:

$p = \frac{1}{700} \times 210$

$p = \frac{210}{700}$

$p = \frac{3}{10}$

Converting to a decimal, $p = 0.3$.

17. **(B)** Draw a vertical line from point B to the line representing the x-axis. The result is −4. Now draw a horizontal line from point B to the line representing the y-axis. The result is −3.

18. **(B)** Draw a vertical line from point B to the line representing the x-axis. The result is −2. Now draw a horizontal line from point B to the line representing the y-axis. The result is −3. The x-coordinate is always written first.

19. **(C)** In Quadrant I, both coordinates are positive. In Quadrant II, the x-coordinate is negative and the y-coordinate is positive. In Quadrant III, both coordinates are negative. In Quadrant IV, the x-coordinate is positive and the y-coordinate is negative.

20. **(C)** Distribute the 4 by multiplying all parts of the equation in the parentheses by 4: $4(7 + i) = (4 \times 7) + (4 \times i) = 28 + 4i$.

21. **(B)** When performing division, the division of two negative numbers results in a positive number.

22. **(D)** $x^2 = 0.49$. Use the square root property: $x = \sqrt{0.49}$, or $x = -\sqrt{0.49}$. Simplify: $x = 0.7$ or $x = -0.7$.

23. **(B)** Simplify the problem: $-13 -7 > k = -20 > k$. Exchange the sides of the inequality and reverse the inequality sign (transformation): $k < -20$.

24. **(A)** A number written in scientific notation is a number between 1 and 10 and a power of 10. The power is negative because the original number was a fraction of 1.

25. **(D)** In a right triangle, the two shortest sides are the legs, and the longest side, which is opposite the right angle, is the hypotenuse. The lengths of the legs are 8 inches and x inches, and the length of the hypotenuse is 13 inches.

    According to Pythagorean theorem, in a right triangle, if a and b are the lengths of the legs and c is the length of the hypotenuse, then $a^2 + b^2 = c^2$.

    Substitute the known values:

    $$7^2 + x^2 = 11^2$$
    $$49 + x^2 = 121$$
    $$x^2 = 72$$
    $$x = \sqrt{72}$$
    $$x = 8.5$$

Chapter 14

Practice Exam 2

•••

*T*he Armed Services Vocational Aptitude Battery (ASVAB) includes four subtests that make up the Armed Forces Qualification Test (AFQT) score: Arithmetic Reasoning, Word Knowledge, Paragraph Comprehension, and Mathematics Knowledge.

The military services use the AFQT score as an initial qualifier to determine whether the military considers you to be "trainable." Each service has established its own minimum score. You can find much more information about how the AFQT is scored, and how the services use those scores, in Chapter 2.

You can't take the AFQT by itself. You have to take the entire ASVAB exam, which includes nine total subtests. All the subtests of the ASVAB are used to determine military job qualifications, while the four subtests that make up the AFQT score are used to determine military qualification.

After you complete the entire sample test, check your answers against the answer key in Chapter 15. On the actual AFQT, hard questions are worth more points than easy questions, so you can't score your test by a simple number correct or number wrong. (Chapter 2 explains how the AFQT is scored.)

Use this test as a progress check after a week or two of study. Adjust your study plan accordingly.

Practice Exam 2 Answer Sheet

Part 1: Arithmetic Reasoning

1. (A) (B) (C) (D)   8. (A) (B) (C) (D)   15. (A) (B) (C) (D)   22. (A) (B) (C) (D)   29. (A) (B) (C) (D)
2. (A) (B) (C) (D)   9. (A) (B) (C) (D)   16. (A) (B) (C) (D)   23. (A) (B) (C) (D)   30. (A) (B) (C) (D)
3. (A) (B) (C) (D)   10. (A) (B) (C) (D)   17. (A) (B) (C) (D)   24. (A) (B) (C) (D)
4. (A) (B) (C) (D)   11. (A) (B) (C) (D)   18. (A) (B) (C) (D)   25. (A) (B) (C) (D)
5. (A) (B) (C) (D)   12. (A) (B) (C) (D)   19. (A) (B) (C) (D)   26. (A) (B) (C) (D)
6. (A) (B) (C) (D)   13. (A) (B) (C) (D)   20. (A) (B) (C) (D)   27. (A) (B) (C) (D)
7. (A) (B) (C) (D)   14. (A) (B) (C) (D)   21. (A) (B) (C) (D)   28. (A) (B) (C) (D)

Part 2: Word Knowledge

1. (A) (B) (C) (D)   8. (A) (B) (C) (D)   15. (A) (B) (C) (D)   22. (A) (B) (C) (D)   29. (A) (B) (C) (D)
2. (A) (B) (C) (D)   9. (A) (B) (C) (D)   16. (A) (B) (C) (D)   23. (A) (B) (C) (D)   30. (A) (B) (C) (D)
3. (A) (B) (C) (D)   10. (A) (B) (C) (D)   17. (A) (B) (C) (D)   24. (A) (B) (C) (D)   31. (A) (B) (C) (D)
4. (A) (B) (C) (D)   11. (A) (B) (C) (D)   18. (A) (B) (C) (D)   25. (A) (B) (C) (D)   32. (A) (B) (C) (D)
5. (A) (B) (C) (D)   12. (A) (B) (C) (D)   19. (A) (B) (C) (D)   26. (A) (B) (C) (D)   33. (A) (B) (C) (D)
6. (A) (B) (C) (D)   13. (A) (B) (C) (D)   20. (A) (B) (C) (D)   27. (A) (B) (C) (D)   34. (A) (B) (C) (D)
7. (A) (B) (C) (D)   14. (A) (B) (C) (D)   21. (A) (B) (C) (D)   28. (A) (B) (C) (D)   35. (A) (B) (C) (D)

Part 3: Paragraph Comprehension

1. Ⓐ Ⓑ Ⓒ Ⓓ   8. Ⓐ Ⓑ Ⓒ Ⓓ   15. Ⓐ Ⓑ Ⓒ Ⓓ
2. Ⓐ Ⓑ Ⓒ Ⓓ   9. Ⓐ Ⓑ Ⓒ Ⓓ
3. Ⓐ Ⓑ Ⓒ Ⓓ   10. Ⓐ Ⓑ Ⓒ Ⓓ
4. Ⓐ Ⓑ Ⓒ Ⓓ   11. Ⓐ Ⓑ Ⓒ Ⓓ
5. Ⓐ Ⓑ Ⓒ Ⓓ   12. Ⓐ Ⓑ Ⓒ Ⓓ
6. Ⓐ Ⓑ Ⓒ Ⓓ   13. Ⓐ Ⓑ Ⓒ Ⓓ
7. Ⓐ Ⓑ Ⓒ Ⓓ   14. Ⓐ Ⓑ Ⓒ Ⓓ

Part 4: Mathematics Knowledge

1. Ⓐ Ⓑ Ⓒ Ⓓ   8. Ⓐ Ⓑ Ⓒ Ⓓ   15. Ⓐ Ⓑ Ⓒ Ⓓ   22. Ⓐ Ⓑ Ⓒ Ⓓ
2. Ⓐ Ⓑ Ⓒ Ⓓ   9. Ⓐ Ⓑ Ⓒ Ⓓ   16. Ⓐ Ⓑ Ⓒ Ⓓ   23. Ⓐ Ⓑ Ⓒ Ⓓ
3. Ⓐ Ⓑ Ⓒ Ⓓ   10. Ⓐ Ⓑ Ⓒ Ⓓ   17. Ⓐ Ⓑ Ⓒ Ⓓ   24. Ⓐ Ⓑ Ⓒ Ⓓ
4. Ⓐ Ⓑ Ⓒ Ⓓ   11. Ⓐ Ⓑ Ⓒ Ⓓ   18. Ⓐ Ⓑ Ⓒ Ⓓ   25. Ⓐ Ⓑ Ⓒ Ⓓ
5. Ⓐ Ⓑ Ⓒ Ⓓ   12. Ⓐ Ⓑ Ⓒ Ⓓ   19. Ⓐ Ⓑ Ⓒ Ⓓ
6. Ⓐ Ⓑ Ⓒ Ⓓ   13. Ⓐ Ⓑ Ⓒ Ⓓ   20. Ⓐ Ⓑ Ⓒ Ⓓ
7. Ⓐ Ⓑ Ⓒ Ⓓ   14. Ⓐ Ⓑ Ⓒ Ⓓ   21. Ⓐ Ⓑ Ⓒ Ⓓ

Part 1: Arithmetic Reasoning

Time: 36 minutes

30 questions

You'll encounter the Arithmetic Reasoning subtest as the second subtest of the ASVAB, right after the General Science subtest. The Arithmetic Reasoning subtest consists of story-type word problems.

Unfortunately, the ASVAB powers-that-be have dictated that you are not allowed to use a calculator. Don't worry — the problems are designed so that they can be solved with the use of pencil and scratch paper.

Each question is followed by four possible answers. Decide which answer is correct and then mark the corresponding space on your answer sheet. Use your scratch paper for any figuring you want to do.

1. Joshua has a jar with 100 marbles. The jar contains twice as many red marbles as yellow marbles, three times as many green as yellow, and twice as many purple as red. How many yellow marbles are in the jar?

   (A) 5
   (B) 8
   (C) 10
   (D) 20

2. Mack travels 1,100 miles during a 40-hour workweek. If he spends two-fifths of his time traveling, how many hours does he spend traveling?

   (A) 16
   (B) 12
   (C) 22
   (D) 8

3. A car headed west for North Platte left at the same time that a car headed east left the same place. The car headed west for North Platte traveled at 55 miles per hour. The car headed east traveled at 70 miles per hour. How many miles apart were the cars at the end of 2.5 hours?

   (A) 212 miles
   (B) 165.5 miles
   (C) 125 miles
   (D) 312.5 miles

4. Twist the preceding problem around a bit: This time assume the cars were traveling in the same direction. How far apart were they at the end of 2.5 hours?

   (A) 37.5
   (B) 62.5
   (C) 73.5
   (D) 87

Go on to next page

5. One more twist. (Isn't this fun?) This time the two cars travel at a right angle (90 degrees) to each other. For example, one car travels west, and the other car travels north. How far apart are the drivers, as the crow flies, after 2.5 hours?

(A) 312.5

(B) 239.3

(C) 222.5

(D) 323.4

6. Dana spent $120.37 on gas in July, $108.45 in August, and $114.86 in September. What was the average monthly cost of Dana's gas?

(A) $343.68

(B) $110.45

(C) $114.86

(D) $114.56

7. A teacher deposited $3,000 in a retirement fund. If she didn't add any more money to the fund, which earns an annual interest rate of 6 percent, how much money would she have in 1 year?

(A) $180

(B) $3,006

(C) $3,180

(D) $6,000

8. A farmer constructs a wooden bin The bin is 6 feet long, 4 feet wide, and 3 feet deep. The bin rests on legs that are 3.5 feet tall to keep the grain away from the damp ground. How much grain can the farmer store in his new bin?

(A) 63 cubic feet

(B) 72 cubic feet

(C) 82 cubic feet

(D) 91 cubic feet

Go on to next page

9. On December 1, the National Weather Service recorded 1.3 inches of rain in Key West, Florida. On December 5, the National Weather Service recorded 0.5 fewer inches of rain than fell on December 1. On December 15, 3 more inches fell in Key West. There was no additional rain during the remainder of the month. How many inches of rain fell in Key West during the month of December?

   (A) 10.9

   (B) 5.1

   (C) 11.4

   (D) 8.7

11. Denise buys a soda for 90¢, a candy bar for $1.20, and a bag of chips for $2.90. Assuming a 3.5 percent sales tax, how much change would she receive from a $10 bill?

   (A) $6.13

   (B) $5.75

   (C) $5.25

   (D) $4.82

10. If it costs $5.50 per square foot to build a new patio, how much would it cost to build a patio that is 9 by 20 feet?

   (A) $647

   (B) $789

   (C) $878

   (D) $990

12. A road map is drawn on the scale of 1 inch equals 10 miles. When planning your trip, you notice that you'll have to travel 10 inches (on the map) to the first turn, 7 inches to the second turn, and then 15 inches to your destination. Your car gets 28 miles per gallon, and gas costs $2.73 per gallon. How much gas money will you need for the round-trip?

   (A) $42.86

   (B) $33.27

   (C) $62.41

   (D) $51.23

Go on to next page

13. The smoke-detector in your house has a malfunction and beeps every 5 minutes. If it first beeps at 10 p.m., how many times will it beep by 4 a.m., when you finally give up and take a hammer to it?

(A) 72

(B) 73

(C) 82

(D) 83

14. Little Tommy spends 15 percent of each day reading. How many hours of the day is Tommy not reading?

(A) 6.2

(B) 4.1

(C) 20.4

(D) 19.5

15. Your first sergeant instructs you to requisition some paint from supply and paint a room. The room has a ceiling that is 8 feet high. The length of the room is 10 feet, and the width of the room is 5 feet. The room has no windows, and you are to paint the doors as well. Assuming that one can of paint will cover 145 square feet of space, how many cans of paint will you need to get from supply?

(A) 1

(B) 2

(C) 3

(D) 4

16. You're moving across town and constructing boxes to put your goodies into. You begin with a sheet of cardboard that forms an 8-x-6-foot rectangle, and cut 2-x-2-foot squares out of each corner in order to fold the box (see the diagram).

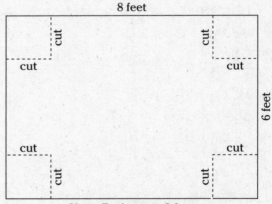

Note: Each cut is 2 feet

When you complete the box, how many cubic feet of knickknacks will it hold?

(A) 8

(B) 10

(C) 16

(D) 18

Go on to next page

17. A display selling bunches of bananas contains six dozen banana bunches when the display is full. The manager of the produce department is supposed to make sure the display is restocked when it is one-quarter full. How many bunches of bananas will be on display when it's time to restock?

    (A) 10

    (B) 18

    (C) 20

    (D) 24

18. A used-car salesperson earns 20 percent commission on the cars that she sells. Fifteen percent is withheld from her weekly paycheck for taxes and other deductions. On Monday, the salesperson sold three cars, totaling $45,000. For the remainder of the week, the salesperson only sold two cars, with a total sales price of $30,000. How much should her weekly paycheck be?

    (A) $12,750

    (B) $13,270

    (C) $13,440

    (D) $14,213

19. A plumber needs four sections of pipe, each 6'3" long to complete a project. Pipe is sold by the foot, for $4.25 per linear foot. How much will the plumber have to pay for the pipe?

    (A) $97.35

    (B) $103.50

    (C) $106.25

    (D) $111.75

20. Rod and Joy own a condo together, which they decide to sell for $200,000. The two decide to split the proceeds according to the ratio of money that each invested in the property. Rod put in the most money, at a ratio of 5:3. How much money should Joy get from the sale?

    (A) $25,000

    (B) $50,000

    (C) $60,000

    (D) $75,000

Go on to next page

21. Referring back to the preceding question, how much money would Rod pocket after repaying the $100,000 he still owes the bank for his share of the condo?

    (A) $15,000
    (B) $25,000
    (C) $30,000
    (D) $35,000

22. On a trip, you drive 350 miles at an average speed of 60 mph. You then return home, driving at an average speed of 70 mph. How long did it take you to complete the trip?

    (A) 8.9 hours
    (B) 9.3 hours
    (C) 10.8 hours
    (D) 11.2 hours

23. The formula used to convert Celsius to degrees Fahrenheit is $F = \frac{9}{5}C + 32$. If the outside temperature is 0 degrees Celsius, what is the temperature in Fahrenheit?

    (A) 0 degrees
    (B) 32 degrees
    (C) –32 degrees
    (D) 14 degrees

24. A store sells Halloween decorations at a 25 percent discount the month of November. If the store is selling a box of decorations for $4.20 in November, what was the original price, before the discount?

    (A) $6.20
    (B) $5.60
    (C) $5.80
    (D) $5.95

Go on to next page

25. A Web site gets 127,750 hits during its first year. How many hits did the Web site average each day?

    (A) 300

    (B) 325

    (C) 350

    (D) 375

26. An empty 50-gallon barrel weighs 35 pounds. When completely filled with water, the barrel weights 455 pounds. Assuming these factors to be true, approximately how much is the weight of 1 gallon of water?

    (A) 5.3 pounds

    (B) 6.5 pounds

    (C) 7.8 pounds

    (D) 8.4 pounds

27. Maloni has 11 more nickels than quarters. How many quarters does she have if the total value of her coins is $2.65?

    (A) 5

    (B) 6

    (C) 7

    (D) 8

28. Dale earns $12.50 per hour. If he works over 40 hours per week, he receives time and a half for any time worked over 40 hours. If Dale worked 8 hours on Monday, 9 hours on Tuesday, 12 hours on Wednesday, 11 hours on Thursday, and 12 hours on Friday, how much did he earn?

    (A) $685

    (B) $725

    (C) $790

    (D) $820

Go on to next page

29. If the average person eats 6.7 pounds of french fries per year, how much would the average person consume in a decade?

    (A) 67 pounds

    (B) 670 pounds

    (C) 6,700 pounds

    (D) 67,000 pounds

30. If you're in a car traveling 50 mph, how far will you travel in 45 minutes?

    (A) 25.8 miles

    (B) 28.3 miles

    (C) 37.5 miles

    (D) 40.4 miles

STOP   DO NOT TURN THE PAGE UNTIL TOLD TO DO SO.
DO NOT RETURN TO A PREVIOUS TEST.

Part 2: Word Knowledge

Time: 11 minutes

35 questions

When you take the ASVAB, you'll encounter the Word Knowledge subtest immediately after the Arithmetic Reasoning subtest. What is "word knowledge"? It's essentially a vocabulary test. You'll be presented with a question with an underlined word — sometimes the word is used in a sentence, and sometimes it isn't. You are to select the choice that best defines the underlined word. If the underlined word is used in a sentence, select the answer as best defines the word, as used in that sentence. Each question is followed by four possible answers. Decide which answer is correct and then mark the corresponding space on your answer sheet.

1. <u>Eclectic</u> most nearly means:

   (A) happy

   (B) varied

   (C) temporary

   (D) permanent

2. The <u>celibacy</u> of priests has often been a controversial topic.

   (A) dedication

   (B) religious views

   (C) abstinence

   (D) persecution

3. I know a stream in which trout <u>abound</u>.

   (A) are numerous

   (B) jump

   (C) swim fast

   (D) are tasty

4. <u>Impromptu</u> most nearly means:

   (A) quick

   (B) timely

   (C) tasty

   (D) unplanned

5. It didn't take the expert long to determine that the painting was a(n) <u>forgery</u>.

   (A) relic

   (B) masterpiece

   (C) fake

   (D) original

6. <u>Lavish</u> most nearly means:

   (A) petty

   (B) ingenious

   (C) generous

   (D) save

7. <u>Genre</u> most nearly means:

   (A) gender

   (B) style

   (C) tender

   (D) close

8. <u>Haughty</u> most nearly means:

   (A) snobbish

   (B) angry

   (C) joyful

   (D) heavy

9. The candidate finally <u>asserted</u> himself about property taxes.

   (A) affirmed

   (B) questioned

   (C) proved

   (D) relinquished

10. The depths of John's <u>depravity</u> were known throughout the community.

    (A) generosity

    (B) ditch

    (C) character

    (D) perverseness

Go on to next page

11. <u>Moratorium</u> most nearly means:

(A) death

(B) participation

(C) suspension

(D) failure

12. <u>Zeal</u> most nearly means:

(A) enthusiasm

(B) zipper

(C) attack

(D) lightning

13. <u>Unkempt</u> most nearly means:

(A) tasty

(B) messy

(C) religious

(D) traitorous

14. <u>Derelict</u> most nearly means:

(A) rebuilt

(B) improved

(C) abandoned

(D) progressive

15. <u>Surmise</u> most nearly means:

(A) guess

(B) fact

(C) rely upon

(D) pay

16. <u>Expedient</u> most nearly means:

(A) disadvantageous

(B) relaxing

(C) fast

(D) appropriate

17. <u>Latent</u> most nearly means:

(A) lasting

(B) invisible

(C) paranormal

(D) adhesive

18. <u>Chronic</u> most nearly means:

(A) powerful

(B) transient

(C) constant

(D) painful

19. The world has not seen a more <u>heinous</u> act than what happened yesterday.

(A) wicked

(B) perplexing

(C) painful

(D) brave

20. John's pants were <u>rent</u> into a thousand pieces

(A) blown up

(B) sewn

(C) torn

(D) painted

21. <u>Divide</u> most nearly means:

(A) pursue

(B) percolate

(C) separate

(D) transfer

22. She has a(n) <u>cohort</u> of admirers.

(A) companion

(B) individual

(C) group

(D) associate

23. The <u>sloth</u> in her disposition was inevitably strong.

(A) enthusiasm

(B) deception

(C) evilness

(D) laziness

24. <u>Embroil</u> most nearly means:

(A) conflict

(B) confuse

(C) genitive

(D) Both (A) and (B)

Go on to next page

25. Jane has always had <u>impeccable</u> manners.

    (A) precise

    (B) friendly

    (C) flawless

    (D) terrible

26. Linda and Dale have always had a(n) <u>static</u> relationship.

    (A) stable

    (B) unchanging

    (C) volatile

    (D) Both (A) and (B)

27. <u>Ingratiate</u> most nearly means:

    (A) good graces

    (B) enthusiasm

    (C) trademark

    (D) Both (A) and (B)

28. He <u>construed</u> her intentions from her gestures.

    (A) interpreted

    (B) guessed

    (C) predicted

    (D) ignored

29. Attacking Iraq set a(n) <u>precedent</u> in American history.

    (A) event

    (B) belief

    (C) tradition

    (D) pastime

30. <u>Affinity</u> most nearly means:

    (A) aversion

    (B) attraction

    (C) stars

    (D) forever

31. The <u>serene</u> background embraced everyone in the group.

    (A) peaceful

    (B) august

    (C) traditional

    (D) loving

32. Tom's dog was actually a(n) <u>hindrance</u> during the hunting trip.

    (A) help

    (B) tradition

    (C) favorite

    (D) obstruction

33. The chandelier began to <u>oscillate</u> for no known reason.

    (A) brighten

    (B) move

    (C) turn on and off

    (D) walk

34. <u>Echelon</u> most nearly means:

    (A) place

    (B) time

    (C) level

    (D) None of the above

35. <u>Emulate</u> most nearly means:

    (A) copy

    (B) protest

    (C) taste

    (D) regret

STOP DO NOT TURN THE PAGE UNTIL TOLD TO DO SO. DO NOT RETURN TO A PREVIOUS TEST.

Part 3: Paragraph Comprehension

Time: 13 minutes

15 questions

You'll encounter the Paragraph Comprehension subtest immediately following the Word Knowledge subtest. This section consists of questions that measure your ability to garner information from a reading passage. Each question is followed by four possible answer choices. Read the paragraph and select the choice that best completes the statement or answers the question. Mark the corresponding choice on your answer sheet.

Patrick claimed to be late because of heavy traffic on the freeway. Even though I have my doubts, his explanation is plausible. I got stuck on the same road just last week. I guess I'll just have to take his word for it.

1. If a statement is plausible,

   (A) you must always believe it

   (B) you should never believe it

   (C) it's hard to understand because it makes no sense

   (D) it's believable enough to possibly be true

The Air Force Aid Society (AFAS) is the official charity of the U.S. Air Force. It promotes the Air Force mission by helping "to relieve distress of Air Force members and their families and assisting them to finance their education." It is rooted in the original Army Air Corps and the World War II Army Air Forces, whose members wanted to "take care of their own." Through the years, AFAS has become increasingly effective in helping individuals with personal emergencies — as well as extremely useful when used by commanders to help solve personnel problems in their units.

2. AFAS is an acronym for:

   (A) Armed Forces Area Assistance

   (B) Armed Forces Achievement System

   (C) Air Force Aid Society

   (D) Air Force Assistance System

3. Which of the following is *not* a goal of the AFAS?

   (A) to assist with urgent personal problems

   (B) to provide affordable home loans

   (C) to provide a means for members to help other members

   (D) to provide educational assistance

4. The AFAS can trace its roots to:

   (A) colonial times

   (B) the Army

   (C) President Roosevelt

   (D) President Reagan

The United States of America is located on the continent of North America. There are 50 states in the U.S., 48 of which form the contiguous United States. The U.S. borders Canada to the north, and Mexico and the Gulf of Mexico to the south. On the east coast, the U.S. is bordered by the Atlantic Ocean, and on the west coast it is bordered by the Pacific Ocean.

5. How many countries share a border with the United States?

   (A) one

   (B) two

   (C) three

   (D) four

6. How many states belonging to the U.S. are not part of the continental United States?

   (A) two

   (B) three

   (C) four

   (D) five

Go on to next page

Living in the United States does not automatically make one an American citizen. Residents of the United States can be aliens, nationals, or citizens. Aliens are people who have emigrated from a foreign country. They have some of the same freedoms and legal rights as U.S. citizens, but they cannot vote in elections. American nationals are natives of American territorial possessions. They have all the legal protections that citizens have, but they do not have the full political rights of U.S. citizens. Persons born in the U.S. or born to U.S. citizens in foreign countries are automatically citizens of the United States. Persons born in other countries who want to become citizens must apply for and pass a citizenship test. Those who become citizens in this manner are naturalized citizens.

7. According to the passage:

    (A) America has the most freedoms of any country in the world.

    (B) Aliens, nationals, and citizens all share the same freedom and political rights.

    (C) American nationals do not share the same political rights as citizens.

    (D) It is very hard to become a citizen of the United States.

War's political nature, physical stress, and agony of combat will outlive any desire to make it bloodless and free of violence, despite a revolution in military affairs caused by technology. The means may change, but the fundamental nature and risks of war will remain.

8. The main point of the passage could be stated as:

    (A) War is hell.

    (B) War will never go away.

    (C) Technology makes war easier.

    (D) None of the above.

Leaders prepare for challenges through their career-long study and application of the art of leadership. Successful leaders generally exhibit common character traits and embrace tried-and-true leadership principles. You should strive to develop and hone your skills, build on expertise in your career specialty, learn from others' experiences, and observe your environment. Throughout your career you should read, observe others' actions, solicit advice, and become attuned to the myriad of social, economic, and political factors that shape your occupation and the world.

9. According to the passage:

    (A) All leaders are different.

    (B) Leadership takes hard work and study.

    (C) Leaders are natural born.

    (D) Timing is of the utmost importance in applying leadership principles.

"When I was 12 years old, Dad sold out his hardware business, intending to put his money in an orange grove at Riverside, but the nicest livery-stable in San Bernardino happened to be for sale just then, so he bought that instead, for he was always crazy about horses."
—Edward Salisbury Field

10. The author's father decided to buy a horse stable because:

    (A) A nice one was available.

    (B) He really liked horses.

    (C) He had just sold his hardware business.

    (D) Both (A) and (B)

Go on to next page

"Standing before the press, which faced the windows, Dr. Pascal was looking for a paper that he had come in search of. With doors wide open, this immense press of carved oak, adorned with strong and handsome mountings of metal, dating from the last century, displayed within its capacious depths an extraordinary collection of papers and manuscripts of all sorts, piled up in confusion and filling every shelf to overflowing. For more than 30 years the doctor had thrown into it every page he wrote, from brief notes to the complete texts of his great works on heredity. Thus, it was that his searches here were not always easy. He rummaged patiently among the papers, and when he at last found the one he was looking for, he smiled."

—Emile Zola

11. Dr. Pascal could best be described as:

   (A) efficient

   (B) unorganized

   (C) carefree

   (D) old

12. According to the passage, Dr. Pascal's approach to the search was:

   (A) hurried

   (B) relaxed

   (C) organized

   (D) enthusiastic

Internships: self-directed learning, a part-time job or an invaluable first step toward a public service career? Internships today go well beyond résumé building. They are about experience building, networking, and learning. Interested in a career in foreign policy? Intern at the State Department and develop research skills and firsthand knowledge. Interested in children's policy? An internship with the Children's Defense Fund will help establish a network of contacts for the future. A truly educational internship offers hands-on experience in the work of a particular profession. You not only perform invaluable support to an agency or organization, but you are learning skills to apply to your future career and your course work.

13. The main subjects(s) of the above paragraph is/are:

   (A) working with the State Department

   (B) working with the Children's Defense Fund

   (C) the advantages of an internship

   (D) Both (A) and (B)

Personal time management is about controlling the use of the most valuable (and undervalued) resource — time. The absence of time management is characterized by last-minute rushes to meet deadlines, meetings that either are double booked or achieve nothing, days that seem somehow to slip unproductively by, and crises that loom unexpectedly from nowhere. This sort of environment leads to inordinate stress and performance degradation. Because personal time management is a management process, it must be planned, monitored, and regularly reviewed.

14. Lack of proper time management can lead to:

   (A) stress

   (B) rushing through projects

   (C) unproductive meetings

   (D) All of the above

15. According to the passage, time management:

   (A) should happen naturally

   (B) should be discussed at all levels of supervision

   (C) is the most important leadership practice of them all

   (D) should be worked out in advance

STOP DO NOT TURN THE PAGE UNTIL TOLD TO DO SO. DO NOT RETURN TO A PREVIOUS TEST.

Part 4: Mathematics Knowledge

Time: 24 minutes

25 questions

The Arithmetic Reasoning subtest measured your ability to solve math word-type problems. The Mathematics Knowledge subtest, on the other hand, tests your knowledge of general mathematics. Again, you aren't allowed to use a calculator, but never fear: These questions can be answered with pencil and paper. You have to work fast, however, because you have a little less than one minute per question — 0.96 minutes per question, to be exact: (Do you like the way I worked math into that?)

1. Which of the following fractions is the largest?

   (A) $\frac{13}{20}$

   (B) $\frac{3}{5}$

   (C) $\frac{13}{16}$

   (D) $\frac{3}{4}$

3. Convert 62 percent into a fraction.

   (A) $\frac{2}{3}$

   (B) $\frac{3}{4}$

   (C) $\frac{7}{10}$

   (D) $\frac{31}{50}$

2. $150 + 173 =$

   (A) 25,950

   (B) 1,721

   (C) 589

   (D) 323

4. The sum of the measures of the angles in the shape below is:

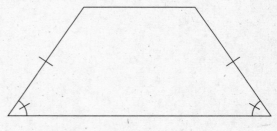

   (A) 180

   (B) 360

   (C) 45

   (D) 90

Go on to next page

5. What is the area of the shape below?

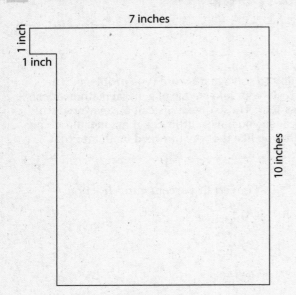

7 inches

1 inch

1 inch

10 inches

(A) 62 square inches

(B) 71 square inches

(C) 102 square inches

(D) 19 square inches

6. $\sqrt{x^2} =$
   (A) x or $-x$
   (B) $2x$
   (C) $x + 2$
   (D) $2x + 2$

7. Convert $\frac{11}{4}$ into a mixed number
   (A) $1\frac{1}{2}$
   (B) 2.75
   (C) $2\frac{3}{4}$
   (D) $3\frac{1}{4}$

8. Convert 317,400,000,000 to scientific notation:
   (A) $3,174^{-11}$
   (B) $3,174^{11}$
   (C) 3.174×10^{11}
   (D) 3.174×10^{-11}

Go on to next page

9. What point is plotted on the chart below?

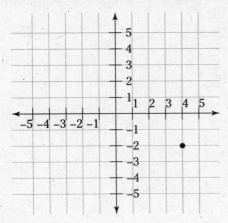

(A) (4, 4)

(B) (−2, 4)

(C) (−2, −2)

(D) (4, −2)

10. Add all the numbers between 1 and 300.

(A) 4,150

(B) 45,150

(C) 7,320

(D) 73,320

11. What is the next number in the following sequence? 1, 8, 27, 64, 125

(A) 250

(B) 216

(C) 175

(D) 185

12. The average of 53, 27, 32, and 41 is:

(A) 38.25

(B) 30.5

(C) 27.3

(D) 61.7

Go on to next page

13. 8 yards + 15 feet =
    (A) 11 yards
    (B) 9 yards
    (C) 24 feet
    (D) 39 feet

14. Find the arithmetic mean of 4 and 9.
    (A) 5.3
    (B) 6.5
    (C) 7.0
    (D) 8.1

15. $y^5 \times y^3 =$
    (A) y^{15}
    (B) y^8
    (C) y^2
    (D) y

16. Find the arithmetic mean of 5 and 25
    (A) 10.3
    (B) 11.2
    (C) 13.4
    (D) 15.0

Go on to next page

17. The shape below is a

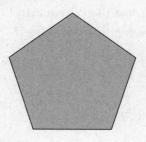

(A) pentagon

(B) polygon

(C) trapezoid

(D) Both (A) and (B)

19. $(4x - 2x^2 - 7xy) + (2x^2 + 5xy) =$

(A) $2x + 4y$

(B) $4xy$

(C) $4x - 2xy$

(D) $4x^2 + 2y^2$

18. $4\frac{1}{2} + 1\frac{2}{5} + 3\frac{3}{10} =$

(A) $9\frac{1}{3}$

(B) $8\frac{1}{2}$

(C) $6\frac{1}{2}$

(D) $9\frac{1}{5}$

20. Solve for x: $(x + 3)^3 + 2(x + 3)^2 - 8(x + 3)^2 = 0$

(A) 2

(B) 4

(C) −7

(D) ±3

Go on to next page ⇨

21. Simplify: $a^2x - bx - a^2y + by + a^2z - bz$

    (A) $a + b + c$

    (B) $a^2 + b - y$

    (C) $(a^2 - b)(x - y + z)$

    (D) The problem can't be reduced further.

22. What is the length of the sides of a square that has an area of 225 square inches?

    (A) 12 inches

    (B) 13 inches

    (C) 14 inches

    (D) 15 inches

23. Translate the following: $N \le 15$

    (A) N is less than or equal to 15.

    (B) N is greater or equal to 15.

    (C) N is less than 15.

    (D) N is greater than 15.

24. 5.12×10^{-5} can also be expressed as

    (A) 512,000,000

    (B) 0.0000512

    (C) 512

    (D) 512,000

Go on to next page

25. 93 percent of 75 is:
    (A) 61.2
    (B) 69.75
    (C) 58.9
    (D) 57.3

STOP DO NOT TURN THE PAGE UNTIL TOLD TO DO SO.
DO NOT RETURN TO A PREVIOUS TEST.

Chapter 15

Practice Exam 2: Answers and Explanations

• •

Two AFQT practice tests down, and two to go! I hope you're starting to get a handle on the test structure and the question types. Ready to find out how you're doing? The answers and explanations in the following sections help you determine how well you performed on the practice test in Chapter 14 — and give you some hints about where you may have dropped a decimal point or two. Don't worry, it happens to the best of us.

Don't focus too much on scores. On the actual AFQT, harder questions are worth more points than easier questions. The AFQT is one of those rare tests on which you can miss some questions and still max out your test score. As always, use the results to decide where you want to concentrate your study time. Do you need more work on math or reading/verbal skills? This chapter helps you find out.

Part 1: Arithmetic Reasoning

The Arithmetic Reasoning subtest is not only one of the important subtests that make up the AFQT, but it's also used as a qualification factor for many of the military jobs you can choose from. You may want to glance at *ASVAB For Dummies* by yours truly (published by Wiley) to see which military jobs require you to do well on this subtest. If you missed more than five or six questions, it's time to dig out that old high school math textbook and wrap your brain around some math problems. Chapters 8 and 10 may also help you out. Some other great books that may help you score better on this subtest include *Math Word Problems For Dummies, Algebra I For Dummies,* and *Algebra II For Dummies,* all by Mary Jane Sterling; *Geometry For Dummies,* 2nd Edition, and *Calculus For Dummies,* both by Mark Ryan; and *SAT II Math For Dummies,* by Scott Hatch, JD, and Lisa Zimmer Hatch, MA — all published by Wiley.

1. **(C)** Let x = the number of yellow marbles. That means red marbles = $2x$, green marbles = $3x$, and purple marbles = $2(2x)$, or $4x$. There are 100 marbles in the jar, so:

   $$x + 2x + 3x + 4x = 100$$
   $$10x = 100$$
   $$x = \frac{100}{10}$$
   $$x = 10$$

2. **(A)** Don't let the number of miles traveled confuse you — you don't use them to solve the problem. Two-fifths of a 40-hour workweek is $\frac{2}{5} \times \frac{40}{1} = \frac{80}{5} = 16$ hours per week spent traveling.

3. **(D)** The distance formula is $d = rt$.

   (1) Car headed west: $d = 55 \times 2.5 = 137.5$

   (2) Car headed east: $d = 70 \times 2.5 = 175$

The cars were $137.5 + 175 = 312.5$ miles apart. Of course, this assumes absolutely straight roads, and no slowdowns or stops along the way, but math word problems often ask you to make such basic assumptions.

4. **(A)** Using the same distance formula you used in the preceding question, you know that one car traveled 137.5 miles and the other 175 miles. Because they were headed in the same direction, subtract the distance traveled by the slower car from the distance traveled by the faster car. The cars were $175 - 137.5 = 37.5$ miles apart.

5. **(C)** The problem forms the parts of a right triangle, each car representing one leg of the triangle (see the following figure).

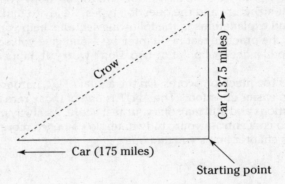

It's time to bring out your old friend, Pythagoras. I think he's in the other room, drinking your coffee. Go ahead and get him — I'll wait.

The Pythagorean theorem states that if you know the length of two sides of a right triangle, you can figure out the length of the third side with the formula $a^2 + b^2 = c^2$. Plug in the known variables:

$$137.5^2 + 175^2 = c^2$$
$$18{,}906.25 + 30{,}625 = c^2$$
$$49{,}513.25 = c^2$$
$$\sqrt{49{,}513.25} = c$$
$$c = 222.5157$$

Go ahead and round this number down to 222.5.

6. **(D)** Add the three monthly amounts to determine the total amount Dana spent on gas: $\$120.37 + \$108.45 + \$114.86 = \$343.68$. Divide the total by 3 to determine the average monthly cost: $\frac{\$343.68}{3} = \$114.56$.

7. **(C)** To determine the amount of interest earned, multiply the principal, $3,000, by the interest rate, 6 percent (or 0.06), and the number of years interest accrues, 1 year: $\$3{,}000 \times 0.06 \times 1 = \$180$. Add the interest earned to the principal to find out how much total money the teacher would have: $\$180 + \$3{,}000 = \$3{,}180$.

8. **(B)** To find the volume of a box, the formula is $v = lwd$, where l = length, w = width, and d = depth. Plug in the known values:

   $v = 6 \times 4 \times 3$

   $v = 72$ cubic feet

The length of the legs doesn't matter.

9. **(B)** 1.3 inches fell on December 1. On December 5, 0.5 inch less rain fell, or $1.3 - 0.5 = 0.8$ inch. On December 15, 3 more inches of rain fell.

   Add the total inches of rain for all three days: $1.3 + 0.8 + 3 = 5.1$ inches of rain.

10. **(D)** Determine the total area of the patio. The area formula is $a = lw$. Plug in the known variables:

    $a = 9 \times 20 = 180$ square feet

    You can now determine the total cost by multiplying the area of the patio, 180 square feet, by the cost per square foot, $5.50 per square foot:

    $180 \times \$5.50 = \$990$

11. **(D)** The total of the purchase is $5 ($0.90 + $1.20 + $2.90 = $5). You know that 3.5 percent of that amount is $5 \times 0.035 = \$0.175$. You have to round this up to 18¢ because it's very hard to give half a cent in change. The total bill comes to $5 + $0.18 = $5.18. Denise should receive in change $10 − $5.18 = $4.82.

12. **(C)** Determine the distance of the trip: 10 inches + 7 inches + 15 inches = 32 inches. On the map, 1 inch = 10 miles, so 32 inches = $32 \times 10 = 320$ miles. This is a round trip, so remember to double that amount: 640 miles.

    Your car travels 28 miles on a gallon of gas, so you'll need $\frac{460}{28} = 22.86$ gallons of gas to complete the trip.

    Gas costs $2.73 per gallon, so you'll need to purchase $\$2.73 \times 22.86 = \$62.41$ worth of gas for the trip.

13. **(B)** The time period between 10 p.m. and 4 a.m. is six hours, which you can convert to 360 minutes ($60 \times 6 = 360$). The smoke detector beeped every five minutes, so you divide the total number of minutes by the time-period that the smoke detector beeped: $\frac{360}{5} = 72$. Now add 1, because it beeped at the beginning of the period: 72 + 1 = 73.

    I'm not actually recommending you beat your smoke detector with a hammer. That would be irresponsible.

14. **(C)** Little Tommy reads for 15 percent of the time, which means he is not reading for 100 percent − 15 percent = 85 percent of the day. And 85 percent of a 24-hour day is $24 \times 0.85 = 20.4$ hours.

15. **(B)** Two of the walls in this room are 8 feet by 10 feet. The other two walls in this room are 8 feet by 5 feet. The ceiling is 10 feet by 5 feet. You are not painting the floor. The area formula for a rectangle is $a = lw$. Plug in the known values:

    (1) 8-x-10-foot wall: $a = 8 \times 10 = 80$. There are two such walls, so double the area: 160 square feet.

    (2) 8-x-5-foot wall: $a = 8 \times 5 = 40$. Again, there are two of these walls, so double the area: 80 square feet

    (3) 10-x-5-foot ceiling: $a = 5 \times 10 = 50$.

    Total the areas to be painted: 160 + 80 + 50 = 290 square feet. Because each can of paint will cover 145 square feet, you'll need $\frac{290}{145} = 2$ cans of paint for the project.

16. **(C)** Mentally construct the box. Once completed, the box will be 4 feet long ($8 - 4 = 4$), by 2 feet wide ($6 - 4 = 2$), by 2 feet deep (the length of the cuts). The volume formula for a rectangle is $v = lwd$. Plug in the known values:

    $v = 4 \times 2 \times 2$

    $v = 16$ cubic feet

17. **(B)** There are 12 bunches of bananas in a stack, which means there are 72 bunches of bananas in 6 dozen ($6 \times 12 = 72$). One-quarter of 72 is $\frac{1}{4} \times \frac{72}{1} = \frac{72}{4} = 18$.

18. **(A)** The salesperson sold $45,000 + $30,000 = $75,000 worth of cars during the week. She earned a 20 percent commission, or $75,000 \times 0.20 = $15,000.

    Fifteen percent of her commission, or $15,000 \times 0.15 = $2,250 is withheld for deductions. The salesperson's paycheck should be $15,000 − $2,250 = $12,750.

    Hmm. . . . Maybe I should become a used-car salesman. Anybody want to buy a nice Chevy?

19. **(C)** Each section of pipe is (6 feet $\times$ 12 inches) + 3 inches = 72 + 3 = 75 inches long. The plumber needs four sections, so he needs 300 inches of pipe. The plumber will have to purchase $\frac{300}{12} = 25$ feet of pipe.

    The plumber needs 25 feet of pipe, and pipe is sold for $4.25 per foot. This means the plumber must pay $25 \times $42.25 = $106.25 for the pipe he needs.

20. **(D)** First, convert the ratio to a set of fractions. The ratio 5:3 can be converted to a fraction by adding the two sides of the ratio together to determine the denominator, while retaining the first side of the ratio as the numerator of the fraction: 5 + 3 = 8, so Rod contributed $\frac{5}{8}$ of the money, meaning Joy contributed $\frac{8}{8} - \frac{5}{8} = \frac{3}{8}$.

    Three-eighths of $200,000 is $\frac{3}{8} \times \frac{\$200,000}{1} = \frac{\$600,000}{8} = \$75,000$.

21. **(B)** From solving the preceding problem, you know that Joy's share of the sale is $75,000. That means Rod's share is $200,000 − $75,000 = $125,000. Because Rod still owes $100,000 to the bank, he only gets to keep $125,000 − $100,000 = $25,000.

22. **(C)** Use the distance formula, $d = rt$, which can be restated as $t = \frac{d}{r}$. Substitute the known values:

    Original trip: $t = \frac{350}{60} = 5.83$ hours

    Return trip: $t = \frac{350}{70} = 5$ hours

    Add the time required for the original trip and the return trip and the sum is 5 + 5.83 = 10.83 hours.

    The time for the complete trip is 10.83 hours, which can be rounded down to 10.8 hours.

23. **(B)** This is an example of a problem where the answer should be obvious after just a quick glance. Since $C = 0$, you know that $F = 32$.

24. **(B)** Let x = the full price. You know that $4.20 has been discounted 25 percent from the full price. Therefore,

    $\$4.20 = 0.75x$

    $x = \frac{\$4.20}{0.75} = \$5.60$

25. **(C)** There are 365 days per year (you have to assume this isn't a leap year). To find the average number of daily hits, divide the total number of hits for the year, by the total number of days in a year: $\frac{127,750}{365} = 350$.

26. **(D)** The weight of the water is the weight of the full barrel minus the weight of the empty barrel: 455 − 35 = 420. Divide the weight of the water, 420, by the number of gallons, 50: $\frac{420}{50} = 8.4$.

27. **(C)** Let q = the number of quarters. That means the number of nickels = $q + 11$.

    Each quarter is worth 25 percent of a dollar, each dime is worth 5 percent of a dollar, and the total amount of change is \$2.65. You now have enough information to set up the equation:

    $$0.25q + 0.05(q + 11) = 2.65$$
    $$0.3q + 0.55 = 2.65$$
    $$q = \frac{2.10}{3}$$
    $$q = 7$$

28. **(B)** Dale worked a total of 52 hours during the week ($8 + 9 + 12 + 11 + 12 = 52$). Forty of those hours were for regular pay and $52 - 40 = 12$ hours were for overtime pay.

    Dale earns \$12.50 per hour for regular pay and $\$12.50 \times 1.5 = \$18.75$ for overtime pay.

    Dale earned $40 \times \$12.50 = \$500$ for his regular hours and $18.75 \times 12 = \$225$ in overtime pay. Dale earned $\$500 + \$225 = \$725$ total during the week.

29. **(A)** You know that a decade is ten years. So, multiply the number of years by the total french fries eaten in a year: $6.7 \times 10 = 67$.

30. **(C)** The rate formula is $d = rt$, so you can use this formula to solve the problem. However, in the problem, the rate is expressed in miles per hour and the distance is expressed in minutes. In math, as in other areas of life, you can't compare applies to oranges. Either you have to convert the miles per hour to miles per minute or you have to convert the minutes to a fraction of the hour.

    $$45 \text{ minutes} = \frac{45}{60} = 0.75 \text{ hours}$$

    You can now use the rate formula. Plug in the known variables:

    $$d = 0.75 \times 50$$
    $$d = 37.5$$

Part 2: Word Knowledge

The Word Knowledge subtest is nothing more than a vocabulary test. However, it can be hard for some people. The good news is that vocabulary isn't an innate talent. It's something that everyone can improve. If you find you need to improve your vocabulary, see Chapter 4. A couple of other great study references are *Vocabulary For Dummies* by Laurie E. Rozakis (Wiley) and *SAT Vocabulary For Dummies* by Suzee Vlk (Wiley). Additionally, see Chapter 5 for more practice questions.

1. **(B)** *Eclectic* is an adjective that means to select from various sources.

2. **(C)** Used as a noun, *celibacy* means abstention from sex.

3. **(A)** Used as a verb, *abound* means to exist in great numbers.

4. **(D)** *Impromptu* is an adjective that means done without preparation.

5. **(C)** *Forgery* is a noun that means not genuine.

6. **(C)** *Lavish* is an adjective that means bestowed upon in great quantities.

7. **(B)** Used as a noun, *genre* means a particular category or style in any artistic endeavor.

8. **(A)** *Haughty* is an adjective that means arrogant.

9. **(A)** *Assert* is a verb that means to state or express positively.

10. **(D)** Used as a noun, *depravity* means extremely bad character.

11. **(C)** *Moratorium* is a noun that means a temporary stop.

12. **(A)** *Zeal* is a noun that means eager desire.

13. **(B)** Used as an adjective, *unkempt* means uncared for or neglected.

14. **(C)** *Derelict* is an adjective that means left or deserted.

15. **(A)** Used as verb, *surmise* means to conjecture or guess.

16. **(B)** *Expedient* can be used as an adjective or a noun and means an appropriate means to an end.

17. **(B)** *Latent* is used as an adjective and means present but not visible.

18. **(C)** Used as an adjective, *chronic* means persistent or continuing.

19. **(A)** *Heinous* is an adjective that means evil.

20. **(C)** *Rent* is the past tense of the verb *rend,* which means to split or tear.

21. **(C)** Used as a verb, *divide* means to separate into parts or groups.

22. **(C)** *Cohort* is a noun that means group or company. It can also mean a companion or associate, but that wouldn't make sense in the context of the sentence.

23. **(D)** *Sloth* is a noun meaning habitual laziness.

24. **(D)** Embroil is a verb. It can mean either to bring into discord or conflict or to incite confusion.

25. **(C)** *Impeccable* is an adjective that means perfect.

26. **(D)** Used as an adjective *static* means showing little or no change, which is the definition of both stable and unchanging.

27. **(A)** *Ingratiate* is a verb that means to bring into favor or good graces of another.

28. **(A)** *Construed* is a verb that means to analyze or interpret based on observation. Although B, guessed, is close, it's not the best answer in this context.

29. **(C)** *Precedent* is a noun, usually used in common law, that means an act or condition that serves as a guide for future events.

30. **(B)** *Affinity* is a noun that means a natural liking or attraction — not to be confused with *infinity,* which means forever.

31. **(A)** *Serene* is an adjective that means peaceful or calm.

32. **(D)** *Hindrance* is a noun that means an impediment or obstruction.

33. **(B)** Used as a verb, *oscillate* means to swing back and forth or vibrate.

34. **(C)** *Echelon* is a noun that means level of command, such as the top echelon of the military.

35. **(A)** *Emulate* is a verb that means to imitate or copy.

Part 3: Paragraph Comprehension

The Paragraph Comprehension subtest can be a bit tricky, but you need to get a good score on this subtest if you want to ace the AFQT. So pay special attention if you've missed more than a couple of these answers — you need some study time (see Chapter 6). Remember that rereading the paragraph several times to make sure that you have the right answer is perfectly fine. The best method of improving your reading comprehension skills is simply to read more. You can find additional practice questions in Chapter 7.

1. **(D)** The passage makes it obvious that the author believes Patrick's excuse is believable, even though he still has doubts.

2. **(C)** This is explained in the very first sentence of the paragraph.

3. **(B)** The AFAS does not provide home loans, nor does anything in the paragraph indicate that it does.

4. **(B)** The third sentence of the passage states that the mission of the AFAS can be traced back to the original Army Air Corps and World War II Army Air Forces.

5. **(B)** The passage says that the U.S. shares a border with Canada to the north and Mexico to the south.

6. **(A)** The passage says there are 50 states in all, and 48 of them form the contiguous United States. Therefore, two states are separate. (The two states are Alaska and Hawaii, in case you didn't know.)

7. **(C)** This is presented in the sixth sentence of the paragraph. Although American nationals have the same legal protections that citizens have, they don't have the same full political rights.

8. **(A)** The author is saying that even if we want war to be bloodless and free of violence, the dangers and risks of war will stay the same.

9. **(B)** The main point of the paragraph is that you must work, study, observe, read, and prepare in order to become successful as a leader.

10. **(D)** The author gives two reasons for his dad's purchasing a stable: the nicest one in town was for sale, and he was always crazy about horses. The fact that he had just sold his business isn't a factor, because he had already intended to invest in an orange grove at the time he sold the business.

11. **(B)** The good doctor piled every word he had ever written into large confusing piles. (I think maybe I'm related to him.)

12. **(B)** The last sentence of the paragraph states that he "patiently rummaged" through the papers.

13. **(C)** The main subject of the paragraph is the value of internships. The State Department and the Children's Defense Fund are sub-points designed to support the main subject.

14. **(D)** The paragraph lists all these consequences of the absence of time management.

15. **(D)** The last sentence states that time management must be planned.

Part 4: Mathematics Knowledge

Some folks find math to be a breeze and can't understand why the rest of us approach math problems with all the enthusiasm of a trip to the dentist. However, the military considers math skills to be important, and they're right. If you miss more than four or five questions, you should consider brushing up on your basic math skills — Chapter 8 can help with this. As with the Arithmetic Reasoning subtest, the following *For Dummies* books may also be of some help: *Algebra I For Dummies* and *Algebra II For Dummies,* both by Mary Jane Sterling; *Geometry For Dummies,* 2nd Edition, and *Calculus For Dummies,* both by Mark Ryan; and *SAT II Math For Dummies,* by Scott Hatch, JD, and Lisa Zimmer Hatch, MA (all published by Wiley). Chapter 9 also has some additional practice questions.

1. **(C)** To compare fractions with different denominators, take the cross-product. The first cross-product is the product of the first numerator and the second denominator. The second cross-product is the product of the second numerator and the first denominator. If the cross-products are equal, the fractions are equivalent. If the first cross-product is larger, the first fraction is larger. If the second cross-product is larger, the second fraction is larger.

Compare the first two fractions, $\frac{13}{20}$ and $\frac{3}{5}$: $13 \times 5 = 65$: $13 \times 5 = 65$ and $20 \times 3 = 60$. The second fraction, $\frac{3}{5}$, is larger.

Compare the larger fraction, $\frac{3}{5}$, to the next fraction, $\frac{13}{16}$: $3 \times 16 = 48$ and $5 \times 13 = 65$: $3 \times 16 = 48$ and $5 \times 13 = 65$. $\frac{13}{16}$ is the larger fraction.

Compare this fraction, $\frac{13}{16}$, with D, $\frac{3}{4}$: $13 \times 4 = 52$ and $16 \times 3 = 48$: $13 \times 4 = 52$ and $16 \times 3 = 48$. $\frac{13}{16}$ is the largest fraction.

2. **(D)** Surprised to see such an easy question? On the Mathematics Knowledge subtest of the ASVAB, you'll see a few very simple questions. Don't get suspicious and think it might be a trap! Sometimes obvious really is obvious.

3. **(D)** 62 percent $= \frac{62}{100} = \frac{31}{50}$

4. **(B)** The figure shown is a trapezoid, which is a quadrilateral — it has four sides. All quadrilaterals have angles that total 360 degrees.

5. **(B)** The shape is actually a square, measuring 1 inch by 1 inch, and a rectangle measuring 7 inches by 10 inches (see the following figure).

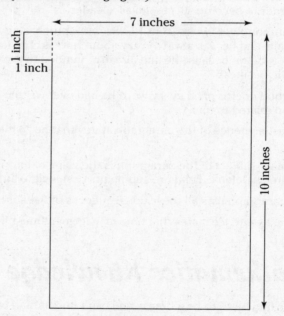

The formula used to find the area of a square or rectangle is $a = lw$. Substitute the known values:

Square: $a = 1 \times 1 = 1$

Rectangle: $a = 7 \times 10 = 70$

Add the area of the square and the area of the rectangle: $70 + 1 = 71$.

6. **(A)** No tricks. The square root of a number squared is the number itself.

Sometimes the obvious answer is the right answer.

7. **(C)** To change an improper fraction into a mixed number, divide the numerator by the denominator. The remainder is the numerator of the fractional part: $11 \div 4 = 2$ with a remainder of 3. Therefore, $\frac{11}{4} = 2\frac{3}{4}$

8. **(C)** Move the decimal point, so that there is only one digit to the left. Count as you move (11 places). Because you moved the decimal point to the left, the powers of 10 are positive.

9. **(D)** The x and y lines intersect at the points of 4 and –2. When plotting, always give the x (horizontal) coordinate first.

10. **(B)** If you have an arithmetic sequence of N numbers and you know the first and last one, you can find the sum by: $s = \frac{N(f+l)}{2}$, where N = the total number of numbers (in this case, 300), f = the first number in the sequence (in this case, 1), and l = the last number in the sequence (here, 300). Plug in the known variables:

$$s = \frac{N\left(\text{First} + \text{Last}\right)}{2}$$

$$s = \frac{300\left(1 + 300\right)}{2}$$

$$s = \frac{300 \times 301}{2}$$

$$s = \frac{90,300}{2}$$

$$s = 45,150$$

11. **(B)** The easiest way to determine number sequences is to factor the numbers and look for relationships among the factors:

$1 = $ no factors

$8 = 2 \times 2 \times 2$

$27 = 3 \times 3 \times 3$

$64 = 2 \times 2 \times 2 \times 2 \times 2 \times 2$ or $4 \times 4 \times 4$

$125 = 5 \times 5 \times 5$

See the pattern? It's $1^3, 2^3, 3^3, 4^3, 5^3$.

The next number in the sequence would obviously be 6^3, or $6 \times 6 \times 6 = 216$.

12. **(A)** Add the numbers and then divide by the number of terms: $53 + 27 + 32 + 41 = 153$ and $\frac{153}{4} = 38.25$.

13. **(D)** Convert the yards to feet by multiplying by 3: $8 \times 3 = 24$. Now simply add the feet together: $24 + 15 = 39$ feet. You can convert the feet to yards, by dividing by 3: $\frac{39}{3} = 13$ yards (but that's not one of the answer choices given).

14. **(B)** The *arithmetic mean* of a series of numbers is the same as the *average* of a series of numbers. To find the average, add the numbers, then divide by the number of terms: $4 + 9 = 13$. Divided by 2, the answer is 6.5.

15. **(B)** If two numbers have the same base, they can be multiplied by keeping the base and adding the powers together.

16. **(D)** *Arithmetic mean* simply means the *average*. So, $15 + 5 = 30$. Divide the sum by 2 and the result is 15.

17. **(D)** A polygon is a closed figure made by joining line segments, where each line segment intersects exactly two others. A pentagon is a five-sided polygon.

18. **(D)** Convert to the lowest common denominator (which is 10), then add:

$$4\frac{1}{2}+1\frac{2}{5}+3\frac{3}{10}=4\frac{5}{10}+1\frac{4}{10}+3\frac{3}{10}=8\frac{12}{10}=9\frac{2}{10}=9\frac{1}{5}$$

19. **(C)** Combine the like terms, then simplify:

$$(4x-2x^2-7xy)+(2x^2+5xy)=$$
$$-2x^2+2x^2-7xy+5xy+4x=$$
$$-2xy+4x=$$

$4x-2xy$

20. **(D)** This problem can be rather confusing if you try directly to solve for x. Instead, think of the term $(x+3)$ as its own entity. In fact, let $y=(x+3)$, and substitute it for $(x+3)$ in the equation:

$$(x+3)^3+2(x+3)^2-8(x+3)^2=0$$
$$y^3+2y^2-8y^2=0$$
$$y^3-6y^2=0$$
$$y^2(y-6)=0$$

At this point, it should be obvious that $y=0$. Since $y=0$, and y also equals $(x+3)$, you could say that $x+3=0$. Therefore, $x=-3$. But $y=6$, too. Replacing the y with 6 in $y=x+3$, you get that $6=x+3$ or $x=3$. So $x=\pm 3$.

21. **(C)** Combine like terms and simplify:

$$a^2x-bx-a^2y+by+a^2z-bz=$$
$$a^2x-a^2y+a^2z-bz+by-bz=$$
$$a^2(x-y+z)-b(x-y+z)=$$
$$(a^2-b)(x-y+z)$$

22. **(D)** The area of a square can be determined by the formula $a=lw$. Because all sides of a square are equal, this can also be stated as $a=s^2$, where s is the length of each side. Plug in the known values:

$$225=s^2$$
$$\pm\sqrt{225}=s$$
$$s=\pm 15$$

You can discard -15, because it isn't logical in this problem.

23. **(A)** The $\leq$ symbol means "less than or equal to."

24. **(B)** Scientific notation is converted to a regular number by moving the decimal point either to the right or left, depending on whether the exponent of 10 is positive or negative. In this case, the exponent is negative, so you move the decimal five places to the left.

25. **(B)** 93 percent $=\frac{93}{100}=0.93$. So, $0.93\times 75=69.75$.

Chapter 16

Practice Exam 3

• •

*B*y now you have two practice AFQT tests under your belt, and I hope you're feeling a bit more confident. If not, don't worry. There are two practice tests left to go. In the sections that follow, you'll find the four subtests of the Armed Services Vocational Aptitude Battery (ASVAB), which make up the Armed Forces Qualification Test (AFQT) score: Arithmetic Reasoning, Word Knowledge, Paragraph Comprehension, and Mathematics Knowledge.

You'll recall from Chapter 2 that the military services use the scores derived from these four subtests to determine your overall AFQT score, and that the AFQT score is the primary factor which decides whether or not you are qualified to enlist in the military branch of your choice. Remember to use the results of the below practice exam to decide which areas you should dedicate

Use the answer key and explanations in Chapter 17 to score your practice exam. Remember not to be too concerned with how many you get right and how many you get wrong. Some of the questions on the practice exam are hard, and others are very easy. When you take the actual subtests as part of the ASVAB, harder questions are awarded more points than easier questions. See Chapter 2 to see exactly how this works, and how it affects your overall AFQT score.

Take this practice exam about a week before you're scheduled to take the actual ASVAB. Use the results to determine which AFQT subjects need a little extra attention.

Practice Exam 3 Answer Sheet

Part 1: Arithmetic Reasoning

1. (A) (B) (C) (D)   8. (A) (B) (C) (D)   15. (A) (B) (C) (D)   22. (A) (B) (C) (D)   29. (A) (B) (C) (D)

2. (A) (B) (C) (D)   9. (A) (B) (C) (D)   16. (A) (B) (C) (D)   23. (A) (B) (C) (D)   30. (A) (B) (C) (D)

3. (A) (B) (C) (D)   10. (A) (B) (C) (D)   17. (A) (B) (C) (D)   24. (A) (B) (C) (D)

4. (A) (B) (C) (D)   11. (A) (B) (C) (D)   18. (A) (B) (C) (D)   25. (A) (B) (C) (D)

5. (A) (B) (C) (D)   12. (A) (B) (C) (D)   19. (A) (B) (C) (D)   26. (A) (B) (C) (D)

6. (A) (B) (C) (D)   13. (A) (B) (C) (D)   20. (A) (B) (C) (D)   27. (A) (B) (C) (D)

7. (A) (B) (C) (D)   14. (A) (B) (C) (D)   21. (A) (B) (C) (D)   28. (A) (B) (C) (D)

Part 2: Word Knowledge

1. (A) (B) (C) (D)   8. (A) (B) (C) (D)   15. (A) (B) (C) (D)   22. (A) (B) (C) (D)   29. (A) (B) (C) (D)

2. (A) (B) (C) (D)   9. (A) (B) (C) (D)   16. (A) (B) (C) (D)   23. (A) (B) (C) (D)   30. (A) (B) (C) (D)

3. (A) (B) (C) (D)   10. (A) (B) (C) (D)   17. (A) (B) (C) (D)   24. (A) (B) (C) (D)   31. (A) (B) (C) (D)

4. (A) (B) (C) (D)   11. (A) (B) (C) (D)   18. (A) (B) (C) (D)   25. (A) (B) (C) (D)   32. (A) (B) (C) (D)

5. (A) (B) (C) (D)   12. (A) (B) (C) (D)   19. (A) (B) (C) (D)   26. (A) (B) (C) (D)   33. (A) (B) (C) (D)

6. (A) (B) (C) (D)   13. (A) (B) (C) (D)   20. (A) (B) (C) (D)   27. (A) (B) (C) (D)   34. (A) (B) (C) (D)

7. (A) (B) (C) (D)   14. (A) (B) (C) (D)   21. (A) (B) (C) (D)   28. (A) (B) (C) (D)   35. (A) (B) (C) (D)

Part 3: Paragraph Comprehension

1. (A) (B) (C) (D)   8. (A) (B) (C) (D)   15. (A) (B) (C)
2. (A) (B) (C) (D)   9. (A) (B) (C) (D)
3. (A) (B) (C) (D)   10. (A) (B) (C) (D)
4. (A) (B) (C) (D)   11. (A) (B) (C) (D)
5. (A) (B) (C) (D)   12. (A) (B) (C) (D)
6. (A) (B) (C) (D)   13. (A) (B) (C) (D)
7. (A) (B) (C) (D)   14. (A) (B) (C) (D)

Part 4: Mathematics Knowledge

1. (A) (B) (C) (D)   8. (A) (B) (C) (D)   15. (A) (B) (C) (D)   22. (A) (B) (C) (D)
2. (A) (B) (C) (D)   9. (A) (B) (C) (D)   16. (A) (B) (C) (D)   23. (A) (B) (C) (D)
3. (A) (B) (C) (D)   10. (A) (B) (C) (D)   17. (A) (B) (C) (D)   24. (A) (B) (C) (D)
4. (A) (B) (C) (D)   11. (A) (B) (C) (D)   18. (A) (B) (C) (D)   25. (A) (B) (C) (D)
5. (A) (B) (C) (D)   12. (A) (B) (C) (D)   19. (A) (B) (C) (D)
6. (A) (B) (C) (D)   13. (A) (B) (C) (D)   20. (A) (B) (C) (D)
7. (A) (B) (C) (D)   14. (A) (B) (C) (D)   21. (A) (B) (C) (D)

Part 1: Arithmetic Reasoning

Time: 36 minutes

30 questions

This subtest asks you to use your mathematical skills to solve real-life problems. When you take the actual ASVAB, the Arithmetic Reasoning subtest will be the second subtest you encounter. You have 36 minutes to correctly answer as many of the questions as you can.

Calculators are not allowed. You're supposed to solve the problems using nothing but your talented brain, a pencil, and a piece of scrap paper.

Each question is followed by four possible answers. Decide which answer is correct and then mark the corresponding space on your answer sheet. Use your scratch paper for any figuring you want to do.

1. Barbara worked 30 hours last week. She earned 422 dollars. If she was paid $455 this week, approximately how many hours did she work?

(A) 32 hours

(B) 35 hours

(C) 37 hours

(D) 39 hours

2. Timothy runs every morning once around a circular track in a park close to his house. If the radius of the circular track is 50 yards, how far does Timothy run every morning?

(A) 250 yards

(B) 285 yards

(C) 314 yards

(D) 380 yards

3. Jack sets up a security camera in his back yard to take automatic pictures every 15 minutes. If the first picture is taken at 10 p.m., and Jack shuts the camera off at 2 a.m., how many pictures will Jack have?

(A) 16 pictures

(B) 132 pictures

(C) 17 pictures

(D) 15 pictures

4. Joy is trying a new weight-loss plan. The theory seems simple: Eat fewer calories and exercise more. The book says that Joy's body burns 2,000 calories per day to maintain her current weight, and every 2,500-calorie deficit is a pound of weight lost. If Joy burns 400 calories per day exercising, and goes on a 1,500-calorie-per-day diet, how many pounds should she lose in one 7-day week?

(A) 3 pounds

(B) $2\frac{1}{2}$ pounds

(C) 4 pounds

(D) 5 pounds

Go on to next page

5. Jimmy B's Diner runs a breakfast special. If a customer buys the special for $2, he can come back on consecutive days and eat again for just $1.25. If a person paid $8.25 for breakfasts during the week, how many consecutive days did he eat the breakfast specials at Jimmy B's?

(A) 7 days

(B) 6 days

(C) 4 days

(D) 5 days

6. Forty soldiers in basic training are to undergo hand-to-hand combat training in a 60-minute training period, but only ten can be trained at one time. In order for each soldier to get the same amount of training time, how many minutes should each soldier be trained?

(A) $1\frac{1}{2}$ minutes

(B) 6 minutes

(C) 30 minutes

(D) 15 minutes

7. Steve can make 9 candles in an hour. How long will it take him to make 126 candles?

(A) 14 hours

(B) 9 hours

(C) 7 hours

(D) 16 hours

8. Your boss gives you a bonus, and you decide to carpet the bedrooms in your house. The house contains one 12-x-14-foot bedroom, one 12-x-10-foot bedroom, and one 8-x-12-foot bedroom. If carpet costs $4.25 per square yard, how much will this project cost?

(A) $181.33

(B) $343.92

(C) $296.87

(D) $630.41

Go on to next page

9. In a manufacturing plant that produces new CD players, there is a 15 percent probability that a CD player will be defective. If five CD players are manufactured, what is the probability that all of them will be defective?

   (A) 7.6 percent

   (B) 60 percent

   (C) 0.42 percent

   (D) 0.0076 percent

11. Paul decides to buy his dad socks for his birthday. He has $30, and the socks he wants sell for $3.95 per pair. Assuming no sales tax, how many pairs of socks can he buy?

    (A) 9

    (B) 7

    (C) 6

    (D) 4

10. A box containing books weighs 60 pounds. If the books weigh 53 pounds, what is the weight of the box alone?

    (A) 2 pounds

    (B) 5 pounds

    (C) 7 pounds

    (D) 8 pounds

12. Penny makes $25.70 in tips on Wednesday, $32.30 in tips on Thursday, and $31.80 in tips on Friday. On Saturday, she spends one-quarter of the money on dinner with her friend. How much money does she have left?

    (A) $89.80

    (B) $22.45

    (C) $44.90

    (D) $67.35

Go on to next page

13. Your mom sends you to the store to buy peas. She says she needs 8 ounces of canned peas to finish the recipe, and tells you to choose the cheapest peas. Which would it be cheapest to buy?

    (A) Two 4-ounce cans of peas at 79¢ each

    (B) One 8-ounce can of peas at $1.49

    (C) Two 3-ounce cans of peas at 59¢ each

    (D) Three 3-ounce cans of peas at 65¢ each

15. A bin of screws at the hardware store contains seven dozen screws when full. The stock clerk is supposed to reorder screws when the bin is one-sixth full. How many screws are in the bin when it's time to reorder?

    (A) 14

    (B) 1

    (C) 84

    (D) 12

14. Two bicyclists head toward each other from the opposite ends of Main Street, which is 6 miles long. The first biker started at 2:05 going 12 mph. The second biker began peddling four minutes later at a rate of 14 mph. What time will they meet?

    (A) 2:13

    (B) 2:21

    (C) 2:29

    (D) 2:34

16. Autumn found a wallet containing $900 in the street. She returned the wallet to its owner, who gave her a $130 reward. What percentage of the $900 was the reward?

    (A) 5 percent

    (B) 9 percent

    (C) 14 percent

    (D) 18 percent

Go on to next page

17. A 12-yard-long string was used to enclose a freshly planted flower garden, forming a square around the garden. If each side of the square used the same amount of rope, how long was one side of the square surrounding the garden?

    (A) 1 yard

    (B) 2 yards

    (C) 3 yards

    (D) 4 yards

19. A rectangle is three times as long as it is wide. The perimeter of the rectangle is 147 inches. What is the length of the rectangle?

    (A) 45 inches

    (B) 55.1 inches

    (C) 68.9 inches

    (D) 70 inches

18. Britney is on her high school track team. This year she placed first in four of her races, second in six of her races, and third in eight of her races. The fraction of races in which she placed first is correctly expressed as:

    (A) $\frac{7}{3}$

    (B) $\frac{3}{7}$

    (C) $\frac{2}{9}$

    (D) $\frac{3}{5}$

20. Lyle bought a trampoline that measures 9 feet by 12 feet. If he wants to surround the trampoline with a fence, so that the fence is 8 feet from each edge of the trampoline, how many feet of chain-link fence will he need?

    (A) 106 feet

    (B) 108 feet

    (C) 110 feet

    (D) 115 feet

Go on to next page

21. A painter has painted a picture on a piece of canvas that measures 10 x 14 inches. In order to accommodate a frame, he has left an unpainted margin of 1 inch all the way around. What part of the canvas has been painted?

    (A) 68.5 percent

    (B) 752 percent

    (C) 25 percent

    (D) 66.1 percent

22. A road map is drawn to a scale of 2 inches = 3 miles. John wants to drive to a point that is $9\frac{1}{2}$ inches away. How many actual miles does this represent?

    (A) $28\frac{1}{2}$ miles

    (B) $14\frac{1}{4}$ miles

    (C) $6\frac{1}{3}$ miles

    (D) 19 miles

23. A field measures 100 yards by 75 yards. If a person wanted to walk diagonally from one corner of the field to the other corner, how far would she walk?

    (A) 100 yards

    (B) 200 yards

    (C) 125 yards

    (D) 60 yards

24. Michael owns a consignment shop, in which he earns 35 percent commission on all the items he sells. If Michael had $8,434.80 worth of sales in the week, how much was his commission?

    (A) $1,843.30

    (B) $2,952.18

    (C) $3,211.14

    (D) $3,343.19

Go on to next page

25. The sum of three consecutive odd numbers is 171. What are the numbers?

    (A) 53, 55, and 57

    (B) 55, 57, and 59

    (C) 57, 59, and 61

    (D) 59, 61, and 63

27. The price of daily admission at Wally World is $27. They do, however, sell season passes for $175. How many trips would you need to make with the season ticket in order for it to cost less than paying the daily admission rate?

    (A) 6

    (B) 7

    (C) 8

    (D) 9

26. Rod smokes $1\frac{1}{2}$ packs of cigarettes per day. Rod buys cigarettes by the carton. There are ten packs of cigarettes in each carton. If Rod pays $35.80 per carton, how much does it cost him for each day of smoking?

    (A) $4.51

    (B) $4.92

    (C) $5.03

    (D) $5.37

28. If eight people can run 16 machines, how many machines can two people run?

    (A) 2

    (B) 4

    (C) 1

    (D) 3

Go on to next page

29. Sam earns three times as much per hour as Bob. Bob earns $2 more per hour than Jeanie. As a group, they earn $55 per hour. What is Jeanie's hourly wage?

    (A) $7

    (B) $8.60

    (C) $9.40

    (D) $10.32

30. A bricklayer charges $12 per square foot to lay a patio. How much would it cost for the bricklayer to lay a 10-x-16-foot patio?

    (A) $960

    (B) $192

    (C) $224

    (D) $1,920

STOP DO NOT TURN THE PAGE UNTIL TOLD TO DO SO.
DO NOT RETURN TO A PREVIOUS TEST.

Part 2: Word Knowledge

Time: 11 minutes

35 questions

The Word Knowledge subtest of the ASVAB is the next subtest that helps make up your AFQT score. This vocabulary subtest gives you only about 20 seconds per question, so you don't want to take too much time to think about each question.

Each question has an underlined word — sometimes that word is used in a sentence, and sometimes it isn't. After the question, you see four possible answer choices. Select the choice that best defines the underlined word, and then mark the corresponding space on your answer sheet. Good luck!

1. The smell that drifted from her kitchen was pure <u>ambrosia</u>.

    (A) deliciousness

    (B) garbage

    (C) chaos

    (D) relaxation

2. <u>Circulate</u> most nearly means:

    (A) trade

    (B) perform

    (C) distribute

    (D) pastime

3. The president <u>vetoed</u> the new law from Congress.

    (A) approved

    (B) disapproved

    (C) enjoyed

    (D) hated

4. <u>Tenacious</u> most nearly means:

    (A) intelligent

    (B) excited

    (C) precious

    (D) stubborn

5. Pop decided to <u>retaliate</u> against the government for the unfair law.

    (A) speak

    (B) write

    (C) protest

    (D) get even with

6. <u>Recur</u> most nearly means:

    (A) happening

    (B) repeat

    (C) treatment

    (D) sentimental

7. Billy was known to be <u>scrupulous</u> in all his undertakings.

    (A) honest

    (B) neglectful

    (C) careful

    (D) Both (A) and (C)

8. <u>Superfluous</u> most nearly means:

    (A) talented

    (B) brilliant

    (C) limited

    (D) excessive

9. The requirement to salute was <u>superseded</u> by the change to the regulation.

    (A) reinforced

    (B) introduced

    (C) supplanted

    (D) None of the above

10. <u>Supplant</u> most nearly means:

    (A) supersede

    (B) reinforce

    (C) introduce

    (D) None of the above

Go on to next page

11. Debbie's attitude <u>piqued</u> me to no end.
    - (A) angered
    - (B) pleased
    - (C) complimented
    - (D) bored

12. <u>Pious</u> most nearly means:
    - (A) irregular
    - (B) mainstay
    - (C) religious
    - (D) unbelieving

13. Everyone, of course, wants the judge to be <u>impartial</u>.
    - (A) discriminating
    - (B) fair
    - (C) intelligent
    - (D) enthusiastic

14. <u>Immense</u> most nearly means:
    - (A) submerged
    - (B) huge
    - (C) mandatory
    - (D) trade

15. The crowd found Linda's speech to be very <u>laudable</u>.
    - (A) funny
    - (B) praiseworthy
    - (C) interesting
    - (D) detailed

16. <u>Originate</u> most nearly means:
    - (A) terminate
    - (B) imitate
    - (C) begin
    - (D) result

17. The police were called out to <u>pacify</u> the rowdy crowd.
    - (A) arrest
    - (B) talk to
    - (C) calm
    - (D) fight

18. <u>Ominous</u> most nearly means:
    - (A) menacing
    - (B) scary
    - (C) peaceful
    - (D) tantalizing

19. <u>Absence</u> most nearly means:
    - (A) immense
    - (B) gone
    - (C) lucky
    - (D) replace

20. Parliament was worried that the king would <u>abdicate</u> the throne.
    - (A) paint
    - (B) replace
    - (C) give up
    - (D) hate

21. <u>Bide</u> most nearly means:
    - (A) patience
    - (B) train
    - (C) temporary
    - (D) wait

22. The <u>apparition</u> in the upstairs hallway confused everyone — even the experts.
    - (A) ghost
    - (B) stain
    - (C) structure
    - (D) window

23. <u>Circumnavigate</u> most nearly means:
    - (A) go through
    - (B) go around
    - (C) plan
    - (D) full speed ahead

24. Tanya was always a <u>clumsy</u> person.
    - (A) graceful
    - (B) awkward
    - (C) depressed
    - (D) happy

Go on to next page

25. <u>Clemency</u> most nearly means:

    (A) mean

    (B) mercy

    (C) accusation

    (D) intolerance

26. After the movie, we went home and had a <u>frugal</u> meal.

    (A) economical

    (B) expansive

    (C) delicious

    (D) tantalizing

27. <u>Generic</u> most nearly means:

    (A) branded

    (B) lifestyle

    (C) not specific

    (D) old

28. The book she gave me had a notably <u>haggard</u> appearance.

    (A) old

    (B) priceless

    (C) new

    (D) worn

29. <u>Improvident</u> most nearly means:

    (A) unwary

    (B) happy

    (C) cautious

    (D) rich

30. Tom felt <u>isolated</u>; he nearly cried.

    (A) sad

    (B) separated

    (C) painful

    (D) depressed

31. <u>Manifesto</u> most nearly means:

    (A) book

    (B) declaration

    (C) performance

    (D) religious belief

32. We thought Paula might be the best person to <u>mediate</u> the contract.

    (A) negotiate

    (B) read

    (C) sign

    (D) rewrite

33. <u>Packet</u> most nearly means:

    (A) preliminary

    (B) poise

    (C) pencil

    (D) bundle

34. <u>Perhaps</u> this book will help you score well on the AFQT.

    (A) definitely

    (B) possibly

    (C) likely

    (D) truly

35. <u>Venerate</u> most nearly means:

    (A) cherish

    (B) old

    (C) perish

    (D) delicate

STOP DO NOT TURN THE PAGE UNTIL TOLD TO DO SO.
DO NOT RETURN TO A PREVIOUS TEST.

Part 3: Paragraph Comprehension

Time: 13 minutes

15 questions

In the Paragraph Comprehension subtest, you're presented with a paragraph of reading material and asked one to four questions about the information contained in the paragraph.

Read the paragraph and select the choice that best completes the statement or answers the question. Mark the corresponding choice on your answer sheet.

In the eyes of his classmates, Sam Smith was a nerd, but in the eyes of the faculty, he was a stellar scholar and proof that Jefferson High was a citadel of superior education. Sam's intellectual image was enhanced by his wavy, overgrown hair, thick glasses, and sharp tongue. What no one realized, though, was that Sam was a budding entrepreneur and an excellent potential fundraiser for the senior class trip. The senior class found out about the fundraiser during history class. Sam was in his usual front-row seat, sitting alert and straight as if good posture could further polish his perfect 4.0 average. Mr. Date told his class about getting orders for Christmas wreaths by going door to door, and then he handed out glossy brochures. Sam had great determination to make the most of this fundraiser because the senior who sold the most wreaths earned a free movie pass for a month! After class, Sam stopped by the library to tell Miss Dewey, the school librarian, all about their fundraising project. The lonesome, steely-eyed book organizer and the brilliant, solitary student huddled together over a notepad like two ancient alchemists hovering over a bubbling pot creating potions. Miss Dewey was surprisingly shrewd. She did all the calculations for library fines as well as the renewal dates for books in her head. If anyone could figure out how to raise money, she could.

1. Sam's grade average is:

    (A) A+

    (B) A–

    (C) B

    (D) B+

2. Where is Sam at the beginning of the story?

    (A) in history class

    (B) at home studying wreath brochures

    (C) at the library

    (D) selling wreaths to Mrs. Macmillan

3. The librarian can best be described as:

    (A) married and smart

    (B) single and smart

    (C) stingy and old

    (D) generous and old

4. What was the reward for handing out the most brochures?

    (A) a movie pass

    (B) $500

    (C) a field trip

    (D) None of the above

Water pollution is a major national concern and a high priority in environmental programs. The introduction of pollutants to our rivers, streams, lakes, and watersheds has caused many previous sources of fresh water to become contaminated. Major water pollutants include untreated wastewater, storm-water runoff from industrial activities, and pollutants from nonpoint sources like airfield and agricultural runoff. Water pollution can result from any chemical used on, disposed of, or leaked onto the ground. Many underground storage tanks have leaked and contaminated the groundwater. Overuse of

Go on to next page

pesticides and fertilizers has also caused contamination. The growing population, expanding industry, and increasing agricultural production have created an increasing demand for fresh water. Thus, conserving water is rapidly becoming the way of life in many communities.

5. According to the above passage:

    (A) There is plenty of fresh water available.

    (B) Rain is an important supplier of fresh water.

    (C) Water conservation is an important political agenda.

    (D) The need for fresh water is increasing.

Inspector General (IG) teams evaluate a military unit's management of nuclear resources against approved safety, security, and reliability standards. Teams evaluate logistics airlift units with nuclear weapons transport missions by observing loading, transporting, unloading, and custody transferring procedures of representative types of weapons. The unit's proficiency is determined by using war reserve (WR) weapons when possible. Training weapons or weapon system simulations are used when WR assets are not available. The final rating is based on the nature, severity, and number of findings noted during the inspection. The unit will be assigned a rating of Satisfactory; Satisfactory (Support Unsatisfactory), for deficiencies outside the control of the commander; or Unsatisfactory. If a unit receives an overall Unsatisfactory, the unit will be reinspected within 90 days.

6. A good name for the inspection discussed above would be:

    (A) NSI, or Nuclear Surety Inspection

    (B) ORI, or Operational Readiness Inspection

    (C) MEI, or Management Efficiency Inspection

    (D) HSI, or Heath Services Inspection

7. Military units that fail the discussed inspection must be:

    (A) put on probation

    (B) disbanded

    (C) reinspected

    (D) discussed at the commander's meeting

Sports and recreational activities provide an opportunity for escape from the daily routine. By nature, some sports and recreational activities have hazards that cannot be eliminated. Officials, coaches, and athletes should become familiar with the injury potentials of recreational activities and learn how to avoid them. Each person who participates in sports or recreational activities must exercise good judgment. A complete, progressive warm-up and stretching program is essential before engaging in sports or vigorous recreational activities. Many injuries occur because people are out of shape or have not warmed up properly. Injury prevention is primarily a participant's responsibility. Peer pressure is often the cause of sports and recreational injuries. A good rule to know and follow is to recognize and respect individual limitations.

8. What is the main focus of the above paragraph?

    (A) getting in shape

    (B) escaping from life's problems

    (C) the importance of warming up properly

    (D) avoiding sport and recreational injuries

9. Who is responsible for avoiding sports injuries?

    (A) officials

    (B) coaches

    (C) athletes

    (D) All of the above

Katie took one more look at her homework through tired, bleary eyes. The report was due next week, and she hadn't started on it yet. She blew back her overgrown bangs that fell across her face and wondered what to do next. She had already cleaned the house and took some chicken out of the freezer to thaw for dinner. Nothing she did that day, however, gave her inspiration for her report. She thought about asking her friend Rod for help, but he was out of town. Katie was proud of her high GPA and was worried about this project, lest she should be taken off the dean's list. Her cellphone rang, giving her an excuse to ignore Reaganomics for a few more minutes. She reached for her phone like a hungry kid who had just seen a piece of candy. In the process, she almost scared her pet cat, Whiskers to death. She took a second to soothe Whiskers (who lost most of his whiskers in a catfight), but the task proved to be impossible. The call was from her friend, Autumn.

Go on to next page

10. For what course was Katie most likely studying?

    (A) math

    (B) economics

    (C) general science

    (D) English

11. Which of the following statements can be inferred from the passage?

    (A) Katie has just finished breakfast.

    (B) Katie likes candy.

    (C) Katie's friend, Rod knows a lot about the subject she's studying.

    (D) Katie likes dogs.

I know you're now interested, so I'll continue the story:

Autumn had long, blond hair that perfectly matched her somewhat frazzled and dizzy personality. Katie, on the other hand, had a halcyon temperament. Katie secretly wondered if all those blond curls affected Autumn's brain. Autumn bubbled on about her boyfriend and then dropped a bomb that changed Katie's day. Katie's friend Rod was planning a cruise next month, and he asked Autumn if she wanted to go! Autumn's melodious voice was triumphant. The only smooth thing about Autumn was her euphonious voice. Katie felt a whole gamut of emotions about Autumn's surprise. She felt jealous because she wanted to go on a cruise, too, but she also felt excited because the entire cruise situation gave her an idea for her report. She quickly made excuses and hung up. She was usually garrulous, but she wanted to start her project right away. She couldn't bear to hear Autumn's drivel about cruise minutiae. She knew it was petty, but she couldn't bear to hear Autumn's chatter for one more second.

12. In the passage, halcyon means:

    (A) excited

    (B) calm

    (C) perplexing

    (D) joyful

13. How did Katie feel about Autumn's news?

    (A) resentful

    (B) distrusting

    (C) stimulated

    (D) Both (A) and (C)

"The difference in affection, of parents towards their several children, is many times unequal; and sometimes unworthy; especially in the mothers; as Solomon saith, A wise son rejoiceth the father, but an ungracious son shames the mother. A man shall see, where there is a house full of children, one or two of the eldest respected, and the youngest made wantons; but in the midst, some that are as it were forgotten, who many times, nevertheless, prove the best. The illiberality of parents, in allowance toward their children, is an harmful error; makes them base; acquaints them with shifts; makes them sort with mean company; and makes them surfeit more when they come to plenty."

—Francis Bacon

14. The author believes that a parent's favorite child is often:

    (A) the youngest

    (B) the oldest

    (C) the middle child

    (D) None of the above

15. According to the author, who is the most biased in their affections toward their children?

    (A) mothers

    (B) fathers

    (C) both equally

STOP DO NOT TURN THE PAGE UNTIL TOLD TO DO SO. DO NOT RETURN TO A PREVIOUS TEST.

Part 4: Mathematics Knowledge

Time: 24 minutes

25 questions

This next subtest measures your basic mathematics knowledge. Usually, you're asked to solve a math problem. Sometimes, you may be asked about a mathematical fact, such as identifying a geometry shape or expanding on a mathematical law.

As on the Arithmetic Reasoning subtest, you're not allowed to use a calculator. However, the questions are designed so that they can be solved using pencil and paper. Aren't you glad Mrs. Gladys pounded all those multiplication tables into your head in the third grade?

You don't have much time, so you have to work fast.

1. $3^3 + (-2)^2 =$
   (A) 27
   (B) 31
   (C) 25
   (D) 24

2. $5! =$
   (A) 5
   (B) 120
   (C) 0.05
   (D) 0.120

3. What is the volume of a cylinder with a radius of 4 inches and a height of 6 inches?
   (A) 144.4 inches
   (B) 250.5 inches
   (C) 301.4 inches
   (D) 355.8 inches

4. In the logarithm 4.83723, what is the 4 called?
   (A) property
   (B) mantissa
   (C) whole log
   (D) characteristic

Go on to next page

5. Solve for x: $\frac{3}{4}(68) + \frac{1}{4}x = 70$

   (A) 42

   (B) 76

   (C) 53

   (D) 81

6. What is the sum of the angle measures of a hexagon?

   (A) 360°

   (B) 540°

   (C) 720°

   (D) 900°

7. In order to determine the diagonal of a rectangle, the formula is $d^2 = l^2 + w^2$, where d = the diagonal, l = the length of the rectangle, and w = the width. If $d = 5$ and $l = w + 1$, what is the width (w) of the rectangle?

   (A) 3

   (B) 4

   (C) 5

   (D) 6

8. What is the length of the hypotenuse of a right triangle, if the legs are 5 inches and 6 inches?

   (A) 6.7 inches

   (B) 7.8 inches

   (C) 8.1 inches

   (D) 9 inches

Go on to next page

9. $\dfrac{4!}{3!} =$

   (A) 2

   (B) 4

   (C) 6

   (D) 8

11. $4^{-2} =$

    (A) 16

    (B) −16

    (C) $\dfrac{1}{4}$

    (D) $\dfrac{1}{16}$

10. Solve for x: $x - 31\dfrac{3}{4}\%(x) = 174$.

    (A) 174.7

    (B) 155.3

    (C) 255.5

    (D) 261.8

12. If $3^n = 9$, and $4x - n = 6$, what is the value of x?

    (A) 2

    (B) 3

    (C) 4

    (D) 5

Go on to next page

13. Solve for x: $5x + 7 = 6(x - 2) - 4(2x - 3)$
    - (A) 1
    - (B) −1
    - (C) −2
    - (D) 2

14. $\left(\dfrac{3}{4}\right)^3 =$
    - (A) 3
    - (B) $\dfrac{1}{16}$
    - (C) 2
    - (D) $\dfrac{27}{64}$

15. Convert 6.39×10^{-4} to standard notation.
    - (A) $(6.39)^5 \times 10$
    - (B) 639,000
    - (C) 639.10
    - (D) 0.000639

16. Ten thousand may be represented as
    - (A) 10^4
    - (B) 10^5
    - (C) 10^6
    - (D) 10^7

Go on to next page

17. What is the area of a room that is 6 feet by 8 feet?

   (A) 24 square feet

   (B) 32 square feet

   (C) 48 square feet

   (D) 52 square feet

19. What is the approximate area of the shape below? Assume the triangle portion is a right triangle. The diameter of the semi-circle is one leg of a right triangle.

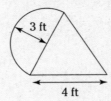

3 ft

4 ft

   (A) 26.1 square feet

   (B) 30.2 square feet

   (C) 31.1 square feet

   (D) 34.3 square feet

18. $(-3)^3 =$

   (A) 27

   (B) −27

   (C) −9

   (D) 9

20. Simplify: $\dfrac{x-2}{x^2-6x+8}$

   (A) $\dfrac{1}{x}$

   (B) $\dfrac{1}{x-4}$

   (C) $\dfrac{1}{x+4}$

   (D) $\dfrac{1}{6}$

Go on to next page

21. Simplify: $-7(4x + 5) - 8$
    (A) $14x - 1$
    (B) $-28x - 43$
    (C) $30x + 4$
    (D) $7x + 32$

23. What is the diameter of a circle with a radius of 2 inches?
    (A) 3.14 inches
    (B) 7 inches
    (C) 6 inches
    (D) 4 inches

22. What is the area of the shaded portion of the shape below?

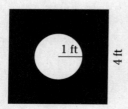

    (A) 8.9 square feet
    (B) 10.3 square feet
    (C) 12.9 square feet.
    (D) 13.2 square feet

24. What is the circumference of the circle described in the preceding question?
    (A) 8.3 inches
    (B) 9 inches
    (C) 12.6 inches
    (D) 13 inches

Go on to next page

25. The expression "$4x$ is greater than 7" can be expressed as

   (A) $7 < 4x$.

   (B) $7 > 4x$.

   (C) $4x \geq 7$.

   (D) $4x \leq 7$.

STOP DO NOT TURN THE PAGE UNTIL TOLD TO DO SO.
DO NOT RETURN TO A PREVIOUS TEST.

Chapter 17

Practice Exam 3: Answers and Explanations

· ·

Are you getting tired of math and English yet? I certainly hope not. You still have one full-length AFQT practice test to go. Then, if you still want more practice, I recommend you jog on down to your neighborhood bookstore and pick up a copy of *ASVAB For Dummies,* written by yours truly (published by Wiley).

Use the answer keys in the following sections to find out how you did on the AFQT practice exam in Chapter 16. The accompanying explanations will tell you how to get to the correct answer if you got somewhat lost along the way.

Part 1: Arithmetic Reasoning

If you already took three practice AFQT exams, and the temperature is a steady 87 degrees, what is the probability that you got most of the questions right on all four subtests? Okay, that's not a real arithmetic reasoning question (insufficient data, as my computer friends say), but I'm betting you've done pretty well. Now it's time to see how you did on this Arithmetic Reasoning practice subtest.

If you need more practice doing arithmetic reasoning–type problems, Chapters 8 and 10 are a good place to start. You can also check out *Math Word Problems For Dummies, Algebra I For Dummies,* and *Algebra II For Dummies,* all by Mary Jane Sterling; *Geometry For Dummies,* 2nd Edition, and *Calculus For Dummies,* both by Mark Ryan; and *SAT II Math For Dummies,* by Scott Hatch, JD, and Lisa Zimmer Hatch, MA — all published by Wiley.

1. **(A)** You can set up this problem as a ratio: $422 is to 30 hours as $455 is to x hours. Mathematically, this is stated as

$$\frac{422}{30} = \frac{455}{x}$$

$$\frac{422}{30}x = 455$$

$$14.07x = 455$$

$$x = \frac{455}{14.07}$$

$$x = 32.33 \text{ hours}$$

2. **(C)** The *circumference* (length around) a circle can be determined by the formula, $c = \pi d$. The diameter of a circle is twice its radius, so this circle has a diameter of 100 yards. Plug in the known values:

$c = 100\pi$

$c = 100 \times 3.14$

$c = 314$ yards

3. **(C)** The time between 10 p.m. and 2 a.m. is 4 hours, or $60 \times 4 = 240$ minutes. Divide the total number of minutes in the time period by 15 minutes, the interval in which the camera takes the pictures. Then add 1 because the first picture is taken at the beginning of the period: $\frac{240}{15} + 1 = 17$.

4. **(B)** In order to maintain her current weight, Joy's body needs $7 \times 2,000 = 14,000$ calories during the week. Joy is taking in $7 \times 1,500 = 10,500$ calories per week in food, and is burning up $7 \times 400 = 2,800$ calories per week while exercising.

That means Joy is taking in a total of $10,500 - 2,800 = 7,700$ calories per week. Subtract her total calorie intake from the number of calories in a week that her body needs to maintain her weight, and you have a deficit of $14,000 - 7,700 = 6,300$ calories.

Since a deficit of 2,500 calories equals 1 pound of weight loss, divide the calorie deficit by the number of calorie deficit needed for 1 pound of weight loss: $6,300 \div 2,500 = 2.52$). Joy will have lost about $2\frac{1}{2}$ pounds.

5. **(B)** Subtract the first day's breakfast charge from the total: $\$8.25 - \$2 = \$6.25$. Then divide the remainder by $\$1.25$ to determine the number of additional consecutive days the customer ate breakfast: $\frac{\$6.25}{\$1.25} = 5$. Add those five days to the first day the special was eaten to find out that the customer ate the breakfast special for six consecutive days.

6. **(D)** Divide the group of 40 soldiers by the number of basic trainees who can be trained at the same time: $40 \div 10 = 4$. This means that four groups of soldiers have to share the 60 minutes, or 60 minutes $\div 4 = 15$ minutes. Thus, each soldier gets 15 minutes of training time.

7. **(A)** This problem can be expressed as a ratio: 9 candles is to 1 hour as 126 candles is to x hours. Mathematically, this can be written

$\frac{9}{1} = \frac{126}{x}$

$9 = \frac{126}{x}$

$9x = 126$

$x = \frac{126}{9}$

$x = 14$

8. **(A)** The formula to determine the area of a rectangle is $a = lw$. Find the area of each bedroom and add them together:

$12 \times 14 = 168$

$12 \times 10 = 120$

$8 \times 12 = 96$

$168 + 120 + 96 = 384$ square feet

Then, because 3 feet make up a yard, there are 9 square feet to a square yard. Divide the total area in square feet by 9 to determine the number of square yards needed: $\frac{384}{3} = 42.66$ square yards. Multiply this by the cost per square yard of carpet: $\$4.25 \times 42.66 = \$181.33$.

9. **(D)** First, convert the 15 percent to a decimal by dividing it by 100: $\frac{15}{100} = 0.15$. The probability that all five CD players will be defective is $0.15 \times 0.15 \times 0.15 \times 0.15 \times 0.15 = 0.0000759$ (round up to 0.000076). Now convert this back to a percentage by multiplying it by 100: $0.000076 \times 100 = 0.0076$.

10. **(C)** This is an easy one. (Don't look so surprised — you'll see a few easy ones on the AFQT.) Simply subtract the weight of the books from the total weight of the box with books: $60 - 53 = 7$.

11. **(B)** Divide $30 by $3.95. The whole number is the number of pairs of socks he could buy: $\frac{\$30}{\$3.95} = 7.59$, or 7 pairs of socks. (Don't round up to 8, because he can't afford eight pairs.)

12. **(D)** Add the sales amounts together: $\$25.70 + \$32.30 + \$31.80 = \$89.80$. Then multiply the total sales by 0.75 to determine how much money she has left: $\$89.80 \times 0.75 = \$67.35$.

13. **(B)** Calculate each answer option and compare:

    A: $2 \times \$0.79 = \$1.58$.

    B: $1.49.

    C: Two 3-ounce cans don't equal 8 ounces, so this answer can't be correct.

    D: $3 \times \$0.65 = \$1.95$.

    B is the cheapest option.

14. **(B)** The first bike got a $12 \times \frac{4}{60} = \frac{4}{5}$-mile head start. Therefore, by the time the second bike leaves, there are $6 - \frac{4}{5} = 5\frac{1}{5}$ miles between them. Their combined rate of travel is $12 + 14 = 26$ mph. Let t = the number of hours the second bike travels.

$$26t = 5\frac{1}{5}$$
$$26t = \frac{26}{5}$$
$$t = \frac{26}{5} \div \frac{26}{1}$$
$$t = \frac{26}{5} \times \frac{1}{26}$$
$$t = \frac{1}{5}$$

$\frac{1}{5}$ of an hour = 12 minutes. The second bike left at 2:09, so both bikes will meet at 2:21.

15. **(A)** First, find how many screws a full bin contains: $7 \times 12 = 84$ screws. Then multiply the total number of screws in a full bin by $\frac{1}{6}$ to find how many screws are in the bin when it's $\frac{1}{6}$ full: $\frac{84}{1} \times \frac{1}{6} = \frac{84}{6} = 14$ screws.

16. **(C)** Divide $130 by $900 to determine the percentage of $900 that the reward comprised: $\$130 \div \$900 = 0.14 = 14.4$ percent.

17. **(C)** A square has four equal sides. Divide the total length of the rope by 4 to find out how long each side of the square will be: $12 \div 4 = 3$.

18. **(C)** The total number of races is 18: $4 + 6 + 8 = 18$. If she placed first in four of her races, the fraction would be expressed as $\frac{4}{18}$, which can be reduced to $\frac{2}{9}$.

19. **(B)** The formula for the perimeter of a rectangle is $p = 2l + 2w$. In this case, $p = 147$, w is unknown, and $l = 3w$. Plug in the known values:

$$147 = 2(3w) + 2w$$

$$147 = 6w + 2w$$

$$147 = 8w$$

$$w = \frac{147}{8}$$

$$w = 18.375$$

The width of the rectangle is 18.375 inches. Because the length is 3 times the width, $3 \times 21 =$ 55.125. Round this down to 55.1.

20. **(A)** Take a look at the following figure. As you can see, the measurements of the chain-link enclosure will be 25 feet by 28 feet.

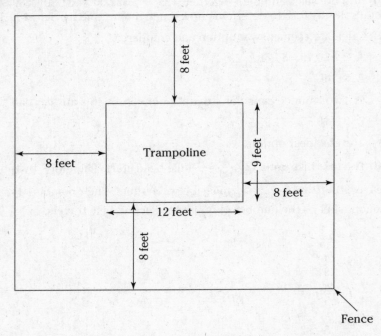

The perimeter formula for a rectangle is $p = 2l + 2w$. Plug in the known values:

$$P = (2 \times 25) + (2 \times 28)$$

$$P = 50 + 56$$

$$P = 106$$

Lyle will need 106 feet of fence.

21. **(A)** The area of the entire piece of canvas is 10 inches × 14 inches = 140 square inches. The portion painted is 8 inches × 12 inches = 96 square inches. (You determine this by subtracting 1 inch from the length of each side to account for the margin.) The portion used for painting can be expressed as a fraction: $\frac{96}{140}$. Reduce this fraction (divide 96 by 140) to determine that 68.5 percent of the canvas is covered with paint.

22. **(B)** If 2 inches = 3 miles, then 1 inch equals $1\frac{1}{2}$ miles. Multiply $1\frac{1}{2} \times 9\frac{1}{2}$ inches to determine the actual distance: $1.5 \times 9.5 = 14.25$, or $14\frac{1}{4}$ miles.

23. **(C)** The formula to determine the diagonal of a rectangle is $d^2 = l^2 + w^2$. Plug in the known values:

$$d^2 = 100^2 + 75^2$$

$$d^2 = 10,000 + 5,625$$

$$d^2 = 15,625$$

$$d = \sqrt{15,625}$$

$$d = 125 \text{ yards}$$

24. **(B)** Multiply his total sales by his percent commission to find his commission: $8,434.80 × 0.35 = $2,952.18.

25. **(B)** The fastest way to solve this would be to simply add the numbers in the possible answer choices: 55 + 57 + 59 = 171.

However, you can also find the answer by using algebra. Let x = the first number. That means the second number is $x + 2$, and the third number is $x + 4$. The sum of these three numbers is 171. The formula becomes:

$$x + (x + 2) + (x + 4) = 171$$

$$3x + 7 = 171$$

$$3x = 165$$

$$x = \frac{165}{3}$$

$$x = 55$$

The first number is 55. That means the second number is $x + 2 = 55 + 2 = 57$, and the third number is $x + 4 = 55 + 4 = 59$.

26. **(D)** There are 10 packs of cigarettes in each carton, and a carton costs $35.80. That means each pack of cigarettes costs $35.80 ÷ 10 = $3.58. Rod smokes $1\frac{1}{2}$ packs of cigarettes each day. It costs Rod $1.5 × $3.58 = $5.37 per day to support his habit.

Don't be like Rod. If you smoke, quit. Besides, they won't let you smoke in basic training anyway.

27. **(B)** Let x equal the number of daily tickets you would purchase. Then $27x$ = the daily ticket cost.

$$175 < 27x$$

$$\frac{175}{27} < x$$

$$6.48 < x$$

You would need to use the ticket more than 6.48 times (or 7 times) in order for it to be cheaper to use the season ticket.

28. **(B)** Two people is $\frac{1}{4}$ as many as eight people: $2 \div 8 = \frac{1}{4}$. Multiply the number of machines that eight people can run by $\frac{1}{4}$ to determine how many machines two people can run: $16 \times \frac{1}{4} = 4$.

29. **(C)** Let x equal Jeanie's hourly wage. Then $x + 2$ would represent Bob's hourly wage, and $3(x + 2)$ would represent Sam's hourly wage.

$$x + (x + 2) + 3(x + 2) = 55$$

$$x + x + 2 + 3x + 6 = 55$$

$$5x + 8 = 55$$

$$5x = 47$$

$$x = \frac{47}{5}$$

$$x = 9.4$$

Jeanie's hourly wage is $9.40.

30. **(D)** The formula to determine the area of a rectangle is $a = lw$. Plug in the known values:

$$a = 10 \times 16$$

$$a = 160 \text{ square feet}$$

Multiply this number by the cost per square foot to determine what the brick layer charges: $160 \times \$12 = \$1,920$.

Part 2: Word Knowledge

Scoring well on the Word Knowledge subtest is crucial to scoring high on the AFQT and getting into the military branch of your choice. If your score is weak in this area, spend time reviewing the material and improving your vocabulary (see Chapter 4).

Other great references that can help you improve your score in this area are *Vocabulary For Dummies,* by Laurie E. Rozakis, and *SAT Vocabulary For Dummies,* by Suzee Vlk (both published by Wiley). Plus, see Chapter 5 for more practice questions.

1. **(A)** *Ambrosia* is a noun that means something divinely sweet, fragrant, or delicious.

2. **(C)** *Circulate* is a verb that means to disseminate or distribute.

3. **(B)** When used as a verb, *veto* means to withhold approval (disapprove).

4. **(D)** *Tenacious* is an adjective that means unyielding.

5. **(D)** *Retaliate* is a verb that means repay bad with bad.

6. **(B)** Used as a verb, *recur* means to happen again or repeatedly, especially at regular intervals.

7. **(D)** Used as an adjective, *scrupulous* means extremely careful. It can also mean very honest. It's impossible to tell from the context of this sentence which meaning was implied.

8. **(D)** *Superfluous* is an adjective that means more than is needed.

9. **(C)** *Supersede* is a verb that means to replace. This is also the definition of the verb *supplant.*

10. **(A)** If you got the preceding question right, you should have gotten this one right — unless you were looking for a trap. No tricks. You won't find tricks and traps on the AFQT. Often, the obvious answer is the correct one.

11. **(A)** Used as a verb, *pique* means to anger or irritate.

12. **(C)** *Pious* is an adjective. It means religious or sincerely devout.

13. **(B)** *Impartial* is an adjective that means unbiased.

14. **(B)** *Immense* is an adjective. It means very great in size or quantity.

15. **(B)** *Laudable* is an adjective that means deserving of praise.

16. **(C)** *Originate* is a verb. It means to create or begin something.

17. **(C)** *Pacify* is a verb that means to make peaceful.

18. **(A)** *Ominous* is an adjective that means threatening or foreboding. Scary is close, but not the closest definition.

19. **(B)** *Absence* is a noun that means state of being not present.

20. **(C)** *Abdicate* is a verb that means to give up royal power.

21. **(D)** *Bide* is a verb that means to await.

22. **(A)** *Apparition* is used as a noun. It means a supernatural appearance.

23. **(B)** *Circumnavigate* is a verb that means to sail or go around an obstacle or area.

24. **(B)** *Clumsy* is an adjective that means without skill or grace.

25. **(B)** *Clemency* is a noun that means forgiveness or mercy.

26. **(A)** *Frugal* is an adjective. It means meager or inexpensive.

27. **(C)** Used as an adjective, *generic* means not pertaining to a specific brand or item.

28. **(D)** *Haggard* is an adjective. It means worn or gaunt. You may have chosen (A), but something can be old and still not be haggard (or worn).

29. **(A)** *Improvident* is an adjective that means lacking in foresight or unwary.

30. **(B)** *Isolate* is a verb that means to separate from others of its kind.

31. **(B)** Used as a noun, *manifesto* means a public declaration of one's intentions or motivations.

32. **(A)** *Mediate* can be used as an adjective or a verb. In the example sentence, it's used as a verb. It means to negotiate between parties.

33. **(D)** *Packet* is a noun that means a group or a bundle.

34. **(B)** *Perhaps* is an adverb that means maybe or possibly. Personally, I think this book will definitely help you score well on the AFQT, but that's another topic.

35. **(A)** *Venerate* is a verb that means to cherish reverentially.

Part 3: Paragraph Comprehension

Those ASVAB folks sure don't give you much time to read all those paragraphs, do they? But, with a little practice, anyone can improve his reading speed and comprehension skills. The material in Chapter 6 can be helpful in these endeavors. There are also more practice questions in Chapter 7.

1. **(A)** In the fourth sentence, the author describes Sam's 4.0 grade-point average. A 4.0 GPA is a perfect grade-point average.

2. **(A)** The entire senior class found out about the fundraiser in history class. That's the setting for the story's beginning.

3. **(B)** The last sentence describes Miss Dewey as shrewd. "Miss" implies that she is not married.

4. **(D)** There was no reward for handing out brochures. The reward of a movie pass goes to the student who sells the most wreaths.

5. **(D)** The paragraph states, "the growing population, expanding industry, and increasing agricultural production have created an increasing demand for fresh water." Although B and C may be true, in general, the topics are not mentioned in the passage.

6. **(A)** The primary purpose of the inspection discussed is to ensure the proper management of nuclear weapons, when compared to approved safety, security and reliability standards. The title "Nuclear Security Inspection" best describes this goal.

7. **(C)** The last sentence discusses what happens if a unit is given an unsatisfactory rating.

8. **(D)** The author talks about the importance of avoiding sports and recreational injuries. A, B, and C are subpoints to support the main point.

9. **(D)** The third sentence in the paragraph lists those who should learn how to avoid such injuries.

10. **(B)** As Katie's report was about "Reaganomics," the most likely choice is economics.

11. **(C)** The author makes it obvious that Katie wants to keep her GPA up and is worried about this report. She considers calling her friend Rod for help, which indicates that Katie must think he's pretty smart about her homework topic.

12. **(B)** The author states that Katie's "halcyon" personality was in contrast to Autumn's "frazzled and dizzy" personality. The answer choice that is the best antonym for frazzled and dizzy is *calm*.

13. **(D)** Katie was jealous because she wanted to go on a cruise, but she was excited because it gave her an idea for her report.

14. **(B)** In the second sentence, the author states that in a house full of children one or two of the eldest are respected, but the youngest are made wantons and the middle children are often forgotten.

15. **(A)** The author's belief that the mother's affections are most unequal is stated in the first sentence.

Part 4: Mathematics Knowledge

Many people find the mathematics knowledge subtest to be more difficult than the Arithmetic Reasoning subtest, but doing well on this subtest is just as important. If you missed more than a few answers, or you ran out of time before you finished, you have a date with the books (Chapter 8 is a great place to start). Getting in touch with a math teacher at your high school or a local community college (or at least finding a good basic-algebra textbook) can help. You can also try out the following Dummies books: *Algebra I For Dummies* and *Algebra II For Dummies,* both by Mary Jane Sterling; *Geometry For Dummies,* by Wendy Arnone; *Calculus For Dummies,* by Mark Ryan; and *SAT II Math For Dummies,* by Scott Hatch (all published by Wiley). Chapter 9 also has some additional practice questions.

1. **(B)** $3^3 + (-2)^2 = (3 \times 3 \times 3) + (-2 \times -2) = 27 + 4 = 31$. Multiplying two negative numbers results in a positive number.

2. **(B)** 5! means the factorial of five. It's equivalent to $5 \times 4 \times 3 \times 2 \times 1 = 120$.

3. **(C)** The formula to find out the volume of a cylinder is $\pi r^2 h$. Plug in the known variables: $3.14 \times 4^2 \times 6 = 3.14 \times 16 \times 6 = 50.24 \times 6 = 301.44$. Round down to 301.4.

4. **(D)** The whole-number part of a logarithm is called the *characteristic*. This part of the logarithm shows the position of the decimal point in the associated number. (The decimal part of a logarithm is called the *mantissa,* just in case you were wondering.)

5. **(B)**

$$\frac{3}{4}(68)+\frac{1}{4}x = 70$$

$$51+\frac{x}{4}=70$$

$$\frac{x}{4}=19$$

$$x = 4 \times 19$$

$$x = 76$$

6. **(C)** The sum of the angles for any polygon can be determined by the formula $s = (n-2) \times 180$, where s = the sum of angles and n = the number of sides. A hexagon has six sides. Plug in the known values:

$$s = (6-2) \times 180$$

$$s = 4 \times 180$$

$$s = 720$$

7. **(A)** Plug the known values into the formula, $d^2 = l^2 + w^2$:

$$5^2 = (w+1)^2 + w^2$$

$$25 = (w+1)(w+1) + w^2$$

$$25 = w^2 + 2w + 1 + w^2$$

$$25 = 2w^2 + 2w + 1$$

$$0 = 2w^2 + 2w + 1 - 25$$

$$0 = 2w^2 + 2w - 24$$

$$\frac{1}{2}(0) = \frac{1}{2}\left(2w^2 + 2w - 24\right)$$

$$0 = w^2 + w - 12$$

This is a quadratic equation, which can be factored as:

$$0 = (w-3)(w+4)$$

$$w - 3 = 0 \text{ and } w + 4 = 0$$

$$w = 3 \text{ and } w = -4$$

You can't have a rectangle with a width of –4, so 3 is the only possible answer.

8. **(B)** Remember that brilliant Greek mathematician, Pythagoras, from Chapter 8? He said that if you know the length of any two sides of a triangle, you can find the length of the third side by applying the Pythagorean theorem, $a^2 + b^2 = c^2$. Plug in the known values:

$$5^2 + 6^2 = c^2$$

$$25 + 36 = c^2$$

$$61 = c^2$$

$$c = \sqrt{61}$$

$$c = 7.81$$

Round down do 7.8.

9. **(B)**

$$\frac{4!}{3!} = \frac{4 \times 3 \times 2 \times 1}{3 \times 2 \times 1} = \frac{24}{6} = 4$$

10. **(B)** The problem is asking you to subtract $31\frac{3}{4}$ percent of the value of x from the value of x:

$$x - 31\frac{3}{4}\%(x) = 174.4$$

$$x - 0.3175x = 174.4$$

$$x(1 - 0.3175) = 174.4$$

$$0.6825x = 174.4$$

$$x = \frac{174.4}{0.6825}$$

$$x = 255.53$$

Round this up to 255.5

11. **(D)** A negative exponent just means that the base is on the wrong side of the fraction line, so you need to flip the base to the other side. For example, $x^{-2} = \frac{x^{-2}}{1} = \frac{1^2}{x}$.

$$4^{-2} = \frac{1^2}{4} = \frac{1}{4} \times \frac{1}{4} = \frac{1}{16}$$

12. **(A)** $n = 2$ because $3^2 = 9$. Now that you know the value of n, simply plug it into the equation, $4x - n = 6$:

$$4x - 2 = 6$$

$$4x = 8$$

$$x = \frac{8}{4}$$

$$x = 2$$

13. **(B)** $5x + 7 = 6(x - 2) - 4(2x - 3)$

$$5x + 7 = 6x - 12 - 8x + 12$$

$$5x + 7 = -2x$$

$$7x + 7 = 0$$

$$7x = -7$$

$$x = -1$$

14. **(D)**

$$\left(\frac{3}{4}\right)^3 = \frac{3}{4} \times \frac{3}{4} \times \frac{3}{4} = \frac{3 \times 3 \times 3}{4 \times 4 \times 4} = \frac{27}{64}$$

15. **(D)** To convert scientific notation to regulation notation, move the decimal place to the left (for a negative exponent), the same number of spaces as the exponent (in this case, 4).

16. **(A)** $10,000 = 10 \times 10 \times 10 \times 10 = 10^4$.

17. **(C)** The area of a rectangle can be determined by using the formula, $a = lw$. Plug in the known values:

$$a = 6 \times 8$$

$$a = 48$$

18. **(B)** $(-3)^3 = -3 \times -3 \times -3 = -27$. If the exponent (power) of a negative number base is odd, the result will be a negative number. If the exponent of a negative number base is even, the result will be a positive number.

19. **(A)** You have to figure the area of two shapes: a half-circle and a triangle. The formula to determine the area of a triangle is $A = \frac{1}{2}bh$, where b = the base of the triangle and h = the height of the triangle. The radius of the half-circle is 3 feet, which means the base of the triangle is 6 feet (twice the radius of the circle). Plug in the known values:

$$A = \frac{1}{2}\left(6 \times 4\right)$$

$$A = \frac{1}{2}\left(24\right)$$

$$A = 12$$

The area of the triangle is 12 square feet.

The formula to determine the area of a circle is $A = \pi r^2$, where r = the radius of the circle. But you only want the radius of one-half of the circle, so the formula becomes $A = \frac{1}{2}\pi r^2$. Plug in the known values:

$$A = \frac{1}{2}\pi 3^2$$

$$A = \frac{1}{2}\left(3.14 \times 9\right)$$

$$A = \frac{1}{2} \times 28.26$$

$$A = 14.13 \text{ feet}$$

The area of the half-circle is 14.13 square feet. Add the two areas together: 14.13 + 12 = 26.13. Round this down to 26.1 square feet.

20. **(B)**

$$\frac{x-2}{x^2-6x+8} = \frac{x-2}{\left(x-4\right)\left(x-2\right)} = \frac{1}{x-4}$$

21. **(B)** $-7(4x + 5) - 8 = -7(4x) - (7 \times 5) - 8 = -28x - 35 - 8 = -28x - 43.$

22. **(C)** You have to compute the areas of two shapes: a square and a circle. The area of the shaded portion is the area of the square minus the area of the circle.

The formula to determine the area of a square is $A = s^2$, where s = the length of one side of the square. Plug in the known value:

$$A = 4^2$$

$$A = 4 \times 4 = 16$$

The area of the square is 16 square feet.

To determine the area of the circle, use the formula, $A = \pi r^2$. Plug in the known values:

$$A = 3.14 \times 1$$

$$A = 3.14$$

Subtract the area of the circle from the area of the square: 16 − 3.14 = 12.86. Round this up to 12.9 square feet.

23. **(D)** The diameter of a circle is twice its radius. This circle has a radius of 2 inches, so its diameter is 4 inches.

24. **(C)** To determine the circumference of a circle, use the formula, $c = \pi d$. Plug in the known values: $c = 3.14 \times 4 = 12.56$. Round this up to 12.6 inches.

25. **(A)** If $4x$ is greater than 7, that means 7 is less than $4x$.

Chapter 18

Practice Exam 4

· ·

Congratulations! You made it to the final AFQT practice exam. By now you should be ready to tackle the actual Armed Services Vocational Aptitude Battery (ASVAB) and impress all those military recruiters when you ace the four subtests that make up the AFQT. If you still want some more practice after this exam, or you want to study for the other ASVAB subtests as well, might I humbly suggest *ASVAB For Dummies* (Wiley)?

The four sections that follow represent the four subtests of the ASVAB that make up your all-important AFQT score. This is the score that determines whether you're qualified to join the military branch of your choice (see Chapter 2). The four subtests are: Arithmetic Reasoning, Word Knowledge, Paragraph Comprehension, and Mathematics Knowledge.

Use the answer key and explanations in Chapter 19 to score the following sections. *Remember:* On the actual ASVAB, harder questions are worth more points than easier questions when you determine your AFQT score.

Take the final practice exam a day or two before the ASVAB to make sure you're ready, and to boost your confidence. If you don't score well, you may wish want to consider asking your recruiter to reschedule your ASVAB test for a later date, to give you more time to study.

Ready to get started? Okay, hold your No. 2 pencil in the air. (Not really — your friends might start talking about you). Ready, set, go!

Practice Exam 4 Answer Sheet

Part 1: Arithmetic Reasoning

1. A B C D   8. A B C D   15. A B C D   22. A B C D   29. A B C D
2. A B C D   9. A B C D   16. A B C D   23. A B C D   30. A B C D
3. A B C D   10. A B C D   17. A B C D   24. A B C D
4. A B C D   11. A B C D   18. A B C D   25. A B C D
5. A B C D   12. A B C D   19. A B C D   26. A B C
6. A B C D   13. A B C D   20. A B C D   27. A B C D
7. A B C D   14. A B C D   21. A B C D   28. A B C D

Part 2: Word Knowledge

1. A B C D   8. A B C D   15. A B C D   22. A B C D   29. A B C D
2. A B C D   9. A B C D   16. A B C D   23. A B C D   30. A B C D
3. A B C D   10. A B C D   17. A B C D   24. A B C D   31. A B C D
4. A B C D   11. A B C D   18. A B C D   25. A B C D   32. A B C D
5. A B C D   12. A B C D   19. A B C D   26. A B C D   33. A B C D
6. A B C D   13. A B C D   20. A B C D   27. A B C D   34. A B C D
7. A B C D   14. A B C D   21. A B C D   28. A B C D   35. A B C D

Part 3: Paragraph Comprehension

1. Ⓐ Ⓑ Ⓒ Ⓓ   8. Ⓐ Ⓑ Ⓒ Ⓓ   15. Ⓐ Ⓑ Ⓒ Ⓓ
2. Ⓐ Ⓑ Ⓒ Ⓓ   9. Ⓐ Ⓑ Ⓒ Ⓓ
3. Ⓐ Ⓑ Ⓒ Ⓓ   10. Ⓐ Ⓑ Ⓒ Ⓓ
4. Ⓐ Ⓑ Ⓒ Ⓓ   11. Ⓐ Ⓑ Ⓒ Ⓓ
5. Ⓐ Ⓑ Ⓒ Ⓓ   12. Ⓐ Ⓑ Ⓒ Ⓓ
6. Ⓐ Ⓑ Ⓒ Ⓓ   13. Ⓐ Ⓑ Ⓒ Ⓓ
7. Ⓐ Ⓑ Ⓒ Ⓓ   14. Ⓐ Ⓑ Ⓒ Ⓓ

Part 4: Mathematics Knowledge

1. Ⓐ Ⓑ Ⓒ Ⓓ   8. Ⓐ Ⓑ Ⓒ Ⓓ   15. Ⓐ Ⓑ Ⓒ Ⓓ   22. Ⓐ Ⓑ Ⓒ Ⓓ
2. Ⓐ Ⓑ Ⓒ Ⓓ   9. Ⓐ Ⓑ Ⓒ Ⓓ   16. Ⓐ Ⓑ Ⓒ Ⓓ   23. Ⓐ Ⓑ Ⓒ Ⓓ
3. Ⓐ Ⓑ Ⓒ Ⓓ   10. Ⓐ Ⓑ Ⓒ Ⓓ   17. Ⓐ Ⓑ Ⓒ Ⓓ   24. Ⓐ Ⓑ Ⓒ Ⓓ
4. Ⓐ Ⓑ Ⓒ Ⓓ   11. Ⓐ Ⓑ Ⓒ Ⓓ   18. Ⓐ Ⓑ Ⓒ Ⓓ   25. Ⓐ Ⓑ Ⓒ Ⓓ
5. Ⓐ Ⓑ Ⓒ Ⓓ   12. Ⓐ Ⓑ Ⓒ Ⓓ   19. Ⓐ Ⓑ Ⓒ Ⓓ
6. Ⓐ Ⓑ Ⓒ Ⓓ   13. Ⓐ Ⓑ Ⓒ Ⓓ   20. Ⓐ Ⓑ Ⓒ Ⓓ
7. Ⓐ Ⓑ Ⓒ Ⓓ   14. Ⓐ Ⓑ Ⓒ Ⓓ   21. Ⓐ Ⓑ Ⓒ Ⓓ

Part 1: Arithmetic Reasoning

Time: 36 minutes

30 questions

The following questions are designed to measure your ability to solve math word problems. Each question is followed by four possible answers. Decide which answer is correct and then mark the corresponding space on your answer sheet. Use your scratch paper for any figuring you want to do.

You may not use a calculator.

1. Kirsten is standing in the middle of a circular track with a diameter of 150 feet. How far away is Kirsten from the runners on the track?

   (A) 150 feet

   (B) 300 feet

   (C) 75 feet

   (D) 25 feet

2. A famous breakfast cereal has a content of 0.125 percent vitamin C. The recommended daily allowance of vitamin C is 18 mg. How many grams of cereal would a person have to eat to get 100 percent of his daily allowance of vitamin C?

   (A) 10.3

   (B) 11.8

   (C) 14.4

   (D) 15.1

3. Allison bought a pair of jeans for $53, a blouse for $39.95, and two pair of stockings for $9.95 each. Sales tax in her state is 7 percent. How much did Allison spend on her shopping trip?

   (A) $112.85

   (B) $110.94

   (C) $110.53

   (D) $120.75

4. Jackie and Kim took identical trips in their cars. They both drove 300 miles, and Jackie averaged 10 mph faster than Kim. If took Jackie $4\frac{1}{2}$ hours to make the trip, what was Kim's speed?

   (A) 55.4 mph

   (B) 56.7 mph

   (C) 66.7 mph

   (D) 66.4 mph

Go on to next page

5. Manny had a coupon for 10 percent off one oil change. The regular oil-change price is $21.95, including parts and labor. If Manny brought his car and his mom's car in for oil changes, how much did he spend?

   (A) $41.70

   (B) $53.92

   (C) $55.23

   (D) $57.11

7. Train A is headed north at 65 mph. Train B is also heading north on an adjacent track at 72 mph. At the end of four hours, how much farther will Train B have traveled than Train A?

   (A) 20 miles

   (B) 22 miles

   (C) 26 miles

   (D) 28 miles

6. A carpenter needs seven pieces of wood, each 3 feet 6 inches long. If the boards are only sold in 8-foot lengths, how many boards will she have to buy?

   (A) 4 boards

   (B) 3 boards

   (C) 5 boards

   (D) 8 boards

8. You decide to build a bookshelf for your sister's birthday, because she has 225 books, all scattered around her room. If four books will fit on a 1-foot length of bookshelf, how many total feet of shelving space should the new bookshelf include, at a minimum?

   (A) 50.35 feet

   (B) 56.25 feet

   (C) 58.36 feet

   (D) 59. 75 feet

Go on to next page

9. Merle needs 65 gallons of paint to paint his house. He would like to purchase all the paint he needs for the least amount of money possible. Which of the following should he buy?

(A) two 25-gallon buckets at $550 each

(B) eleven 5-gallon buckets at $108 each

(C) six 10-gallon buckets at $215 each

(D) None of the above

10. A truck driver is hauling a load from Reno to Kansas City. The distance between the two cities is 1,650 miles. The law says that truckers must sleep eight hours for each ten hours of driving. If the trucker can average 50 miles per hour (and obeys the law), how many hours will it take him to deliver his load?

(A) 57 hours

(B) 45 hours

(C) 33 hours

(D) 24 hours

11. When making a budget, Dana discovered that she had spent $1,565.16 for groceries during the year. What was Dana's average monthly grocery expense?

(A) $101.93

(B) $125.17

(C) $130.43

(D) $149.19

12. Becky is excited because she qualifies for a 0 percent five-year loan for a new car through her local dealership. She buys a new car for $1,500 down, and payments of $379 per month for five years. How much did Becky spend on the new car?

(A) $24,240

(B) $28,190

(C) $30,158

(D) $31,222

Go on to next page

13. Daytona Beach averaged 7.5 inches of rain each month for the months of April, May, and June. How much rain in total did Daytona Beach receive during these three months?

   (A) 18.1 inches

   (B) 18.2 inches

   (C) 20.3 inches

   (D) 22.5 inches

14. A carpenter earns $12.30 an hour for a 40-hour week. His overtime pay is $1\frac{1}{2}$ times his base pay. His federal tax withholdings is 23 percent. He also has $150 per week deducted for child support. If he puts in a 46-hour week, how much weekly pay will he receive?

   (A) $602.70

   (B) $314.08

   (C) $413.90

   (D) $273.43

15. Mark is in the Air Force and stationed in Germany. The military shipped his Ford Mustang over for him, and he's driving it on the autobahn (the German interstate). The speed limit in Germany is stated in kilometers per hour, but Mark's speedometer is calibrated in miles per hour. Mark knows that a kilometer is about $\frac{5}{8}$ of a mile. If the speed limit on the autobahn is 120 kmph, what should Mark's speedometer read, if he is traveling the speed limit?

   (A) 70 mph

   (B) 65 mph

   (C) 75 mph

   (D) 80 mph

16. A man bought a total of 40 chickens and ducks. He paid $2 per chicken, and $1 per duck. He paid $44 in all. How many chickens did the man buy?

   (A) 2

   (B) 4

   (C) 6

   (D) 8

Go on to next page

17. Davy has three times as many Nintendo games as Alex. If he gives Alex six games, he will then have twice as many as Alex has. How many Nintendo games did Alex start with?

    (A) 14
    (B) 16
    (C) 18
    (D) 20

18. Milk that has 5 percent butterfat is mixed with milk that has 2 percent butterfat. How much of the 5 percent butterfat milk will be needed to produce 60 gallons of milk that has 3 percent butterfat?

    (A) 14 gallons
    (B) 16 gallons
    (C) 18 gallons
    (D) 20 gallons

19. A roadside stand in Georgia sells boiled peanuts for $2.49 per bag, and roasted peanuts for $3.29 per bag. If you want to buy three bags of boiled peanuts and four bags of roasted peanuts, how much will you spend?

    (A) $12.86
    (B) $16.94
    (C) $20.63
    (D) $24.80

20. A teacher deposited $3,000 in a retirement fund. If she didn't add any more money to the fund, which earns an annual interest rate of 6 percent, how much money would she have in 1 year?

    (A) $3,180
    (B) $3,223
    (C) $3,225
    (D) $3,321

Go on to next page

21. Paula is taking the Arithmetic Reasoning subtest. She wants to get at least 25 of the questions right in order to score well on the AFQT. What percent of the questions does she need to answer correctly?

    (A) 83 percent

    (B) 82 percent

    (C) 81 percent

    (D) 80 percent

22. Janet left Jacksonville, Florida (eastern time), on a train to visit her grandfather in New Orleans, Louisiana (central time), at 6 a.m. If the trip took 12 hours, what time (New Orleans time) did she arrive?

    (A) 5 p.m.

    (B) 6 p.m.

    (C) 7 p.m.

    (D) 8 p.m.

23. It takes Simon 30 minutes to walk eight city blocks. How long would it take him to walk six city blocks?

    (A) 19.3 minutes

    (B) 22.5 minutes

    (C) 23 minutes

    (D) 26 minutes

24. Mick bought five cases of ramen noodles on sale for $3.75 a case. The regular price is $5.20 a case. How much money did Mick save?

    (A) $6.50

    (B) $6.75

    (C) $7.00

    (D) $7.25

Go on to next page

25. David has 20 pies. He gives $\frac{1}{4}$ of his pies to his son, $\frac{1}{3}$ of his pies to his brother, and $\frac{1}{6}$ of his pies to his friend. How many pies does he have left?

    (A) 5

    (B) 0

    (C) 4

    (D) 6

26. Mark and Mickey are heading for the same place. Mark is 120 miles away and traveling at an average speed of 50 mph. Mickey is 135 miles away and traveling at an average speed of 45 mph. Who will arrive first?

    (A) Mark

    (B) Mickey

    (C) Both will arrive at the same time

27. Penelope delivers pizzas after school. She makes $8.35 per hour, plus $1.50 for each delivery. If her boss gives her a 15 percent per hour raise, how much will she make per hour?

    (A) $8.90

    (B) $9.60

    (C) $11.10

    (D) $11.80

28. A business cleans area rugs for 75¢ per square foot. How much would it cost to clean an area rug that measures 8 by 10 feet?

    (A) $55

    (B) $75

    (C) $60

    (D) $65

Go on to next page

29. Joy is a waitress in a popular eatery. She makes $4.90 per hour, plus tips. If she had sales of $623 one night, and made $127 in tips, what was her average percentage of tips during the night?

(A) 15 percent

(B) 18 percent

(C) 20 percent

(D) 22 percent

30. If four bricks of equal length measure 44 inches when placed end-to-end, how long is each brick?

(A) 10 inches

(B) 11 inches

(C) 12 inches

(D) 13 inches

STOP DO NOT TURN THE PAGE UNTIL TOLD TO DO SO.
DO NOT RETURN TO A PREVIOUS TEST.

Part 2: Word Knowledge

Time: 11 minutes

35 questions

The Word Knowledge subtest measures how well you've mastered the English language in terms of vocabulary. Sometimes the words are used in a sentence; other times they aren't. After the question, you see four possible answer choices. Select the choice that best defines the underlined word, and then mark the corresponding space on your answer sheet.

1. The tour included a stop at the Johnson Abyss.

    (A) house

    (B) building

    (C) hole

    (D) park

2. Try as he might, he wasn't able to stifle his sneezes.

    (A) suppress

    (B) record

    (C) ignore

    (D) suffocate

3. Ben planned to move the unwieldy piano up the stars.

    (A) loud

    (B) heavy

    (C) awkward

    (D) broken

4. We'll put the wee bird back into the nest.

    (A) excited

    (B) dead

    (C) sleeping

    (D) tiny

5. According to the prophecy, you'll have a happy life.

    (A) story

    (B) prediction

    (C) tradition

    (D) wise man

6. Purloin most nearly means:

    (A) steal

    (B) borrow

    (C) old

    (D) worn

7. Refract most nearly means:

    (A) eye

    (B) bend

    (C) glasses

    (D) imprison

8. Paul and Gary planned to take the old skiff on their camping trip.

    (A) tent

    (B) truck

    (C) boat

    (D) fishing pole

9. Speculate most nearly means:

    (A) preliminary

    (B) jump

    (C) train

    (D) think

10. Subjugate most nearly means:

    (A) fight

    (B) play

    (C) conquer

    (D) king or queen

Go on to next page

11. His patience was taxed to the <u>utmost</u>.
   (A) nearest
   (B) anticlimax
   (C) moderate
   (D) maximum

12. <u>Vertigo</u> most nearly means:
   (A) upright
   (B) dizzy
   (C) horizontal
   (D) excited

13. <u>Writhe</u> most nearly means:
   (A) shrink
   (B) wrinkle
   (C) twist
   (D) fold

14. Penny recited the <u>sonnet</u> with such passion, we almost cried.
   (A) poem
   (B) story
   (C) bible verse
   (D) speech

15. The pot was <u>teeming</u> with delicious home-made soup.
   (A) fragrant
   (B) boiling
   (C) filled
   (D) heavy

16. <u>Technique</u> most nearly means:
   (A) build
   (B) feather
   (C) method
   (D) forever

17. <u>Bequeath</u> most nearly means:
   (A) give
   (B) bury
   (C) grave
   (D) funeral

18. We were told not to worry, as timidity was a <u>characteristic</u> of the animals on display.
   (A) abnormal
   (B) unnatural
   (C) cursory
   (D) feature

19. <u>Deceit</u> most nearly means:
   (A) lie
   (B) truth
   (C) perplexing
   (D) confuse

20. <u>Conveyance</u> most nearly means:
   (A) scenery
   (B) transport
   (C) playful
   (D) management

21. He gave us the entire speech again, in its <u>entirety</u>.
   (A) brevity
   (B) loudness
   (C) completeness
   (D) None of the above

22. We drove all over town, but Tammy continued to <u>elude</u> us.
   (A) find
   (B) evade
   (C) call
   (D) follow

23. <u>Stiletto</u> most nearly means:
   (A) violin
   (B) razor blade
   (C) knife
   (D) theatrical performance

24. <u>Protagonist</u> most nearly means:
   (A) villain
   (B) character
   (C) leader
   (D) superficial

Go on to next page

25. Private Jones was sent back for more <u>ord-nance</u>.

    (A) ammunition

    (B) food

    (C) water

    (D) reinforcements

26. The committee voted to <u>oust</u> Pickard at sunset.

    (A) execute

    (B) reward

    (C) honor

    (D) kick out

27. <u>Mutilate</u> most nearly means:

    (A) repair

    (B) destroy

    (C) disfigure

    (D) transfer

28. <u>Loath</u> most nearly means:

    (A) unwilling

    (B) hate

    (C) like

    (D) gravel

29. <u>Litigious</u> most nearly means:

    (A) likeable

    (B) quarrelsome

    (C) complaisant

    (D) court

30. <u>Reciprocity</u> most nearly means:

    (A) compensation

    (B) fine

    (C) damage

    (D) punishment

31. We attempted to <u>reassure</u> Nemo about the facts of the case.

    (A) convince

    (B) discourage

    (C) tell

    (D) lie to

32. He tried to <u>tarnish</u> my reputation, but I wouldn't let him.

    (A) enhance

    (B) corrupt

    (C) embellish

    (D) fix

33. Paula promised me a <u>tremendous</u> birthday present.

    (A) expensive

    (B) cheap

    (C) amazing

    (D) pretty

34. Last week's sermon was about the <u>sanctity</u> of the church.

    (A) privacy

    (B) holiness

    (C) teachings

    (D) apathy

35. <u>Constrict</u> most nearly means:

    (A) expand

    (B) release

    (C) unblock

    (D) inhibit

STOP DO NOT TURN THE PAGE UNTIL TOLD TO DO SO.
DO NOT RETURN TO A PREVIOUS TEST.

Part 3: Paragraph Comprehension

Time: 13 minutes

15 questions

How are your reading skills? That's what the questions on the Paragraph Comprehension subtest are designed to measure. You'll be presented with a paragraph of information followed by one to four questions. Read the paragraph and select the choice that best completes the statement or answers the question. Mark the corresponding choice on your answer sheet.

Trust is essential in forming any good relationship. Teamwork requires good relationships with a high degree of trust. Team members must share mutual confidence in the integrity and ability of teammates. They also need to feel comfortable enough to take risks, think outside the box, and share their thoughts and ideas without fear of being shut down or discounted. Freedom to communicate openly, honestly, and directly with people within the group is the hallmark of a team that has trust. Dr. Suzanne Zoglio, an organizational consultant and founder of the Institute for Planning and Development, states in her book entitled *Teams at Work,* "Nothing reduces trust in a group faster than members saying one thing within the group and something else outside the group. When members are assertive enough to say what they need to say directly to the appropriate people and to refrain from talking behind each other's backs, trust is enhanced."

1. According to Dr. Zoglio, the fastest way to destroy trust in a group is to:

   (A) try to control the group

   (B) steal from your co-workers

   (C) talk behind other people's backs

   (D) complain about others to the boss

The Freedom of Information Act (FOIA) provides access to federal agency records (or parts of these records) except those protected from release by nine specific exemptions. FOIA requests are written requests that cite or imply the FOIA. The law establishes rigid time limits for replying to requesters and permits assessing fees in certain instances. The FOIA imposes mandatory time limits of 20 workdays for advising requesters of releasability determinations for requested records. The law permits an additional ten-workday extension in unusual circumstances specifically outlined in the FOIA.

2. The FOIA applies to:

   (A) all records

   (B) state and federal records

   (C) federal records only

   (D) state records only

3. What is the <u>maximum</u> time the government has to respond to FOIA requests?

   (A) 20 workdays

   (B) 10 workdays

   (C) 30 workdays

   (D) 30 calendar days

4. FOIA requests:

   (A) are always free

   (B) may require a fee in some cases

   (C) always require a fee

   (D) cost $1.25 per page.

Go on to next page

"When a thing is old, broken, and useless we throw it on the dust-heap, but when it is sufficiently old, sufficiently broken, and sufficiently useless we give money for it, put it into a museum, and read papers over it, which people come long distances to hear. By-and-by, when the whirligig of time has brought on another revenge, the museum itself becomes a dust-heap, and remains so till after long ages it is rediscovered, and valued as belonging to a neo-rubbish age—containing, perhaps, traces of a still older paleo-rubbish civilization. So when people are old, indigent, and in all respects incapable, we hold them in greater and greater contempt as their poverty and impotence increase, till they reach the pitch when they are actually at the point to die, whereon they become sublime. Then we place every resource our hospitals can command at their disposal, and show no stint in our consideration for them." —Samuel Butler

5. The author believes:

    (A) the world needs more museums

    (B) the world needs more hospitals

    (C) the world makes no sense

    (D) the world treats old people much like it treats old things

The winds of spring were blowing briskly through Becky's hair. This was her favorite time of year, the browns and tan colors of winter had turned into the deep green of spring. Her recruiter gave her a sympathetic smile as they got out of the car and walked to the three-story stone building on the corner. Becky was visiting the Military Entrance Processing Station (MEPS) in order to take her ASVAB test. Even though Sergeant Evans assured her that she would do fine, she couldn't help but be a little worried. This test would decide her future. The AFQT portion of the test would decide whether she could even get in the military, and the other portions of the test would determine what jobs she would qualify for. Becky tried to dispel her pessimism by imagining how she would tell her friends and family the great news that she had aced the test. They would all yell and scream and tell her how happy they were for her. Becky wished she felt more energetic for this test. She felt tired from the weeks of studying *ASVAB For Dummies* and *ASVAB AFQT For Dummies*. She hoped all that studying would help. She was glad it was a multiple-choice test.

6. From the information in the paragraph, it's obvious that Becky is:

    (A) hungry

    (B) planning to join the military

    (C) happy

    (D) highly intelligent

7. Who is Sergeant Evans?

    (A) Becky's recruiter

    (B) Becky's father

    (C) Becky's mother

    (D) Becky's brother

8. According to the passage, how long did Becky study for the ASVAB?

    (A) over a year

    (B) weeks

    (C) two days

    (D) a week

Domestic violence involves unjustified physical aggression and verbal assaults within a family unit. Years ago, people considered domestic violence to be a private matter, and nobody wanted to get involved in stopping it. Today, spouse and child abuse is against the law in all 50 states.

9. According to the passage, domestic violence is:

    (A) a crime

    (B) a private matter

    (C) a situation that can only be resolved by the courts

    (D) always unjustified

10. Which of the following would *not* be considered domestic violence?

    (A) calling your wife a bad name

    (B) slapping your child in the face

    (C) hitting your spouse

    (D) punching your teacher

Go on to next page

Many people confuse Memorial Day and Veterans Day. Memorial Day is a day for remembering and honoring military personnel who died in the service of their country, particularly those who died in battle or as a result of wounds sustained in battle. While those who died are also remembered on Veterans Day, Veterans Day is the day set aside to thank and honor *all* those who served honorably in the military — in wartime or peacetime.

11. The primary purpose of the passage is to:

    (A) honor veterans

    (B) explain the differences between two holidays

    (C) describe veteran ceremonies

    (D) honor the American flag

The Institute of Medicine has released a report urging the Department of Defense (DOD) to announce a mandatory date when smoking will no longer be allowed in the military. The report also urges DOD officials to immediately cease selling tobacco products on military installations. The DOD has long been engaged in a project to reduce smoking in the military. In fact, 51 percent of military personnel smoked in 1980, and that number decreased to less than 30 percent by 1998. However, from 1998 to 2005 (the latest year in which the DOD conducted a study), the rate crept up again to more than 32 percent. Among the services (as of 2005), 32 percent of soldiers, 32.4 percent of sailors, 23.3 percent of Air Force personnel, and 36.3 percent of marines reported that they smoked.

12. Which service has the most smokers?

    (A) Army

    (B) Navy

    (C) Air Force

    (D) Marine Corps

13. The Institute of Medicine wants to:

    (A) reduce smoking rates in the military

    (B) eliminate smoking in the military

    (C) force Congress to pass a law barring smoking in the military

    (D) ban smoking in military hospitals

14. When is the last time the Department of Defense conducted a smoking survey?

    (A) 1998

    (B) 2001

    (C) 2005

    (D) 2008

Shylinn and Kiley were inseparable, but Shylinn was the leader of the two. They were not biological sisters, but they shared everything from middle school classes to CDs. Shylinn was tall, blond, and very pretty. Additionally, her self-assurance made her stand out in a crowd. Kiley had dark hair and was quiet and rather thoughtful. Another thing the friends shared, but not happily, was a crush on Billy. Billy was in their sixth-grade class and seemed to enchant both girls. Shylinn always knew just what to say when she saw him, but Kiley just stood there, silently blushing.

15. Which of the girls had a crush on Billy?

    (A) Shylinn

    (B) Kiley

    (C) Both girls

    (D) Neither girl

STOP DO NOT TURN THE PAGE UNTIL TOLD TO DO SO. DO NOT RETURN TO A PREVIOUS TEST.

Part 4: Mathematics Knowledge

Time: 13 minutes

15 questions

The Mathematics Knowledge subtest measures your ability to perform basic math problems, identify and work with geometrical shapes, and state basic math rules. You have less than a minute per question, so try not to waste time.

You can't use a calculator on this subtest , so you'll want to have that scratch pad handy.

1. If the sum of two angles equal 90 degrees, what are they called?

    (A) right angles

    (B) complementary angles

    (C) obtuse angles

    (D) parallel angles

2. Round 10,335.48787 to the nearest whole number.

    (A) 10,335

    (B) 10,336

    (C) 10,334

    (D) None of the above

3. The sum of the measures of the angles of the shape below is:

    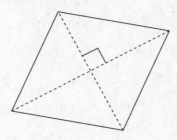

    (A) 90 degrees

    (B) 45 degrees

    (C) 180 degrees

    (D) 360 degrees

4. In an equilateral triangle, if two sides have the sum of 50 inches, what is the length of the third side?

    (A) 30 inches

    (B) 25 inches

    (C) 50 inches

    (D) 55 inches

Go on to next page

5. What is the volume of an aquarium that measures 18 inches long, by 6 inches wide, by 11 inches high?

(A) 1,100 square inches

(B) 1,188 cubic inches

(C) 1,233 square inches

(D) 1,238 cubic inches

6. What is the circumference of a circle that has a radius of 5 feet?

(A) 3.39 feet

(B) 33.9 feet

(C) 3.14 feet

(D) 31.4 feet

7. What is the perimeter of the right triangle below?

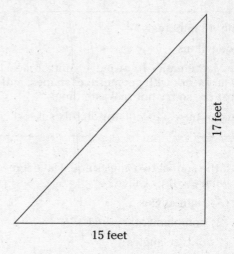

15 feet

17 feet

(A) 48.3 feet

(B) 54.7 feet

(C) 61.1 feet

(D) 65.3 feet

8. If $2 + x \geq 8$, what is the value of x?

(A) greater than or equal to 6

(B) less than or equal to 6

(C) 6

(D) 4

Go on to next page

9. Which of the following fractions is the largest?

    (A) $\frac{2}{5}$

    (B) $\frac{3}{8}$

    (C) $\frac{7}{10}$

    (D) $\frac{13}{16}$

11. $x^4 \times x^5 \times x^{-3} =$

    (A) x^6

    (B) x^{12}

    (C) x

    (D) x^{23}

10. $\sqrt{25} \times \sqrt{64} =$

    (A) 35

    (B) 40

    (C) 45

    (D) 50

12. $(y^2 y^3)^6 =$

    (A) $2y^2$

    (B) $2y^{30}$

    (C) y^2

    (D) y^{30}

Go on to next page

13. If $(5 + 3)(6 \div 2)(8 - 1) = (3 + 7)x$, then $x =$
    (A) 10.3
    (B) 14
    (C) 16.8
    (D) 17.4

15. $\dfrac{900 \times 3}{2} =$
    (A) 920
    (B) 960
    (C) 1,240
    (D) 1,350

14. If $x = 3$, then $x^3 \times x =$
    (A) 73
    (B) 81
    (C) 35
    (D) 38

16. Seven horses are running a race. How many different ways could the horses finish the race?
    (A) 54
    (B) 150,400
    (C) 5,040
    (D) 50,400

Go on to next page

17. $(7^2)^2 =$
    (A) 1,953
    (B) 1,593
    (C) 2,041
    (D) 2,401

18. $(x + 4)(x + 2) =$
    (A) $x^2 + 6x + 6$
    (B) $x^2 + 8x + 8$
    (C) $x^2 + 8x + 6$
    (D) $x^2 + 6x + 8$

19. 7 yards + 14 feet =
    (A) 30 feet
    (B) 35 feet
    (C) 38 feet
    (D) 40 feet

20. What is 14 percent of 42?
    (A) 6.2
    (B) 4.8
    (C) 5.9
    (D) 6.3

Go on to next page

21. What is the mean of the numbers 10, 28, 50, 71, and 91?

    (A) 28

    (B) 50

    (C) 55

    (D) 57

23. What is the sum of the angles of the shape below?

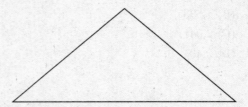

    (A) 90 degrees

    (B) 45 degrees

    (C) 180 degrees

    (D) 360 degrees

22. $\dfrac{-14}{7} =$

    (A) –2

    (B) 2

    (C) Either (A) or (B)

    (D) –7

24. 72 is what percent of 108?

    (A) 34 percent

    (B) 53 percent

    (C) 66.6 percent

    (D) 71.3 percent

Go on to next page

25. Solve for *b*: 3*b* = 3
    (A) 1
    (B) 2
    (C) 4
    (D) 5

STOP DO NOT TURN THE PAGE UNTIL TOLD TO DO SO.
DO NOT RETURN TO A PREVIOUS TEST.

Chapter 19

Practice Exam 4:
Answers and Explanations

. . . .

Are you ready to take the actual ASVAB yet and max out the AFQT score? I sure hope so. I hope you're feeling confident as well. If you still don't feel ready, you may want to look over the practice exams again, until you're comfortable with the types of questions that will be presented on the real test. You may also want to consider reading *ASVAB For Dummies* for another full-length AFQT practice exam, as well as three full-length ASVAB practice tests.

The answer keys in the following sections tell you how well you did on the final AFQT practice exam. *Remember:* Don't be too concerned about the percent right or wrong. On the actual test, harder questions are worth more points than easier questions when computing your AFQT score, so it's entirely possible to miss a few questions and still max out your AFQT score.

Part 1: Arithmetic Reasoning

How'd you do on this subtest? If you don't feel so good about the results, you may want to postpone taking the real ASVAB until you've gotten some more study time under your belt, and perhaps taken a math course or two at your neighborhood community college. You may also want to take another look at Chapters 8 and 10.

Other great resources to improve your math skills are *Math Word Problems For Dummies, Algebra I For Dummies,* and *Algebra II For Dummies,* all by Mary Jane Sterling; *Geometry For Dummies,* 2nd Edition, and *Calculus For Dummies,* both by Mark Ryan; and *SAT II Math For Dummies,* by Scott Hatch, JD, and Lisa Zimmer Hatch, MA — all published by Wiley.

1. **(C)** Kirsten is standing in the middle of a circular track, which means the distance between her and the outside of the circle is the radius. The radius of a circle equals half of the diameter, so Kirsten is 75 feet away from the runners on the track.

2. **(C)** If the foodstuff is 0.125 percent vitamin C, then there are 0.125 grams of vitamin C for every 100 grams of the foodstuff. This follows from the definition of percent (percent means part of 100). That means there are 0.00125 grams of vitamin C in every gram of the cereal.

   A milligram (mg) is $\frac{1}{1,000}$ of a gram, so 0.00125 grams is equivalent to $1,000 \times 0.00125 = 1.25$ mg. In other words, for each gram of cereal one eats, he is getting 1.25 mg of vitamin C.

   The goal is 18 mg of vitamin C. $\frac{18 \text{ mg}}{1.25 \text{ mg}} = 14.4$ grams of cereal.

3. **(D)** First add the cost of the clothes: $53.00 + $39.95 + $9.95 + $9.95 = $112.85.

   Allison's state has a sales tax of 7 percent, and 7 percent of $112.85 is $112.85 \times 0.07 = $7.899. Round this up to $7.90, and add it to the total shopping bill: $112.85 + $7.90 = $120.75.

4. **(B)** The distance formula is $d = rt$. This can also be expressed as $r = \frac{d}{t}$.

Let Jackie's rate $= r$. That means Kim's rate of speed is $r - 10$.

Compute Jackie's rate of travel:

$$r = \frac{d}{t}$$
$$r = \frac{300}{4.5}$$
$$r = 66.7$$

Jackie traveled at an average speed of 66.7 mph. That means Kim's rate of speed was 66.7 − 10 = 56.7 mph.

5. **(A)** Manny's coupon was only good for 10 percent off one oil change. Therefore, Manny paid full price for one oil change, and the discounted rate for the second oil change. Set up your equation as follows:

$21.95 + ($21.95 − [$21.95 × 0.10]) =

$21.95 + ($21.95 − $2.20) =

$21.95 + $19.75 = $41.70

Note that $21.95 × 0.10 = $2.195, but I rounded that up to $2.20.

6. **(A)** Each 8-foot length of board will provide two pieces of wood, 3 feet by 6 inches long, with 1 foot of board left over for scrap (2 × 3 feet, 6 inches = 7 feet). Thus, he will need $\frac{7}{2} = 3.5$ individual boards. Because the carpenter can only buy boards in 8-foot lengths, she will need to purchase four boards.

7. **(D)** The distance formula is $d = rt$. Plug in the known values:

Train A: $d = 65 \times 4 = 260$ miles.

Train B: $d = 72 \times 4 = 288$ miles. Train B traveled 288 − 260 = 28 miles farther than Train A.

8. **(B)** Divide the number of books by 4 to determine how many feet of shelving space will be required: $\frac{225}{4} = 56.25$. Personally, I would build it even bigger. Anyone who owns 225 books is going to buy some more, sooner or later.

9. **(D)** Hopefully, you got this one at a glance. None of the options would provide the amount of paint required (65 gallons).

10. **(A)** The distance formula is $d = rt$. This can also be expressed as $t = \frac{d}{r}$. Plug in the known values:

$$t = \frac{1,650}{50} = 33 \text{ hours}$$

The trucker will be driving a total of 33 hours, but must sleep eight hours for each ten hours of driving. That means the trucker must sleep three times during the trip ($\frac{33}{10} = 3.3$). That equates to $3 \times 8 = 24$ hours of sleep. Add this to the total driving time, and you see it will take the trucker 33 + 24 = 57 hours to deliver his load.

11. **(C)** Divide the total yearly expense by the number of months in a year: $1,565.16 ÷ 12 = $130.43.

12. **(A)** Becky must pay $379 per month for $5 \times 12 = 60$ months. Therefore, she will make a total of $379 × 60 = $22,740 in monthly payments. Add this to the $1,500 she made as a down payment, and you see that Becky paid $24,240 for her new car ($22,740 + $1,500 = $24,240).

13. **(D)** Multiply the average rainfall for each month by the total number of months: 7.5 × 3 = 22.5.

14. **(B)** The carpenter's base pay is $12.30 an hour and his overtime pay is $12.30 × 1.5 = $18.45 per hour. The carpenter earned $12.30 × 40 = $492.00 in base pay, and $18.45 × 6 = $110.70 in overtime pay, for a total of $110.70 + $492.00 = $602.70 in weekly pay.

His federal tax deduction is $602.70 × 0.23 = $138.62, and he has deducted $150 in child support for total deductions of $138.62 + $150 = $288.62.

Subtract his total deductions from his weekly earned pay, and you get $602.70 − $288.62 = $314.08.

15. **(C)** A kilometer is $\frac{5}{8}$ of a mile, so multiply $120 \times \frac{5}{8}$, or $\frac{120}{1} \times \frac{5}{8} = \frac{600}{8} = 75$. Mark's speedometer should read 75 mph.

16. **(B)** You solve this problem by using two separate equations. Let c = the number of chickens, and d = the number of ducks.

You know the total number of chickens and ducks together is 40. Mathematically, you express this as $c + d = 40$.

You also know that the cost per chicken is $2, the cost per duck is $1, and the total cost is $44. That translates to ($2 × c) + ($1 × d) = $44. For simplicity's sake, this can also be stated as $2c + d = 44$.

You need to express one of the equations so that it can be used as a definition of one of the variables in the other equation. Use $c + d = 40$, because it's easier — $c + d = 40$ can also be expressed as $d = 40 - c$.

Substitute this with the value of d in the second equation:

$$2c + d = 44 = 2c + (40 - c) = 44$$

$$2c - c + 40 = 44$$

$$c = 44 - 40$$

$$c = 4$$

The man bought four chickens.

17. **(C)** Let x = the number of Nintendo games that Alex has initially; then $3x$ is the number that Davy has at the start. If Davy gives six games to Alex, the Davy has $3x - 6$ games and Alex has $x + 6$ games. After the transfer, Davy has twice as many games as Alex, so you can write down an equation to represent this fact:

$$3x - 6 = 2(x + 6)$$

$$3x - 6 = 2x + 12$$

$$3x - 2x = 12 + 6$$

$$x = 18$$

18. **(D)** Let x = the milk with 5 percent butterfat, and y = the milk with 2 percent butterfat. You know that you need to add these together to come up with 60 gallons of milk. This can be expressed as $x + y = 60$.

You also know that 5 percent of x, plus 2 percent of y needs to equal 3 percent of the 60 gallons. Express this as $5\%x + 2\%y = 3\%(60)$. You can convert this equation to decimals to make it easier to work with:

$$0.05x + 0.02y = 0.03 \times 60$$

$$0.05x + 0.02y = 1.8$$

This equation will be much easier to work with if you get rid of the decimals by multiplying the whole equation by 100:

$$5x + 2y = 180$$

You now have two equations to work with: $x + y = 60$ and $5x + 2y = 180$.

Solve the first equation in terms of y: $x + y = 60$ can be expressed as $y = 60 - x$. Substitute this value for y in the second equation:

$$5x + 2(60 - x) = 180$$

$$5x + 120 - 2x = 180$$

$$5x - 2x = 180 - 120$$

$$3x = 60$$

$$x = 20$$

The solution will require 20 gallons of the 5 percent milk.

19. **(C)** Three bags of boiled peanuts cost $3 \times \$2.49 = \$7.47$. Four bags of roasted peanuts cost $4 \times \$3.29 = \$13.16$. Add these numbers together to arrive at $\$20.63$.

20. **(A)** To determine the amount of interest earned, multiply the principal ($\$3,000$) by the interest rate (6 percent) and the number of years interest accrues (1 year): $\$3,000 \times 0.06 \times 1 = \$180$. Add the interest earned to the principal to show how much total money the teacher would have: $\$180 + \$3,000 = \$3,180$.

21. **(A)** *Remember:* There are 30 questions on this subtest. Divide the number of questions she must get right (25) by the total number of questions (30) to reach 0.833 or 83.3 percent.

22. **(A)** Simply add 12 hours to 6 a.m. to arrive at 6 p.m. Central time is one hour earlier than eastern time, so she arrived at 5 p.m. New Orleans time.

23. **(B)** You can solve this by expressing the problem as a ratio. 30 minutes is to 8 city blocks, as x minutes is to 6 city blocks. Mathematically, this would be:

$$\frac{30}{8} = \frac{x}{6}$$

$$\frac{30}{8} \times 6 = x$$

$$\frac{180}{8} = x$$

$$x = 22.5$$

24. **(D)** The price of five cases of ramen noodles at regular price is $5 \times \$5.20 = \$26$. Mick bought five cases for $5 \times \$3.75 = \$18.75$. Mick saved $\$26 - \$18.75 = \$7.25$ on this purchase.

25. **(A)** Convert the fractions so that they all have a common denominator. To do this, you must find a denominator that all the original denominators can divide evenly into. The numbers 4, 3, and 6 all divide evenly into 12.

$$\frac{1}{4} = \frac{3}{12}$$

$$\frac{1}{3} = \frac{4}{12}$$

$$\frac{1}{6} = \frac{2}{12}$$

You can now add these fractions together:

$$\frac{3}{12} + \frac{4}{12} + \frac{2}{12} = \frac{3+4+2}{12} = \frac{9}{12}$$

$\frac{9}{12}$ can be reduced to $\frac{3}{4}$, which means there are $\frac{1}{4}$ or 25 percent of the lures left, and 25 percent of 20 is 5 ($20 \times 0.25 = 5$).

26. **(A)** This should be obvious after a quick glance. Mark is closer and traveling at a faster speed than Mickey, so, of course, he will arrive first.

27. **(B)** Penelope's raise is $8.35 × 0.15 = $1.25 per hour. Add the raise to her original per hour salary: $8.35 + $1.25 = $9.60. Don't get confused by her per-delivery bonus. It's a distracter and has nothing to do with the question asked.

28. **(C)** The formula to determine the area of a rectangle is $A = lw$. Plug in the known values:

    $A = 8 × 10$

    $A = 80$ square feet

    It costs 75¢ per square foot to clean the rug, so it would cost a total of $80 × $0.75 = $60 to clean the rug.

29. **(C)** Divide Joy's tip amount by her total sales to determine her average tip: $\frac{\$127}{\$623} = 0.203 = 20$. Her hourly wage is not a factor in solving this problem.

30. **(B)** Because each brick is of equal length, simply divide the total length (44 inches) by the number of bricks (4): $44 ÷ 4 = 11$.

Part 2: Word Knowledge

The Word Knowledge subtest, as with all the AFQT subtests, determine whether you qualify for enlistment. If you're not seeing the improvement in your scores that you need to see, work with a partner who can quiz you on vocabulary. Review your vocabulary words intensely, even several times a day, to ensure your success on this subtest. You may also want to reread the information in Chapter 4.

Also check out *Vocabulary For Dummies,* by Laurie E. Rozakis, and *SAT Vocabulary For Dummies,* by Suzee Vlk (both published by Wiley). Finally, see Chapter 5 for more practice questions.

1. **(C)** *Abyss* is a noun that means a deep, immeasurable space, gulf, or cavity.

2. **(A)** *Stifle* is a verb that means to suppress, curb, or withhold. It can also mean to suffocate, but that's not the best choice in the context of the sentence.

3. **(C)** *Unwieldy* is an adjective that means not easily handled, or awkward.

4. **(D)** Used as an adjective, *wee* means very small.

5. **(B)** *Prophecy* is a noun that means a prediction about the future. Choice A is close, because prophecies are often told in the form of a story, but B is the more exact definition.

6. **(A)** Used as a verb, *purloin* means to take dishonestly.

7. **(B)** *Refract* is used as a verb. It means to bend or change the path of something (usually light). If you chose A or C, it's probably because you heard your eye doctor talk about refraction of the eye, which is basically how your eye refracts (or bends) light.

8. **(C)** *Skiff* is a noun that means a small boat, usually propelled with oars.

9. **(D)** *Speculate* is a verb that means to engage in thought or conjecture.

10. **(C)** Used as a verb, *subjugate* means to take complete control of.

11. **(D)** In this sentence, *utmost* is used as a noun, meaning the absolute limit.

12. **(B)** *Vertigo* is a noun that means a sensation of dizziness.

13. **(C)** *Writhe* is a verb. It means to twist or wriggle about.

14. **(A)** *Sonnet* is a noun; a sonnet is a specific type of poem.

15. **(C)** *Teeming* is a verb (participle) that means filled to the point of overflowing.

16. **(C)** *Technique* is a noun that describes a particular way of doing something.

17. **(A)** *Bequeath* is a verb that means to give by way of a will, or to pass on to heirs.

18. **(D)** *Characteristic* is a noun that means a distinguishing feature.

19. **(A)** *Deceit* is used as a noun. It means a lie or falsehood.

20. **(B)** *Conveyance* is a noun that means any means of transportation.

21. **(C)** Used as a noun, *entirety* means the whole thing.

22. **(B)** *Elude* is a verb that means to hide from.

23. **(C)** *Stiletto* is a noun that means a small dagger.

24. **(C)** *Protagonist* is a noun that means person who takes the lead. You may have been tempted to choose B, but although the protagonist in a story is the lead character, he or she is not always the hero.

25. **(A)** *Ordnance* is a noun; it is any kind of weapon, ammunition, or explosive used in warfare.

26. **(D)** *Oust* is used as a verb. It means to eject.

27. **(C)** *Mutilate* is a verb that means to damage or disfigure.

28. **(A)** You may have gotten this one wrong. Don't worry — it's a hard one. *Loath* is an adjective meaning unwilling, whereas *loathe* is a verb meaning to dislike intensely.

29. **(B)** *Litigious* is an adjective that means argumentative.

30. **(A)** *Reciprocity* is a noun that means repayment.

31. **(A)** *Reassure* is used as a verb. It means to certify, or restore confidence.

32. **(B)** *Tarnish* is a verb that means to dirty, defame, or corrupt.

33. **(C)** *Tremendous* is an adjective that means overwhelming or awe-inspiring.

34. **(B)** *Sanctity* is used as a noun; it means holiness or godliness.

35. **(D)** *Constrict* is a verb that means to confine, squeeze, or inhibit.

Part 3: Paragraph Comprehension

If you're still struggling with this subtest, remember to take your time when you read the passages. And, after you read each question, you can quickly reread the passage just to make sure you're on the money. The information is in the paragraph; you just have to concentrate to pull it out. Turn to Chapter 6 if you still need additional help to pull off a good score on this subtest. You can also find more practice questions in Chapter 7.

1. **(C)** The next-to-the-last sentence in the passage says, "Nothing reduces trust in a group faster than members saying one thing within the group and something else outside the group."

2. **(C)** The first sentence explains that the FOIA provides access to federal agency records.

3. **(C)** According to the paragraph, the FOIA imposes a mandatory time limit of 20 workdays to respond, but permits an additional 10 workdays in unusual cases.

4. **(B)** The third sentence in the paragraph says that the law allows assessing fees in some cases.

5. **(D)** The paragraph likens the life cycle of old things to the life cycle of an elderly person.

6. **(B)** Becky is going to MEPS with her recruiter; she is obviously planning to join the military. Personally, I think the correct answer should be D. Becky showed great intelligence by reading *ASVAB For Dummies* and *ASVAB AFQT For Dummies*.

7. **(A)** Although the passage doesn't come straight out and say this, because Becky is visiting MEPS with her military recruiter, this answer is the most likely choice.

8. **(B)** The author states that Becky was tired from weeks of study.

9. **(A)** The final sentence of the paragraph states that domestic violence is a crime.

10. **(D)** Domestic violence is unjustified physical or verbal abuse *within a family unit.* Your teacher is (usually) not a member of your family.

11. **(B)** The paragraph explains the difference between Memorial Day and Veterans Day.

12. **(D)** According to the passage, 36.3 percent of Marines smoke, which is more than in any other service branch.

13. **(B)** The first paragraph states that the IOM wants DOD to ban smoking entirely in the military.

14. **(C)** According to the paragraph, the latest military smoking statistics are as of 2005.

15. **(C)** The author states that both girls had a crush on Billy, but Kiley was always shy around him.

Part 4: Mathematics Knowledge

If you're still missing too many math questions, you may need to take more drastic measures like enrolling in a basic algebra class at a local community college. If your scores are improving, keep hitting the books and testing yourself up until the day of the ASVAB. Chapter 8 will also be a good review.

If you want to increase your math skills, the following Dummies books will help: *Algebra I For Dummies* and *Algebra II For Dummies,* by Mary Jane Sterling; *Geometry For Dummies,* by Wendy Arnone; *Calculus For Dummies,* by Mark Ryan; and *SAT II Math For Dummies,* by Scott Hatch (all published by Wiley). Chapter 9 also has some additional practice questions.

1. **(B)** If the sum of two angles equals 90 degrees, they're called complementary angles.

2. **(A)** Determine what your rounding digit is and look to the right side of it. If the digit is 0, 1, 2, 3 or 4, do not change the rounding digit. If the digit is 5, 6, 7, 8 or 9, the rounding digit rounds up by one number.

3. **(D)** The shape shown is a rhombus, which is a *quadrilateral* (a shape with four sides). All quadrilaterals have angles that total 360 degrees.

4. **(B)** An equilateral triangle has three sides that are all equal in length. If the sum of two sides is 50 inches, each side is 25 inches long.

5. **(B)** The formula to determine volume of a rectangular box is $v = lwh$. Plug in the known variables:

   $v = 18 \times 6 \times 11$

   $x = 1{,}188$

   Volume is always expressed in cubic measurement.

6. **(D)** The formula to calculate the *circumference* (distance around) a circle is $c = \pi d$. Because the diameter of a circle is twice its radius, the formula can also be stated as $c = \pi 2r$. Plug in the known variables:

   $c = \pi \times 2 \times 5$

   $c = \pi 10$

   $c = 3.14\,\pi\,10$

   $c = 31.4$ feet

7. **(B)** The triangle shown is a *right triangle* — one of its angles is 90 degrees. The Pythagorean theorem says that if you know the lengths of any two sides of a right triangle, you can find the length of the third side with the formula, $a^2 + b^2 = c^2$. Plug in the known values:

$$a^2 = 15^2 + 17^2$$
$$a^2 = 225 + 289$$
$$a^2 = 514$$
$$a = \sqrt{514}$$
$$a = 22.7$$

The perimeter of a triangle is the sum of all three sides: $15 + 17 + 22.7 = 54.7$ feet.

8. **(A)** Solve an inequality as you would for any unknown:

$$2 + x \geq 8$$
$$2 - 2 + x \geq 8 - 2$$
$$x \geq 6$$

9. **(D)** Find a common denominator for the fractions. In this case, 80 works for all the fractions. Convert all the fractions: $\frac{2}{5} = \frac{32}{80}$, $\frac{3}{8} = \frac{30}{80}$, $\frac{7}{10} = \frac{56}{80}$, and $\frac{13}{16} = \frac{65}{80}$. Comparing the fractions, you can see that $\frac{13}{16}\left(\frac{65}{80}\right)$ is the largest fraction.

However, finding a common denominator can sometimes be difficult and painstakingly slow. Another way to compare fractions with different denominators is to use the cross-product method.

The first cross-product is the product of the first numerator and the second denominator. The second cross-product is the product of the second numerator and the first denominator. If the cross-products are equal, the fractions are equivalent. If the first cross-product is larger, the first fraction is larger. If the second cross-product is larger, the second fraction is larger.

Compare the first two fractions, $\frac{2}{5}$ and $\frac{3}{8}$: $2 \times 8 = 16$ and $5 \times 3 = 15$. The first fraction is larger.

Compare the larger fraction $\left(\frac{2}{5}\right)$ to the third fraction $\left(\frac{7}{10}\right)$: $2 \times 10 = 20$ and $5 \times 7 = 35$. The third fraction is larger.

Compare the largest fraction $\left(\frac{7}{10}\right)$ with the last fraction $\left(\frac{13}{16}\right)$: $7 \times 16 = 112$ and $10 \times 16 = 160$.

The final fraction $\left(\frac{11}{16}\right)$ is the largest of the group.

10. **(B)** $\sqrt{25} = 5$, $\sqrt{64} = 8$, and $8 \times 5 = 40$.

11. **(A)** Whenever you multiply two terms with the same base, you can add the exponents: $x^4 \times x^5 \times x^{-3} = x^{4 + 5 + (-3)} = x^6$.

12. **(D)** Whenever you multiply two terms with the same base, you can add the exponents: $(y^2 y^3)^6 = (y^5)^6$.

Whenever you have an exponent expression that is raised to a power, you can multiply the exponent and power: $(y^5)^6 = y^5 \times 6 = y^{30}$.

13. **(C)** Simplify, then isolate x:

$$(5 + 3)(6 \div 2)(8 - 1) = (3 + 7)x$$
$$8 \times 3 \times 7 = 10x$$
$$10x = 168$$
$$\frac{10x}{10} = \frac{168}{10}$$
$$x = 16.8$$

14. **(B)** Substitute 3 for all the x's in the equation:

$x^x \times x = 3^3 \times 3 = 27 \times 3 = 81$.

15. **(D)**

$$\frac{900 \times 3}{2} = \frac{2,700}{2} = 1,350$$

16. **(C)** To determine all the possible ways in which the horses could finish the race (called per-mutations), solve for factorial. 7 factorial ($7! = 7 \times 6 \times 5 \times 4 \times 3 \times 2 \times 1 = 5,040$).

17. **(D)** Whenever you have an exponent expression that is raised to a power, you can multiply the exponent and power: $(7^2)^2 = 7^2 \times^2 = 7^4 = 7 \times 7 \times 7 \times 7 = 2,401$.

18. **(D)** Multiply the first number in the first set of parentheses with the first number in the second set of parentheses. Then multiply the first number in the first set of parentheses with the first and second number in the second set of parentheses, respectively:

$(x + 4)(x + 2) =$

$[(x \times x) + (x \times 2)] + [(4 \times x) + (4 \times 2)] =$

$x^2 + 2x + 4x + 8 =$

$x^2 + 6x + 8$

19. **(B)** Convert the yards to feet. There are 3 feet to a yard, so $7 \times 3 = 21$ feet and 21 feet + 14 feet =35 feet.

20. **(C)** First, convert 14 percent to a decimal by dividing it by 100: $\frac{14 \text{ percent}}{100} = 0.14$. Multiply this by 42 to determine what 14 percent of 42 is: $42 \times 0.14 = 5.88$. Round this number up to 5.9.

21. **(B)** *Mean* is another word for *average*. To find the mean of a series of numbers, add the numbers together, and then divide sum by the number of items: $10 + 28 + 50 + 71 + 91 = 250$ and $\frac{250}{5} = 50$.

22. **(A)** In division, if one number is positive and the other is negative, the result is negative.

23. **(C)** The sum of angles for a triangle is always 180 degrees.

24. **(C)** Begin by putting the problem into a fraction: $\frac{72}{108}$. Now convert the fraction to a decimal: 0.666. Because *percent* means "part of 100," move the decimal place two spaces to the right to get the number expressed as a percent: 66.6 percent.

25. **(A)** You didn't expect to see such an easy one, did you? I got tired of writing harder problems. (Not really. You'll see a few very easy problems on the mathematics knowledge subtest. It's not a trick.)

$3b = 3$

$\frac{3b}{3} = \frac{3}{3}$

$b = 1$

Part V
The Part of Tens

The 5th Wave   By Rich Tennant

"It's an Armed Services aptitude test taken on a computer, and you're telling me my hours of experience playing World of Warcraft count for <u>nothing</u>?!"

In this part . . .

You can put down your pencil now — no more quizzes or practice tests. You've made it to the Part of Tens. There is no way I could write a *For Dummies* book and not include this part. The Part of Tens features my personal AFQT top-ten lists. I give you important information for getting the best score possible on the AFQT and point you in the right direction for finding more information if you need it.

Good luck! And I hope you get stationed in Hawaii. Save a place for me on the beach.

Chapter 20

Ten Tips for a Better AFQT Score

The U.S. military enlists around 317,000 new troops each and every year. And all those men and women share one thing in common: They all earned a qualifying score on the AFQT. (See Chapter 2 for qualifying AFQT scores for each service.)

Many people score very high, which makes their mothers proud and their recruiters smile. It also opens up a new world of special enlistment programs and enlistment incentives that are available only to those who score well on the AFQT.

I'm sure you want to be counted among the group who score well on the AFQT. Otherwise, why would you be reading this book? If so, this chapter will be a big help. Here I list ten sure-fire ways to maximize your AFQT score and get you on your way to a satisfying and successful military career.

Take Your Time

Don't cram. I don't care whether you call it a "power study," "mega-brain feeding," or "mugging" — it doesn't work. Study after study has shown this. For example, a 2007 study conducted by University of South Florida psychologist Doug Rohrer determined that last-minute studying reduces retention of material and may hinder the learning process.

Rome wasn't built in a day, but it took only a few hours for the city to crash and burn. If you develop a solid study-plan and stick with it for six to eight weeks, you'll score much higher on the AFQT than if you try to pack four subjects' worth of knowledge into your brain in one or two days. Plus, you won't walk into the testing center with your eyes red and your brain fried.

Make a Study Plan

You wouldn't expect the U.S. military to fight a war without a plan, would you? It would be disorganized chaos, and probably nothing would be achieved. The same is true when studying for the AFQT (or doing anything else, for that matter). If you try to study without a plan, you'll wind up wandering here and there, reading this and that, but you won't really accomplish anything.

Start by studying the subjects you find the hardest, and spend extra time on those areas. It's human nature to want to read about things and study areas that you're good at. Remember that, so you can counteract this instinct.

Use the Practice Exams to Your Advantage

If you bought this book expecting the practice exams to include the exact same questions you'll see on the ASVAB, I'm afraid I have bad news: You won't see the same questions on the ASVAB that I include in this book (or any other ASVAB/AFQT preparation guide). Giving you the actual questions and answers in advance would be cheating — and illegal. The military classifies ASVAB tests as "official use only." That means only those with an official "need to know" have access to the test questions and answers — and that certainly does not include authors of ASVAB AFQT prep books.

The best I can do is to provide you with practice questions that are *very similar* to the ones you'll see on the ASVAB. In short, don't waste your time trying to memorize the questions and answers on the practice exams.

Even so, the practice exams are a *very* valuable study tool. Not only do they give you an idea about the *type* of questions you'll see, as well as the test format, but they're useful in determining what AFQT subject areas you need to spend the most time on.

Here are my recommendations for taking the exams:

- **Practice Exam 1:** Take this test before you set up your study plan. You can use the results of Practice Exam 1 to determine which areas of the AFQT you need to spend the most time on.

- **Practice Exam 2:** Use this test as a progress check after a week or two of study. Adjust your study plan accordingly.

- **Practice Exam 3:** Take this practice exam about a week before you're scheduled to take the actual ASVAB. Use the results to determine which AFQT subjects need a little extra attention.

- **Practice Exam 4:** Take the final practice exam a day or two before the ASVAB to make sure you're ready, and to boost your confidence.

If you've already taken some or all of the exams and you didn't follow this schedule, that's okay, too. The key is to take the exams and learn from them.

Memorize Basic Math Formulas

The Arithmetic Reasoning and Mathematics Knowledge subtests require you to know many standard mathematical formulas used in geometry and algebra. As a minimum, you should have the following committed to memory by the time you sit down to take the ASVAB:

- **Perimeter of a square:** $p = 4s$, where s = one side of the square

- **Area of a square:** $a = s^2$

- **Diagonal of a square:** $d = s\sqrt{2}$

- **Perimeter of a rectangle:** $p = 2l + 2w$, where l = the length and w = the width of the rectangle
- **Area of a rectangle:** $a = lw$
- **Diagonal of a rectangle:** $d = \sqrt{l^2 + w^2}$
- **Perimeter of a triangle:** $p = s_1 + s_2 + s_3$, where s = the length of each side of the triangle
- **Area of a triangle:** $a = \frac{1}{2}bh$, where b = the length of the triangle's base (bottom) and h = the height of the triangle
- **Radius of a circle:** $r = \frac{1}{2}d$, where d = the diameter of the circle
- **Diameter of a circle:** $d = 2r$
- **Circumference of a circle:** $c = 2\pi r$
- **Area of a circle:** $a = \pi r^2$
- **Volume of a cube:** $v = s^3$, where s = the length of one side of the cube
- **Volume of a rectangular box:** $v = lwh$, where l = the length, w = the width, and h = the height of the box
- **Volume of a cylinder:** $v = \pi r^2 h$, where r = the radius of the cylinder and h = the height of the cylinder
- **Surface area of a cube:** $SA = 6s^2$
- **Surface area of a rectangular box:** $SA = 2lw + 2wh + 2lh$
- **Distance formula:** $d = rt$, where d = distance, r = rate, and t = time
- **Interest formula:** $I = prt$, where I = interest, p = principal, r = rate, and t = time

Memorize the Math Order of Operations

When a math problem asks you to perform more than one operation, you need to perform the operations in the set-in-stone correct order:

1. **Start with calculations in brackets or parentheses.**

   Note: When you have nested parentheses or brackets — parentheses or brackets inside other parentheses or brackets — do the inner ones first and work your way out.

2. **Work on terms with exponents and roots.**

3. **Do all the multiplication and division, in order from left to right.**

4. **Finish up with addition and subtraction, also in order from left to right.**

Boost Your Vocabulary

The Word Knowledge subtest is nothing more than a vocabulary test. This subtest contains questions that ask you to find the word that is "closest in meaning" to a given word. The more words you know, the better you'll do on this subtest. It's that simple. (For more on how to boost your vocabulary, check out Chapter 4.)

Comprehending What You Read

To do well on the Paragraph Comprehension subtest, you must be able to read a paragraph, pick out the main point(s), find implied meanings, and analyze what you've read.

Practice this task daily by reading a paragraph in a newspaper or magazine, and then asking a friend to question you about information included in that paragraph.

Arriving at the Test Site Refreshed and Prepared

Don't let the recruiter schedule you to take the ASVAB until you're sure that you're ready. Recruiters sometimes have a habit of trying to get you tested as soon as possible so they can fill their recruiting goals. However, if you don't achieve a qualifying AFQT score, you waste your time, your recruiter's time, and the military's time. *Remember:* You may have to wait for up to *six months* for a retest. (For more on retesting, turn to Chapter 2.)

The ASVAB test takes about two and a half hours, and by the time you're finished, you'll have answered 216 questions. Give yourself a head start against the fatigue factor by arriving well rested and motivated. Get a good night's sleep on the night before the test. If you're traveling to the test site in a bus or car, try to get a quick catnap during the journey — as long as you're not the one doing the driving, of course!

Try to eat a light meal or snack just before the test. You don't want your grumbling stomach to distract you from solving a quadratic equation.

Watching the Clock

You only have a limited amount of time to complete each subtest, but don't worry about it. The more you panic, the more likely you are to make mistakes. Just work at a steady pace, and you'll do fine.

If you're taking the computerized version of the ASVAB, there will be a counter on the screen, counting down the time remaining on the subtest. If you're taking the paper version of the ASVAB, a clock will be clearly visible on the wall and the test proctor will post the start and stop time of the subtest, where you can easily see them.

Here's how the time breaks down for the subtests that make up your AFQT score:

- **Arithmetic Reasoning:** 30 questions in 36 minutes. That's 72 seconds per question.
- **Word Knowledge:** 35 questions in 11 minutes. That works out to 18 seconds per question.
- **Paragraph Comprehension:** 15 questions in 13 minutes. That's 52 seconds per question.
- **Mathematics Knowledge**: 25 questions in 24 minutes. That's 57 seconds per question.

Don't spend too much time on one question. If you're drawing a blank, make a guess and move on (see the next section).

Guessing Smart

If you're stuck on a question, before making a wild guess, first try to eliminate any answers that you know to be wrong. If you can eliminate even *one* wrong answer, you increase your chances of guessing the right answer from one in four to one in three. If you can eliminate *two* wrong answers, your chances increase to 50/50. (For more tips on intelligent guessing, see Chapter 3.)

Chapter 21

Ten Topics to Explore

In This Chapter
▶ Getting to know the military
▶ Boosting your math and communicative skills
▶ Exploring other ways to study for the AFQT

1'll be the first to admit, *ASVAB AFQT For Dummies* is a great book. Quite possibly the greatest book ever to be published (my well-known modesty aside). However, I can't pack everything there is to know about math, vocabulary, reading, and joining the military into 336 pages. You may have to rely on some outside help.

If you need to brush up on some of your skills before taking the ASVAB and maxing out your AFQT score, reading the appropriate chapters in this book is a great place to start. But you may need or want even more work in a particular subject area, or you may want to know more about the military, or even the entire ASVAB. This chapter helps you find what you need. Here I list places you can get additional information if the chapters of this book leave you wanting more.

For More about the ASVAB

This book is about boosting your Armed Forces Qualification Test (AFQT) score, but this score is only comprised of four of the nine ASVAB subtests. Although the AFQT score is very important — because it determines whether you're qualified to join the military (see Chapter 2) — the other subtests of the ASVAB are used to determine which military jobs you qualify for.

If you want to brush up on all the ASVAB subtests, an excellent resource is my very own *ASVAB For Dummies* (Wiley), if I do say so myself. You can pick up a copy at your favorite bookstore or at www.dummies.com.

For More about the Military

If you're thinking about joining the military, presumably you want to learn more about how the military operates. The following Web sites are great resources:

✔ **About.com:** Much as I would like to, I don't spend all my time writing *For Dummies* books. I spend much of my time running a military information Web site. Here you can find a huge vault of invaluable information about military careers, including what basic training is like, military job descriptions, promotion tips, assignments, and military pay and benefits. There is even a discussion board where you can get your questions answered, and talk with current military members and veterans from all the service branches. Point your browser to http://usmilitary.about.com.

- ✔ **DefenseLINK:** To figure out what the military is up to, you can stop by the official Web site of the Department of Defense. The site is a treasure trove of military information articles and photos. Go to www.defenselink.mil.

- ✔ **Army recruiting:** If you're thinking about joining the Army, the Army's recruiting Web site is an essential first stop. Here you can read about Army enlistment qualification and Army careers, and even chat online with an Army recruiter. Visit www.goarmy.com.

- ✔ **Air Force recruiting:** If you want to soar with the eagles (F-15 Eagles, of course), you should check out the Air Force recruiting Web site at www.airforce.com.

- ✔ **Navy recruiting:** If you aren't the claustrophobic type, and you're thinking of a career aboard a submarine (or maybe an aircraft carrier), check out the official Navy site at www.navy.com.

- ✔ **Marine Corps recruiting:** The Marines have a few good men (and women) standing by at the Marine Corps recruiting Web site to help you become one of the proud few. Check them out at www.marines.com.

- ✔ **Coast Guard recruiting:** The Coast Guard is a military service, but it doesn't belong to the Department of Defense. Instead, it falls under the organization of the Department of Homeland Security. You can find out about joining the Coast Guard at www.gocoastguard.com.

For More about Math

The Mathematical Knowledge and Arithmetic Reasoning subtests on the ASVAB make up half of your AFQT score. If you want to do well on these tests but haven't had to use your math skills since you got that nifty calculator, check out the following resources:

- ✔ **A slew of *For Dummies* math books:** *Algebra I For Dummies* and *Algebra II For Dummies,* both by Mary Jane Sterling; *Geometry For Dummies,* 2nd Edition, and *Calculus For Dummies,* both by Mark Ryan; and *SAT II Math For Dummies,* by Scott Hatch, JD, and Lisa Zimmer Hatch, MA — all published by Wiley — are great places to start. Check your favorite bookstore or visit www.dummies.com.

- ✔ **AAA Math:** AAA Math can help you review math problems from kindergarten through eighth grade. The Web site features a comprehensive set of interactive arithmetic lessons, with unlimited free online practice. Visit www.aaamath.com.

- ✔ **High School Ace Math:** Designed specifically to help high school students ace those frustrating high school math tests, High School Ace Math is an excellent study reference for those who want to do well on the Mathematics Knowledge subtest. Give it a try at http://highschoolace.com/ace/math.cfm.

For More about Math Word Problems

Solving math word problems requires a special set of skills. You not only have to know basic math, but you must analyze the problem, determine how to set up an equation, and then solve it. *Algebra I For Dummies, Algebra II For Dummies,* and *Geometry For Dummies* (see the preceding section) can be a great help in understanding word problems, but you may want to start with *Math Word Problems For Dummies,* by Mary Jane Sterling (Wiley). Also, check out Purple Math at www.purplemath.com/modules/index.htm.

For More about Vocabulary

You can't get a good score on the AFQT without doing well on the Word Knowledge subtest. These resources can help you boost your vocabulary knowledge:

- ✔ *Vocabulary For Dummies,* **by Laurie E. Rozakis, and** *SAT Vocabulary For Dummies,* **by Suzee Vlk (both published by Wiley):** Head to your favorite bookstore or www.dummies.com.
- ✔ **FreeVocabulary.com:** This site has over 5,000 free vocabulary words along with their definitions — a great resource for anyone looking to improve his vocabulary.
- ✔ **ImprovingVocabulary.org:** This site offers free tips for improving your vocabulary. If you want, you can purchase their software program, which is designed to make you a word wizard in no time.

For More about Reading Comprehension

If you need to brush up on your reading skills for the Paragraph Comprehension subtest, or even if you just want to speed-read your way through *War and Peace,* try these sites:

- ✔ **MrNussbaum.com:** Dozens of reading comprehension exercises at your fingertips. Take a look at www.mrnussbaum.com/readingpassageindex.htm.
- ✔ **Resource Room:** This site offers tips, techniques, and exercises to help improve your reading comprehension skills. Go to www.resourceroom.net/comprehension.

For More about Test Taking

The best way to prepare for the AFQT is to develop a sound study plan and make sure you're prepared for the test. However, even with the best preparation, a question or two may trip you up. Chapter 2 has some great tips to help you take the test. Here are some other resources:

- ✔ **TestTakingTips.com:** This site offers tips and techniques about studying, note taking, reducing test anxiety, and taking tests.
- ✔ **Study Guides and Strategies:** This site gives ten great tips for terrific test taking. Take a look at www.studygs.net/tsttak1.htm.

Playing at Public Libraries

Remember when you learned math and English in high school? You were taught from standard textbooks. It turns out, those same textbooks are a great resource to help you review. However, have you ever priced a standard textbook in a bookstore? Holy cow! No wonder our education system always seems to be out of money.

If only there were a place where you could borrow math and English high school and college textbooks for free. . . . Wait a minute! There *is* such a place! It's the public library, and most towns and cities have one. Not only can you borrow standard textbooks, but libraries offer you a calm and quiet place to study, away from the hustle and bustle and demands of daily life.

Consorting with Colleges

Some people are just not good at studying on their own. They prefer organized classrooms, specific assignments, and teachers to explain things. If you're one of these people, you may want to consider enrolling in a math, vocabulary, or reading course at your local community college. Who knows? You may even qualify for state or federal student aid and be able to take college courses for free!

Supplementing your AFQT knowledge through college courses offers a couple big advantages:

- ✔ If you have a GED and get at least 15 college credits, you boost your chances of being accepted for enlistment by a factor of at least 10.
- ✔ If you get over 30 college credits, you may qualify for advanced enlistment rank.

Trying Out a Tutor

Another great thing about colleges and universities: They usually have a group of highly intelligent students who are anxious to supplement their incomes by tutoring other students in a variety of subjects. Even if you decide not to enroll in college courses yourself, what could be better than having some cute girl or guy help you prepare for the AFQT subtests?

To find a tutor in your area, visit the administration office of your local college or university. Or just walk around campus and look at the bulletin boards — students often advertise their tutoring services on fliers.

Index

Notes

BUSINESS, CAREERS & PERSONAL FINANCE

Accounting For Dummies, 4th Edition*
978-0-470-24600-9

Bookkeeping Workbook For Dummies†
978-0-470-16983-4

Commodities For Dummies
978-0-470-04928-0

Doing Business in China For Dummies
978-0-470-04929-7

E-Mail Marketing For Dummies
978-0-470-19087-6

Job Interviews For Dummies, 3rd Edition*†
978-0-470-17748-8

Personal Finance Workbook For Dummies*†
978-0-470-09933-9

Real Estate License Exams For Dummies
978-0-7645-7623-2

Six Sigma For Dummies
978-0-7645-6798-8

Small Business Kit For Dummies, 2nd Edition*†
978-0-7645-5984-6

Telephone Sales For Dummies
978-0-470-16836-3

BUSINESS PRODUCTIVITY & MICROSOFT OFFICE

Access 2007 For Dummies
978-0-470-03649-5

Excel 2007 For Dummies
978-0-470-03737-9

Office 2007 For Dummies
978-0-470-00923-9

Outlook 2007 For Dummies
978-0-470-03830-7

PowerPoint 2007 For Dummies
978-0-470-04059-1

Project 2007 For Dummies
978-0-470-03651-8

QuickBooks 2008 For Dummies
978-0-470-18470-7

Quicken 2008 For Dummies
978-0-470-17473-9

Salesforce.com For Dummies, 2nd Edition
978-0-470-04893-1

Word 2007 For Dummies
978-0-470-03658-7

EDUCATION, HISTORY, REFERENCE & TEST PREPARATION

African American History For Dummies
978-0-7645-5469-8

Algebra For Dummies
978-0-7645-5325-7

Algebra Workbook For Dummies
978-0-7645-8467-1

Art History For Dummies
978-0-470-09910-0

ASVAB For Dummies, 2nd Edition
978-0-470-10671-6

British Military History For Dummies
978-0-470-03213-8

Calculus For Dummies
978-0-7645-2498-1

Canadian History For Dummies, 2nd Edition
978-0-470-83656-9

Geometry Workbook For Dummies
978-0-471-79940-5

The SAT I For Dummies, 6th Edition
978-0-7645-7193-0

Series 7 Exam For Dummies
978-0-470-09932-2

World History For Dummies
978-0-7645-5242-7

FOOD, GARDEN, HOBBIES & HOME

Bridge For Dummies, 2nd Edition
978-0-471-92426-5

Coin Collecting For Dummies, 2nd Edition
978-0-470-22275-1

Cooking Basics For Dummies, 3rd Edition
978-0-7645-7206-7

Drawing For Dummies
978-0-7645-5476-6

Etiquette For Dummies, 2nd Edition
978-0-470-10672-3

Gardening Basics For Dummies*†
978-0-470-03749-2

Knitting Patterns For Dummies
978-0-470-04556-5

Living Gluten-Free For Dummies†
978-0-471-77383-2

Painting Do-It-Yourself For Dummies
978-0-470-17533-0

HEALTH, SELF HELP, PARENTING & PETS

Anger Management For Dummies
978-0-470-03715-7

Anxiety & Depression Workbook For Dummies
978-0-7645-9793-0

Dieting For Dummies, 2nd Edition
978-0-7645-4149-0

Dog Training For Dummies, 2nd Edition
978-0-7645-8418-3

Horseback Riding For Dummies
978-0-470-09719-9

Infertility For Dummies†
978-0-470-11518-3

Meditation For Dummies with CD-ROM, 2nd Edition
978-0-471-77774-8

Post-Traumatic Stress Disorder For Dummies
978-0-470-04922-8

Puppies For Dummies, 2nd Edition
978-0-470-03717-1

Thyroid For Dummies, 2nd Edition†
978-0-471-78755-6

Type 1 Diabetes For Dummies*†
978-0-470-17811-9

* Separate Canadian edition also available
† Separate U.K. edition also available

Available wherever books are sold. For more information or to order direct: U.S. customers visit www.dummies.com or call 1-877-762-2974.
U.K. customers visit www.wileyeurope.com or call (0)1243 843291. Canadian customers visit www.wiley.ca or call 1-800-567-4797.

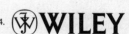

INTERNET & DIGITAL MEDIA

AdWords For Dummies
978-0-470-15252-2

Blogging For Dummies, 2nd Edition
978-0-470-23017-6

**Digital Photography All-in-One
Desk Reference For Dummies, 3rd Edition**
978-0-470-03743-0

Digital Photography For Dummies, 5th Edition
978-0-7645-9802-9

**Digital SLR Cameras & Photography
For Dummies, 2nd Edition**
978-0-470-14927-0

**eBay Business All-in-One Desk Reference
For Dummies**
978-0-7645-8438-1

eBay For Dummies, 5th Edition*
978-0-470-04529-9

eBay Listings That Sell For Dummies
978-0-471-78912-3

Facebook For Dummies
978-0-470-26273-3

The Internet For Dummies, 11th Edition
978-0-470-12174-0

Investing Online For Dummies, 5th Edition
978-0-7645-8456-5

iPod & iTunes For Dummies, 5th Edition
978-0-470-17474-6

MySpace For Dummies
978-0-470-09529-4

Podcasting For Dummies
978-0-471-74898-4

**Search Engine Optimization
For Dummies, 2nd Edition**
978-0-471-97998-2

Second Life For Dummies
978-0-470-18025-9

**Starting an eBay Business For Dummies,
3rd Edition†**
978-0-470-14924-9

GRAPHICS, DESIGN & WEB DEVELOPMENT

**Adobe Creative Suite 3 Design Premium
All-in-One Desk Reference For Dummies**
978-0-470-11724-8

**Adobe Web Suite CS3 All-in-One Desk
Reference For Dummies**
978-0-470-12099-6

AutoCAD 2008 For Dummies
978-0-470-11650-0

**Building a Web Site For Dummies,
3rd Edition**
978-0-470-14928-7

**Creating Web Pages All-in-One Desk
Reference For Dummies, 3rd Edition**
978-0-470-09629-1

**Creating Web Pages For Dummies,
8th Edition**
978-0-470-08030-6

Dreamweaver CS3 For Dummies
978-0-470-11490-2

Flash CS3 For Dummies
978-0-470-12100-9

Google SketchUp For Dummies
978-0-470-13744-4

InDesign CS3 For Dummies
978-0-470-11865-8

**Photoshop CS3 All-in-One
Desk Reference For Dummies**
978-0-470-11195-6

Photoshop CS3 For Dummies
978-0-470-11193-2

Photoshop Elements 5 For Dummies
978-0-470-09810-3

SolidWorks For Dummies
978-0-7645-9555-4

Visio 2007 For Dummies
978-0-470-08983-5

Web Design For Dummies, 2nd Edition
978-0-471-78117-2

Web Sites Do-It-Yourself For Dummies
978-0-470-16903-2

Web Stores Do-It-Yourself For Dummies
978-0-470-17443-2

LANGUAGES, RELIGION & SPIRITUALITY

Arabic For Dummies
978-0-471-77270-5

Chinese For Dummies, Audio Set
978-0-470-12766-7

French For Dummies
978-0-7645-5193-2

German For Dummies
978-0-7645-5195-6

Hebrew For Dummies
978-0-7645-5489-6

Ingles Para Dummies
978-0-7645-5427-8

Italian For Dummies, Audio Set
978-0-470-09586-7

Italian Verbs For Dummies
978-0-471-77389-4

Japanese For Dummies
978-0-7645-5429-2

Latin For Dummies
978-0-7645-5431-5

Portuguese For Dummies
978-0-471-78738-9

Russian For Dummies
978-0-471-78001-4

Spanish Phrases For Dummies
978-0-7645-7204-3

Spanish For Dummies
978-0-7645-5194-9

Spanish For Dummies, Audio Set
978-0-470-09585-0

The Bible For Dummies
978-0-7645-5296-0

Catholicism For Dummies
978-0-7645-5391-2

The Historical Jesus For Dummies
978-0-470-16785-4

Islam For Dummies
978-0-7645-5503-9

**Spirituality For Dummies,
2nd Edition**
978-0-470-19142-2

NETWORKING AND PROGRAMMING

ASP.NET 3.5 For Dummies
978-0-470-19592-5

C# 2008 For Dummies
978-0-470-19109-5

Hacking For Dummies, 2nd Edition
978-0-470-05235-8

Home Networking For Dummies, 4th Edition
978-0-470-11806-1

Java For Dummies, 4th Edition
978-0-470-08716-9

**Microsoft® SQL Server™ 2008 All-in-One
Desk Reference For Dummies**
978-0-470-17954-3

**Networking All-in-One Desk Reference
For Dummies, 2nd Edition**
978-0-7645-9939-2

**Networking For Dummies,
8th Edition**
978-0-470-05620-2

SharePoint 2007 For Dummies
978-0-470-09941-4

**Wireless Home Networking
For Dummies, 2nd Edition**
978-0-471-74940-0